Other Volumes in the International Collection

AUSTRALIA PLAYS
ed. Katharine Brisbane
Jack Davis: *No Sugar*
Alma de Groen: *The Rivers of China*
Michael Gow: *Away*
Louis Nowra: *The Golden Age*
David Williamson: *Travelling North*
ISBN 1 85459 056 1

THE CRACK IN THE EMERALD
New Irish Plays ed. David Grant
Dermot Bolger:
    The Lament for Arthur Cleary
Marina Carr: *Low in the Dark*
Michael Harding: *The Misogynist*
Marie Jones: *The Hamster Wheel*
ISBN 1 85459 237 8

CZECH PLAYS
ed. Barbara Day
Vaclav Havel: *Tomorrow!*
Ivan Klima: *Games*
Josef Topol: *Cat on the Rails*
Daniela Fischerova: *Dog and Wolf*
ISBN 1 85459 074 X

DUTCH PLAYS
ed. Della Couling
Lodewijk de Boer:
    The Buddha of Ceylon
Judith Herzberg:
    The Wedding Party
Arne Sierens: *Drummers*
Karst Woudstra: *Burying the Dog*
Frans Strijards:
    The Stendhal Syndrome
ISBN 1 85459 289 0

GERMAN PLAYS
ed. Elyse Dodgson
Klaus Pohl: *Waiting Room Germany*
Dea Loher: *Stranger's House*
Anna Langhoff: *The Table Laid*
D. Rust: *Jennifer Klemm*
ISBN 1 85459 338 2

HUNGARIAN PLAYS
ed. László Upor
András Nagy. *The Seducer's Diary*
Andor Szilágyi: *Unsent Letters*
Ákos Németh: *Muller's Dances*
Péter Kárpáti: *Everywoman*
ISBN 1 85459 244 0

LATIN AMERICAN PLAYS
ed. Sebastian Doggart
Octavio Paz: *Rapaccini's Daughter*
Jose Triana:
    Night of the Assassins
Griselda Gambaro: *Saying Yes*
Carlos Fuentes:
    Orchids in the Moonlight
Mario Vargas Llosa:
    Mistress of Desires
ISNB 1 85459 249 1

SCOT-FREE
New Scottish Plays
    ed. Alasdair Cameron
John Byrne: *Writer's Cramp*
John Clifford: *Losing Venice*
Anne Marie Di Mambro:
    The Letter-Box
Chris Hannan:
    Elizabeth Gordon Quinn
John McKay: *Dead Dad Dog*
Rona Munro:
    Saturday at the Commodore
Tony Roper: *The Steamie*
ISBN 1 85459 017

SOUTH AFRICA PLAYS
ed. Stephen Gray
Anthony Akerman:
    Somewhere on the Border
Maishe Maponya:
    The Hungry Earth
Susan Pam-Grant:
    Curl Up and Dye
Paul Slabolepszy: *Over the Hill*
Pieter-Dirk Uys: *Just Like Home*
ISBN 1 85459 148 7

STARS IN THE MORNING SKY
ed. Michael Glenny
Alexander Chervinsky:
    Heart of a Dog
Alexander Galin:
    Stars in the Morning Sky
Alexander Gelman:
    A Man with Connections
Grigory Gorin: *Forget Herostratus!*
Ludmila Petrushevskaya:
    Three Girls in Blue
ISBN 1 85459 020 0

SCOTLAND PLAYS

New Scottish Drama

Selected and introduced by Philip Howard

WORMWOOD Catherine Czerkawska

BROTHERS OF THUNDER Ann Marie Di Mambro

PASSING PLACES Stephen Greenhorn

ONE WAY STREET David Greig

QUELQUES FLEURS Liz Lochhead

ONE GOOD BEATING Linda McLean

LAZYBED Iain Crichton Smith

THE INTERNATIONAL COLLECTION

N
H
B

NICK HERN BOOKS

London

in association with

TRAVERSE
THEATRE

A Nick Hern Book

Scotland Plays first published in Great Britain in 1998 as an original paperback by Nick Hern Books Limited, 14 Larden Road, London W3 7ST, in association with the Traverse Theatre, Edinburgh

Typeset by Country Setting, Woodchurch, Kent TN26 3TB
Printed and bound in Great Britain by Cox and Wyman, Reading, Berks

Published in association with the Scottish Consultative Council on the Curriculum

A CIP catalogue record for this book is available from the British Library

ISBN 1 85459 383 8

Contents

Introduction

This new collection of plays testifies to Scotland as a nation of many parts, and to Scotland's playwrights as significant players in what is widely perceived as the current cultural confidence at the end of the century. All the playwrights in this volume share a rigorous determination to avoid being seen as insular or inward-looking, preferring instead to pursue wider concerns. And while it is notoriously foolish to attempt to identify a Golden Age in a nation's playwriting, it is hard not to connect the climate of confidence with that of political and constitutional change as the country acquires its own Parliament.

Scotland's contemporary playwrights have a chameleon-like knack of reinventing themselves in line with cultural and political shifts. They are a robust force who remain phlegmatic in the face of a permanent series of funding crises in Scottish theatre (they are steadfastly un-self-pitying). They find their influences from far and wide – as likely from North America (the Canada/Scotland sympathy is well documented) or Europe as from England. They are always open to dramatic and literary innovations, while being fiercely protective of three distinctively Scottish dramatic traditions: the atavistic, the demotic and the vaudevillian. They share with contemporary English playwrights an impressively agile virtuosity in straddling the personal and the political – the authors represented in this volume are exemplary in this respect.

Perhaps it is the rich diversity of language and regional variation within Scotland which contributes to the writers' fascination with dramatic language: they are certainly as interested in this as they are in form or storytelling. However, it must be said that this volume of plays contains a greater variety of dramatic voices and regional influences than it does of Scotland's distinct languages: neither Doric nor Lallans are represented here – which is a reflection of the fact that contemporary playwrights are more likely to use the language of, say, David Mamet than a pure, uneroded Scots. This should not belie the current renascence of Gaelic playwriting, which has followed increased investment in Gaelic arts and television since the early 1990's.

The strength of the written text in Scottish theatre (at least in the cities and Lowlands of Scotland: the oral tradition of the Highlands being quite distinct) has never been dented by followers of fashion in physical theatre. Instead, there have been a number of young theatre companies, working principally outwith theatre buildings, who have explored new ways of working with text: two such companies are KtC and Suspect Culture (represented in this volume by *One Way Street*) – both of them working with playwrights, but using other theatre artists to create a weave of authorial voices. Another discernible trend is the appetite which the playwrights share to develop their texts with theatre companies and thus work collaboratively.

The plays in this collection show a breadth of subject-matter which stretches far beyond the borders of Scotland – maybe the first benchmark of confidence among a nation's playwrights. *Wormwood* by Catherine Czerkawska (Traverse, 1997) was written in response to the tenth anniversary of the world's worst nuclear accident at Chernobyl, in the Ukraine, on 26 April 1986. The play is based on meticulous research into the events which led up to the catastrophe, including the testimony of survivors and victims; but it is fuelled throughout by the quiet anger of the playwright herself who lives and works in Ayrshire, a part of Scotland affected by the radioactive cloud which spread westwards over Europe. Czerkawska, pregnant at the time, describes this as 'a great force coming towards us which we could do nothing about'.

Wormwood avoids anti-nuclear hectoring by focusing sharply on the flawed logic in the human design behind safety systems; Czerkawska is fascinated by the the potential for disaster in a nuclear environment 'given a particular set of demands on human fallibility'. The setting of the play is Pripyat, the workers' dormitory town adjacent to the Chernobyl plant – but also a moment frozen in time through which the characters move backward and forward. Czerkawska skilfully interweaves the personal and the political: she identifies the good fortune felt by workers employed at the plant, and the irony of Kiev, the centre of power, demanding a surge of electricity on the night of the disaster. More importantly, she homes in on the experience of one family through the eyes of Natalia, a scientist and the family's only survivor, and through Artemis, a contemporary *deus ex machina*. The real achievement of the play is twofold: first, the chain of events at Chernobyl finds dramatic expression in the conflict between the characters; and, secondly,

Czerkawska finds a rare poetry in the science, much of it taken from oral testimony: the heavy metallic taste on Tanya's tongue, the sheer beauty of the nuclear fire, the swaying of the flames, the dragon.

Ann Marie Di Mambro's *Brothers of Thunder* (Traverse, 1994) avoids classification as simply an 'AIDS play' or 'Gay Play' by submerging the issues in strong, steadfast characterisation and a passionate insistence on themes of reconciliation and forgiveness. Within her basic setting of church and bedroom, Di Mambro keeps a shrewd eye on the theatrical possibilities of the church as an auditorium and, conversely, the audience as congregation. She recognises the liturgy and ritual of the Roman Catholic Church as an ideal framework in which to examine some of the thornier questions of sexuality and personal responsibility common to cleric and layman alike.

James (the priest) and John (the young man dying of an AIDS-related illness) twist and turn as the biblical 'brothers of thunder' of the title, before Di Mambro deliberately and boldly injects Simon (a Californian playboy), virus-like, into their hermetically sealed world – and so creating the unlikeliest of trinities. Part of the play's success is that, like Czerkawska's *Wormwood*, the anger at its heart is so carefully controlled that its incisiveness is all the more effective. When the play was revived in Glasgow eighteen months after its Traverse premiere, one critic opined that it seemed more timely now, which was, it seemed to me, a curiously back-handed way of recognising that Di Mambro had been ahead of her time all along.

Passing Places by Stephen Greenhorn (Traverse, 1997) is, in many ways, the ultimate Scotland Play. In telling his story of two young lads from Motherwell who escape the psychopathic Binks and little town blues, and discover much else in the Highlands, Greenhorn achieves a seamless dissection of Scotland and all the differing nations therein. Subtitled 'a road movie for the stage', the play combines the classic filmic form with what is a classic Scottish journey: from the industrialised, maligned, nominally powerful Central Belt to the supposed wilderness and Brigadoon atmosphere of the Highlands. In a *Scottish* road movie, the Going West of the American Dream is, of course, replaced by a Going North; the surfing 'paradise' of Thurso becomes a new *ultima Thule*.

Alex and Brian discover two important things early in their journey, about Scotland and about themselves: first, it's a bigger and more disparate country than they had bargained for. They visit Skye, where you're as likely to find a Canadian as a Scot; they encounter Ukrainian as well as Gaelic; on the same day as Alex sits on the gable end of a ruined croft, they pass Dounreay nuclear power station (Scotland's own 'radioactive dustbin') and meet a man on the far north coast who works for a Californian company via computer: the Electric Croft. Secondly, and with even more significance for the play's emotional heart, it takes each of them the length of the play to stop feeling like 'the wrong person in the wrong place'. Constantly bemused by the seething mix of nationalities and influences in the Highlands, and his own sense of dislocation in general, Alex complains of feeling like a foreigner in his own country, and compares himself and Brian to the mountains of Sutherland: he feels they are nothing to do with anything and wonders how they got there in the first place.

Along the way, the boys' rite of passage is drawn deftly and movingly. Most of the characters are limited in their ambitions: Binks wants to exchange Lanarkshire for Hawaii, but he'll still be drinking Buckie. Brian imagines seventeen words for dogshit in Motherwell, while Alex maintains that 'beautiful' is not a word he can say out loud. Behind the banter, the play is as shy of overt, self-advertising emotion as Alex is himself, but the undertow is all the more heartfelt. Greenhorn roots the boys' yearning in their direct experience of boredom and hardship (which gives the play its grounding), without ever dulling the sheer, exuberant comedy. The familiar gritty realism of the boys' dilemma is never portentous, and so, as (in true road movie style) the journey refuses to end but, rather, heads ever further north, the emotion is all the more unexpected.

One Way Street by David Greig (Suspect Culture, 1995) is another play which avoids wearing its heart on its sleeve, rendering its emotional impact all the more surprising. If the germ of the play is the philosopher Walter Benjamin's insistence that the story of his life should be a street map – more a geography than a biography – then the text, as devised by collaborative company Suspect Culture, presents a literal and metaphorical journey through East Berlin as the anti-hero John Flannery writes his anarchic travelogue: through the historical layers of this city, and indeed through his life. Greig creates a young everyman for his own generation, who flees his suffocatingly silent family in Lancashire, a family where 'words decay', to become a writer. But this writer cannot avoid tainting his travelogue with his own anxieties and anger as the journey through Berlin turns increasingly into a *post mortem* of his fractious affair with Greta, a young German woman.

Flannery's flight from Burnley to Berlin mirrors Greig's own fascination with post-War Europe: Greta is an East Berliner, who is steeped in a culture where friends and relations are always leaving for the West (for her, Friedrichstrasse Station is a 'hall of tears'), who knows all about living at a crossroads of Europe; Flannery and Greta fall in love during a demonstration to protect squatters on the point of eviction, and through her he becomes, briefly, a revolutionary *manqué*. This story of a singularly ordinary Englishman thrust into the melting pot of Europe is told by a variety of characters, but only one performer, and bears all the hallmarks of the pioneering collaborative approach to text by Greig and his principle Suspect Culture partner, Graham Eatough.

Quelques Fleurs by Liz Lochhead (Nippy Sweeties, 1991), like *One Way Street*, has a monologue format, but two characters, compulsive shopper Verena and offshore oilman husband Derek. It is a 'talking heads' play which remains resolutely dramatic through a skilful narrative interplay between the two characters: Verena moving forward in time from Christmas to Christmas as Derek moves backwards. Verena is not new to *Quelques Fleurs*: she was originally written for actor Siobhan Redmond (a long-term collaborator of Lochhead's), and then honed to monologue perfection in Lochhead's own performance poetry (viz. *True Confessions and New Clichés*, Polygon 1985), the woman who 'basically' found herself listening to the central heating turning itself on and off, and who now finds dramatic expression in a play. *Quelques Fleurs* has been produced in a number of versions while Lochhead developed the characters, but this published text is the final one.

Lochhead finds an extraordinary kind of poetry in Verena's material obsessions: she is a doyenne of designer Christmas trees ('less is more'), but can't abide real ones because of pine-needle-drop. Verena's patter sails along, peppered with a liturgy of brand names and domestic details, plus hilarious recreations of her family and friends (even shopping with Moira McVitie on the fateful day), while Derek (a mere offstage character in the original Verena monologues) drinks himself into oblivion on the Aberdeen-Glasgow train – until eventually their dual time-frames collide. Lochhead illustrates a very particular kind of emptiness while at the same time remaining unfailingly hilarious, before she wrongfoots us at the end.

One Good Beating by Linda McLean (Traverse 1996) has the rare virtue of knowing its own length and yet, within thirty-five minutes, conjures up a remarkably vivid picture of one merciless family and three lives. The play belongs to a Scottish vernacular tradition epitomised in this century by Ena Lamont Stewart's *Men Should Weep*, but, in this case, stripped bare of every domestic excrescence barring tea, and plonked inside and outside a coal shed. The jagged, athletic dialogue contains a dense clutch of emotions which leave a bigger dent than a play thrice its length.

The character of Murdo in *Lazybed* by Iain Crichton Smith (Traverse, 1997) is, like Liz Lochhead's Verena, a development from an earlier creation of the author's, notably in his collection of stories *Thoughts of Murdo* (Balnain 1993). *Lazybed* is the story of a man who cannot or will not get out of bed one morning, for 'metaphysical reasons': the impotence of the Will. The play is steeped in the culture and imagery of Scotland's *Gàidhealtachd*: Crichton Smith was born on the Isle of Lewis in 1928, with Gaelic as his first language. This incarnation of Murdo owes something to Goncharov's *Oblomov* (1859), whose title character similarly prefers to stay in bed, from which he holds court to a panoply of Russian archetypes. Both are anti-enterprise figures in their way – Oblomov, the estate-owner, is impossibly ignorant of the modern needs of his rural tenants, while Murdo, the crofter, cannot wield a spade in an age of toryism and spiritual vapidity. The difference, of course, is that Murdo is 'metaphysical' while Oblomov is slothful.

Crichton Smith's Murdo is a spirited cross between a humanist everyman and an absurdist autobiography, though the dramatic character is much less cartoonish than in the book. Behind Murdo's retiral to bed, philosophical investigations and irritable *contretemps*, there is depression and breakdown, but Crichton Smith renders this resolutely comic and, along the way, allows himself several well-aimed assaults (always shrewd but never spiteful) at the ridiculousnesses of modern life. Many familiar pre-occupations from Crichton Smith's *œuvre* are infused in the play: the deep mother-son bond, mistrust of the intellectual, and belated, transcending discovery of love and marriage (Murdo learns to accept life through his encounter with Death). Similarly, his status as one of Scotland's great twentieth-century poets is well evidenced by the signature images of the play: from the blue vase – a sort of mock-philosophical paradigm – to the mouse and the owl ('Nature red in tooth and claw').

The publication of these seven plays follows a recent campaign to 're-brand' Scotland in marketing terms, a campaign to investigate what the country means to the wider world – was this a chance to question the Brigadoon image so relentlessly peddled by tourist boards to international visitors? The culmination was a public ceremony at Edinburgh Castle at which a new logo (Scotland the Brand) was unveiled – in a tartan swirl. So Scotland is now a trademark as well as a small Northern European country. These seven playwrights say more about Scotland, and with greater value, than a new tartan logo, even if they do not command quite the same fee. Scotland's writers remain its best weapon against such kitsch – and the Traverse will continue to pursue vigorously both its role as Scotland's new writing theatre, and its dedication to furthering the climate of confidence for playwrights in Scotland.

Philip Howard
Traverse Theatre, May 1998

WORMWOOD

Catherine Czerkawska

Catherine Czerkawska was born in Leeds of Polish/Irish/English parentage, moved to Scotland as a child, and studied at the Universities of Edinburgh and Leeds.

Her theatre plays include *Heroes and Others* (Scottish Theatre Company) and *Wormwood* (Traverse), and her published poetry includes *White Boats* (with Andy Greig) and *A Book of Men* (Akros) which won an Arts Council New Writing Award.

Her radio work includes: *O Flower of Scotland* (winner of Pye Award), *Bonnie Blue Hen* (winner of Scottish Radio Industries Club Award); for Radio 4: *The Peggers and the Creelers, Running Before the Wind, The Curiosity Cabinet.* For television: *Shadow of the Stone* (STV) and *Strathblair.* Her books include: *Fisherfolk of Carrick, Shadow of the Stone, The Golden Apple.*

She is currently under commission to the Traverse for *The Pebble House.*

For my dear dad,
JULIAN WLADYSLAW CZERKAWSKI
1926-1995

a scientist who knew how to imagine

Wormwood was first performed at the Traverse Theatre,
Edinburgh on 16 May 1997, with the following cast:

ARTEMIS, *youthful though not necessarily young*

	Forbes Masson
NATALIA, *a young science graduate*	Meg Fraser
VIKTOR, *an engineer, Natalia's fiancé*	Stephen Clyde
STEFAN, *a fire-fighter. Older than Viktor*	Liam Brennan
TANYA, *his wife and Natalia's older sister.*	
A schoolteacher	Anne Marie Timoney
ANTON, *Stefan and Tanya's only son. Aged 12 or 13,*	
he is mature for his years.	Anthony O'Donnell

Directed by   Philip Howard
Designed by   Angela Davies
Lighting designed by   Renny Robertson
Assistant director   Rosy Barnes
Music by   Jon Beales

*It would be suitable if all the characters spoke with Scots
accents, rather than assuming some kind of RP. It is worth
bearing in mind that these are Ukrainians, and their whole
demeanour should have a certain energy – overlain also with
a caution because of the political situation in which they find
themselves. But above all they should not sound too English.*

Many thanks are due to Philip Howard, the actors and everyone
else involved in this production – all of them for so much
invaluable help, collaboration and advice, and to family and
friends who were prepared to talk and to listen. Thanks, also, to
all at the Traverse for nurturing the play, and supporting the
playwright, especially Ella Wildridge, John Tiffany and the
actors who took part in script workshops.

ACT ONE

The stage is very light and bright. Some years have passed since the Chernobyl disaster, and we are in the town called Pripyat, which was built close to the plant, for the convenience of the workers. It was, in many senses, a model town: a good place to live.

The set should suggest – perhaps – a children's playground, with swings, miniature roundabout, seesaw, etc. There are wooden park benches at the rear of the stage, and to either side. Perhaps too a picnic table which could be moved and used as necessary. There may be scattered toys: a trike, a doll, a football etc.

There is an air of decay and desolation about the whole place, emphasised by the almost dazzling light. This is not a place that has suffered destruction so much as total abandonment. To quote from an eyewitness account describing Pripyat, five years after the disaster: 'Not a window was broken. The paint on the doors had begun to fade, but in the years since they were last hurriedly closed, none had been damaged. In the fairground, a Ferris Wheel stood motionless, and red and blue dodgem cars were scattered across the floor as though the electricity had only just been turned off.'

The whole place should have the sinister air of a moment frozen in time.

ANTON enters. He is a boy of about thirteen: tall, quite mature looking but with the occasional gesture of childhood still lingering about his actions, his speech. He wanders about, as though slightly confused about where he is and why. There should be a certain detachment about him. He finds the football and begins to fool about with it, hesitantly at first, and then with more surety and enjoyment.

ARTEMIS enters and kicks the ball back to ANTON. ANTON stops, picks up the ball and watches him, clutching it close to his chest.

ARTEMIS is thin, anonymous, and smooth. He should have something of the precise, physical and yet faintly menacing air of a conjuror. At this point the audience should have no idea who he is.

ANTON *wanders away, still preoccupied, still holding the football, giving it the occasional bounce, glancing back at* ARTEMIS. ARTEMIS *sits down on one of the benches, takes out a cigarette and lights it, blowing out the smoke luxuriously.*

NATALIA *enters. She is a woman in her early thirties, smartly but simply dressed. She looks around her at the empty playground and then approaches* ARTEMIS, *surprised to see him.*

ARTEMIS. Excuse me . . .

NATALIA (*coming over to him, but unsure of herself*). Good morning . . .

ARTEMIS. Can I help you?

NATALIA. Are you one of our party?

ARTEMIS (*amused*). Your party? What party would that be?

NATALIA. We're meant to be going in today . . .

ARTEMIS. Ah, that party. No. Not me.

NATALIA. You must be one of the scientists. Aren't you?
I mean nobody else would . . . (*At a loss.*) Why are you here then?

ARTEMIS. So you're going in are you?

NATALIA. I think so. At least, I thought so . . .

ARTEMIS. But now you're not so sure.

NATALIA. I suppose I'll have to go in. I can't change my mind now.

ARTEMIS. Won't it be dangerous? For a young woman like you . . .

NATALIA. No more dangerous than just being here. Besides, things are changing all the time. We need to assess what's happening in there.

ARTEMIS. I should say there's a simple answer to that one.

NATALIA. What?

ARTEMIS. Nobody knows. Nobody knows anything.

NATALIA. That's true enough.

ARTEMIS. But of course they'll give you protective clothing won't they . . . ?

NATALIA. I believe there are plastic suits.

ARTEMIS (*amused by this*). Plastic suits. (*Pauses.*) What about gamma rays?

NATALIA. Well no, they're no protection against . . . listen I thought you weren't a scientist . . .

ARTEMIS. Oh, I do have a little basic knowledge. What about you then? What do *you* specialise in?

NATALIA. Me? I'm a radio ecologist. I don't know if that means anything to you.

ARTEMIS. A little. You study the effects of radiation on the environment.

NATALIA. Plants, animals, people . . .

ARTEMIS. This should be right up your street then. So they've been showing you around have they. Around this – heritage park.

NATALIA. We were being taken round the big greenhouse. The one behind the football pitch.

ARTEMIS. Another experiment. They have every facility here, don't they. So why aren't you with the rest of them. Examining plants . . .

NATALIA. Have you seen some of those plants?

ARTEMIS. Bizarre, aren't they.

NATALIA. They look as if they might just pull up their roots and walk away . . .

ARTEMIS. You have a vivid imagination. For a scientist.

NATALIA. Some scientists know how to imagine . . .

ARTEMIS. Is that a gift or a failing I wonder?

NATALIA. Oh it's a gift.

ARTEMIS. So why aren't you with the others?

NATALIA *gets up, moving about the stage.* ARTEMIS *watches her.*

NATALIA. I slipped away from them. I wanted to look around by myself. I thought I might as well risk it.

ARTEMIS. You're still taking a chance. You must know. You of all people. There are hot spots all over the place. Here. Out in the forest. Everywhere. Well, they're not quite so hot *now* perhaps . . . but all the same . . .

She sits down again.

NATALIA. You know quite a lot, don't you? Hot spots . . . gamma rays . . .

ARTEMIS. I know that most people seem to think that radiation spreads out in a nice regular pattern.

NATALIA. If only it did.

ARTEMIS (*he stands up and paces it out*). Exactly. Then you'd be able to take sensible precautions. Wouldn't you? You scientists. Step it out on the map. Within this radius, so many people will die. Outside this given area, the risk is slight. And at this distance, you'll be quite safe. Only . . .

NATALIA. Only it doesn't work like that.

This should be slightly comic but also uncomfortable. He is always like a magician or master of ceremonies, in charge. A conjuror.

ARTEMIS. Instead it swirls around. The wind picks it up and puts it down again. Drops it at your feet. It comes with the rain. The spring showers. Even the dew. Beware of puddles where the rain collects and dries up and collects again. Beware of your dog's furry coat. Beware of all kinds of nice ordinary things.

NATALIA. Like places where mushrooms grow.

ARTEMIS. Pity so many people round here pick them.

NATALIA. We used to go and pick mushrooms . . . in the forest.

ARTEMIS. Did you?

NATALIA. My fiancé and I. His name was Viktor. Maybe you knew him.

ARTEMIS. Did he work at the plant?

NATALIA. He started work here in the autumn before the . . . before the accident. I was still studying in Kiev. But I saw him here whenever I could. I used to come and stay with my sister and her husband. They used to live not too far from here.

ARTEMIS. And have you been back there yet? To their apartment?

NATALIA. No. No I haven't. I don't think I'd be allowed . . .

ARTEMIS. Strictly speaking you aren't *allowed* to be *here*. But you've come all the same. Anyway, you were saying . . . this Viktor . . .

NATALIA. We met in Kiev. We were both studying . . . Then he got the job here. Which suited me fine . . .

ARTEMIS. I'm sure it did.

NATALIA. No, not just . . . I mean I know it was a good place to live. New apartments. Parks, lakes, gardens. Everyone wanted to live and work here.

ARTEMIS. Of course they did. It was a privilege to work here.

NATALIA. But you see my sister was here. Tanya. And we had always been very close. She was older than me. I was the afterthought. She used to baby me along you know. Then, after she got married and moved . . . I missed her. I missed her a lot. And I really got on with her husband. He was a lovely man, Stefan . . . (*She is lost for a moment in the past.*)

Anyway, Viktor and I used to go for long walks in the forest. It meant we could spend some time together . . . In autumn we went looking for mushrooms. That was our excuse. And then in the spring we just went walking. That year – I remember the weather had got quite warm, quite suddenly. It was a lovely spring.

VIKTOR *enters.* NATALIA *goes to him and they kiss. They walk, his arm around her shoulders.*

VIKTOR. It's so nice to have you all to myself for once.

NATALIA. Not for long.

VIKTOR. Why?

NATALIA. I promised we'd meet Tanya and Stefan later.

VIKTOR (*without enthusiasm*). Did you?

NATALIA. They're bringing a picnic.

VIKTOR. That'll be nice.

NATALIA. Don't worry. You'll have me to yourself all the time soon. You'll be sick of the sight of me.

VIKTOR. No I won't. I'll be glad when we're together. I get sick of managing by myself.

NATALIA. Is that all you want me for?

VIKTOR. I didn't mean that. It's just that I'm not much good at housework.

NATALIA. Oh and I am, I suppose?

VIKTOR. Well you're a lot better than me anyway.

NATALIA. You could always learn . . . besides your landlady does it all for you at the moment . . . what are you complaining about?

VIKTOR (*kisses her*). She doesn't do this.

NATALIA. I should hope not!

VIKTOR. You can teach me to cook. So long as you wash up afterwards . . .

NATALIA. That's big of you Viktor.

VIKTOR. I hate washing up.

NATALIA. I'll be working as well.

VIKTOR. I was just joking.

NATALIA. Were you?

VIKTOR. Of course I was. Anyway, we'll have our own flat soon. Won't it be great?

NATALIA. Mm.

VIKTOR. No more staying with Tanya and Stefan.

NATALIA. I don't mind staying with them. And I'm getting to know Anton. I always felt I'd lost contact with him a bit. He's grown up so much since they moved here.

VIKTOR. He looks more like his dad every day.

NATALIA. He does, doesn't he?

VIKTOR. So long as he doesn't inherit Stefan's warped sense of humour.

NATALIA. It isn't warped. He just winds *you* up because he knows you'll react.

VIKTOR. Hmm.

NATALIA (*hugging him*). Never mind. I love you anyway.

> ARTEMIS *walks across, whispering 'And the third angel sounded, and there fell a great star, burning as it were a lamp, and the name of the star is called Wormwood.'*

NATALIA. What's that noise? Is there a stream near here?

VIKTOR. It's just the wind in the trees . . .

NATALIA. Telling tales.

VIKTOR. Will they be here soon?

NATALIA. Not yet.

VIKTOR. Come on then. Let's go down to the lake.

> *They move off.* VIKTOR *to the back of the stage,* NATALIA *towards the bench from which* ARTEMIS *has been watching.*

NATALIA. I must go. I'll be late.

ARTEMIS. Don't worry. There's plenty of time. So your Viktor worked at the plant did he?

NATALIA. That's right. We were going to live here. After we got married.

ARTEMIS. Here?

NATALIA. Yes. Well it was convenient for work. As soon as I qualified we were going to get married. And I was going to work at the plant too. They'd offered us a wonderful flat. We'd have got nothing like it in Kiev.

ARTEMIS. The workers at the plant were very privileged, weren't they?

NATALIA. *Did* you work there?

ARTEMIS. It's a big place.

NATALIA. I don't remember you . . . Did you know my Viktor? We thought we were so lucky. So lucky to be here together.

> *She goes back to join* VIKTOR. *He comes to meet her and they walk together, close, his arm around her.*

VIKTOR. You know with both of us earning, we could get a car. We might even be able to afford a summer cottage in a few years . . .

NATALIA. By the lake?

VIKTOR. Maybe. A small place. A couple of rooms.

NATALIA. A wooden house. With fretwork. And a veranda for sitting out on.

VIKTOR. And drinking cherry vodka!

NATALIA. Tanya would be green with envy.

VIKTOR. She'd get the benefit of it. Her and Stefan both.

NATALIA. They could use it too. And Anton.

VIKTOR. That's if Stefan could bring himself to accept any favours from me . . . Stefan could invite his mum.

NATALIA. Gosh you are feeling generous.

VIKTOR. She's such an old . . .

NATALIA. Shsh.

VIKTOR. Well. My son the fireman. My son the hero . . .

NATALIA. Honestly. You two. You're always niggling at each other.

VIKTOR. No we're not. Stefan insults me and I keep my mouth shut.

NATALIA. I've told you, that's just his sense of humour.

VIKTOR. Aye . . . warped. Well I don't find him very funny.

NATALIA. I do.

VIKTOR. I know.

NATALIA. Anyway, I think it's something to do with his job. And Tanya worries enough for both of them.

VIKTOR. She's lost weight these last few months.

NATALIA. I know she has. Stefan asked me if I'd noticed. I had of course. I asked her if she'd been dieting but she said no she hadn't.

VIKTOR. Probably living with Stefan. He's enough to wear anybody out.

NATALIA. I wish you liked him more.

VIKTOR. I don't like him flirting with you.

NATALIA. You're jealous.

VIKTOR. I'm not.

NATALIA. Yes you are. Viktor it means nothing. He flirts with everyone. He even flirts with the woman in the butcher's . . .

VIKTOR. What woman in the butcher's?

NATALIA. You know. The big one on the till.

VIKTOR. Christ. He's brave. She's built like a . . .

NATALIA. Mind you, they always get the best cuts of meat, him and Tanya.

VIKTOR. I'm sure they do.

NATALIA. You ought to try it!

VIKTOR. I'd be terrified. Anyway you won't have to buy much meat. I eat in the canteen.

NATALIA. Do you have to be so . . .

VIKTOR. What?

NATALIA. I don't know. So literal.

Anyway, that's just Stefan. That's just the way he is.

VIKTOR. He can't seem to take anything seriously. It surprises me. With a job like he's got you'd think he'd be more . . .

NATALIA. What? Self-important?

VIKTOR. Is that what you think I am?

NATALIA. No. Oh Viktor don't go all huffy on me.

VIKTOR. I'm not huffy.

NATALIA. Let's not argue over Stefan. I just think the reason he makes so many jokes, the reason he's so . . . well, if the place goes up in flames it's all down to him.

He sits down again and she moves back towards ARTEMIS.

ARTEMIS. So. What brings *you* back to this place? After all these years?

NATALIA. I always meant to come back.

ARTEMIS. And how do you feel about it, now that you are back?

NATALIA (*half to him, but half to herself*). It's very strange isn't it? I suppose this is what it would be like if they dropped a neutron bomb. No people but no damage either. It's so empty, and it's fading away quietly. It hurts me to see it. It hurts me, like a real physical pain. Like a betrayal.

ARTEMIS. Perhaps you shouldn't have come.

NATALIA. I thought Viktor might be here. I thought they all might.

ARTEMIS. Maybe they are.

NATALIA. I miss them all so much. Every day. You'd think it would get easier with time, wouldn't you? I thought if I could come back I might find out . . . (*what happened*).

ARTEMIS (*interrupting her*). And do you feel them here?

NATALIA. Perhaps I do. I don't know. But anyway, I had to see for myself. I had to come back and allow myself to remember. The way it was. Before. And after. Funny. The whole calendar of my life is arranged that way. Before and after. You know, we were so happy that we didn't know how happy we were. We had everything to look forward to. We all did.

ARTEMIS. All of you?

NATALIA. Of course! All of us! It was going to be so good!

Enter TANYA *and* STEFAN *and sit with* VIKTOR. *For all that they are older and have been married for some time* STEFAN *and* TANYA *should be physically closer, and happier than* NATALIA *and* VIKTOR *who are slightly ill at ease with each other.* VIKTOR *is often prickly,* NATALIA *trying to placate him. They have all been picnicking together and are at the jokey, congenial stage, perhaps drinking wine.* ARTEMIS *stays where he is, watching.*

ANTON *enters, juggling his football and bouncing it.*

TANYA. Anton – will you go and do that somewhere else.

ANTON. I'm only practising. I have to practise somewhere.

VIKTOR. Are you into football then Anton?

ANTON (*still bouncing*). Yeah. Love it.

STEFAN. He's good. Aren't you son? He's in the school team . . .

VIKTOR. What position do you play?

ANTON. Mid-field.

STEFAN. Ach they all want to be strikers. Too much concentration on goal scoring and not enough on teamwork if you ask me.

ANTON. Oh dad! You always say that!

TANYA. He's right. You do. I don't know what you're talking about, but you do.

STEFAN. It's the truth. You know what I mean, don't you Viktor?

VIKTOR. Not really. I was never into football.

ANTON. Boring!

TANYA. Anton!

VIKTOR. There's plenty more to life than football.

STEFAN. I'm not sure about that son, are you?

ANTON. Can't think of much.

STEFAN. Mind you, that big lad in your team, what's his name – ?

ANTON. Mikhail?

STEFAN. Aye, that's the one. He'd rather see his team lose than help someone else to a goal . . .

ANTON. He's good. He's fast. He's the best player we've got.

STEFAN. So he is but that's not the point . . . Teamwork. That's what you need.

ANTON. Come on then . . . you can give me a few tips.

NATALIA. You dug that hole for yourself Stefan!

TANYA. Go on. You could do with the exercise.

STEFAN. I get plenty of exercise. Besides, I've just eaten.

ANTON. Dad!

STEFAN. Later.

ANTON. Oh all right . . . (*He sits down, unobtrusively, listening.*)

STEFAN. How's the job going then Viktor? How long have you been at the plant now?

Five months is it?

VIKTOR. About that.

STEFAN. And is it all you expected?

VIKTOR. More or less. I mean, nothing's ever quite what you expect is it? But yes, it's good.

TANYA. You don't sound too sure . . .

VIKTOR. Oh I am. I am sure. We're very lucky you know.

NATALIA (*to* VIKTOR). That's what your mum keeps telling me. You don't know how lucky you are, she says . . . (*To* STEFAN.) They're so proud of him. His mum and dad.

STEFAN (*to* VIKTOR). Well they would be, wouldn't they? Have they been here to see you yet?

VIKTOR. I got permission to show them round the plant.

STEFAN. Bet they were impressed.

VIKTOR. Well they were.

STEFAN. Did you show them the still then? Bet that really impressed them.

VIKTOR. What still?

STEFAN. The one they use for making the potato vodka. All the guys who haven't got enough to do.

VIKTOR. What are you talking about? Tanya, what is he talking about?

TANYA. You are joking aren't you?

STEFAN. Do I look as if I'm joking?

VIKTOR. He is. He's having us on.

STEFAN. I'm bloody serious. I don't know which frightens me more – the vodka or those guys lighting up in non-smoking areas.

NATALIA (*pulling at his arm*). Stefan . . .

VIKTOR. Rubbish! He's talking bloody rubbish.

STEFAN. Oh and then there are all the folk who fall asleep on duty . . .

Mind you, that could have something to do with the vodka . . .

NATALIA. Will you shut up!

TANYA. She's right. Shut up! You're upsetting him.

STEFAN *shrugs good humouredly.*

STEFAN. Must be easily bothered then.

NATALIA. He's having you on Viktor.

TANYA. Take no notice of him.

STEFAN (*to* TANYA). *You* know I'm right though. Don't you?

TANYA. I know no such thing.

STEFAN. Well I've told you often enough.

TANYA. Shut up Stefan. You're just doing it to . . .

STEFAN. To what?

TANYA. You know how I feel . . .

STEFAN. I'm sorry, I'm sorry. I do know. I'll stop. Look. I've stopped. I have.

There is a moment between them. A pause. He looks at her, frowning, shaking his head slightly. NATALIA *notices this and leaps in to change the subject.*

NATALIA. I always thought your mum and dad were a bit disappointed Viktor.

VIKTOR. What about?

NATALIA. You know. That you weren't more interested in farming.

VIKTOR. They weren't disappointed!

STEFAN. Not even just a little bit? Christ Viktor you don't need to tell me. I've been there. Mine were just the same. Well my dad really. My mum was on my side. 'Farming runs in the family son.' That's what he kept telling me. Still he managed to con my brother into living off the land so that was all right. I bet your dad was the same. Admit it.

VIKTOR. Well, just at first maybe. But not now.

STEFAN. No. I don't suppose they will be now. Not now they've seen the famous plant. I bet they like the kudos of having someone in the family working here eh?

VIKTOR. And why not? Why are you always so bloody cynical. It's the most up to date power station in the world . . .

ANTON. That's what they keep telling us at school.

STEFAN. Yeah, and if you believe that . . .

TANYA. Shsh!

STEFAN. Why? Who's listening? Is there somebody lurking behind that tree? Come out, come out and show yourself!

TANYA. Anton, will you go and practise your football! Now! (*He goes.*)

NATALIA (*joining in with* STEFAN *out of sheer devilment*). We haven't said anything wrong. Our power stations are the pinnacle of Soviet achievement.

VIKTOR. Stop it you two, will you just stop it!

TANYA. Don't keep tormenting him Stefan. It isn't fair. (*To* NATALIA.) And you're just as bad.

STEFAN. You've changed your tune. That wasn't what you said to me after that last fire . . .

VIKTOR. What fire? (TANYA *again looks warningly at* STEFAN.) We've never had a fire.

STEFAN. Aye you have.

TANYA. There *was* one Viktor . . . he should know. He was there . . .

STEFAN. Why does it always have to be on my shift? Why me?

VIKTOR. Well I never heard about it . . .

STEFAN. You wouldn't, would you? It was before you came to work here. Last summer. In a paint store . . .

VIKTOR. Oh well, there you are then. A paint store.

STEFAN. And we were tripping over bodies trying to get in there with the hoses.

VIKTOR. Bodies?

STEFAN. Surplus employees then!

I'm telling you, there are too many people with too little to do in that plant. And it's folk like me who get to carry the can . . .

NATALIA. Ach you always exaggerate. I'm sure it's safe enough . . .

TANYA. How safe is safe enough?

VIKTOR. Well . . .

NATALIA. Well what?

VIKTOR. There is a problem, but it isn't a big one. It isn't an issue of safety.

STEFAN. What is it an issue of then?

VIKTOR. Just that we're overstaffed in some areas, and overpressed in others.

STEFAN. So why are you overpressed? Tell me that.

VIKTOR. I suppose there's a certain amount of inefficiency.

STEFAN. You mean jobs for the boys and girls. People who wouldn't know a fuel rod from a stair rod. That what you mean? But it's not an issue of safety?

VIKTOR. It's admin. Your brother in law needs a job. You don't put him in the control room. But you might put him in the store room. You know how it is.

STEFAN. No I don't bloody know how it is. The fire service doesn't operate like that Viktor. I have to know what I'm doing . . . and why . . . and what will happen if I fuck up.

TANYA. Stefan!

STEFAN. Sorry, sorry . . .

VIKTOR. Yeah well you wouldn't get knocked down in the rush to join, would you?

TANYA. It all sounds pretty dangerous to me. Nepotism in your industry?

VIKTOR. If it happens at all, it's pretty low key. Store managers, finance, that sort of thing. Not the really important stuff. Those people have to be properly qualified.

STEFAN. Like you.

VIKTOR. Yes, like me!

NATALIA. And me for that matter.

TANYA. I still think it sounds dangerous.

VIKTOR. Tanya we would never ever compromise on safety.

NATALIA. He's right you know . . . he's very conscientious. Aren't you?

STEFAN. I'm sure *he* is . . . It isn't your Viktor that worries me . . .

VIKTOR. If I thought there was any real problem, I'd . . .

STEFAN. What would you do? Blow the whistle?

VIKTOR. I'd give up the job tomorrow . . .

STEFAN. Would you? You'd give up the salary and the nice shops to spend it in and the big flat you'll get once you're married?

NATALIA. He'd have to. If there was any real problem.

STEFAN. Can't he answer for himself?

VIKTOR. I will if you give me the chance. It's the most important thing of all. Safety.

ANTON *returns with his football.*

ANTON. Dad! You promised!

VIKTOR (*half gets up*). Come on. I'll have a kickabout with you.

ANTON. Dad! Are you not going to play?

STEFAN. Don't you bother yourself Viktor. I'm coming son. Sick of sitting on my arse.

NATALIA. Let him play. At least he's offering.

TANYA (*to her sister*). They're like big kids.

VIKTOR. It's all right. I don't mind.

STEFAN (*as he joins* ANTON). I only hope everyone else at that plant has your conscience Viktor.

VIKTOR. We're all concerned about safety.

STEFAN. I'm sure you are. But what comes first? Is it safety, or is it a question of supplying Kiev with all the power it needs?

VIKTOR. Safety every time. It's the most important thing about the job.

ARTEMIS *finds this funny. He stands up and moves to centre stage. There are, from now on, interludes of what should be almost 'reportage' interwoven with the action, so that what we are seeing is a series of first hand accounts from the characters. This might be reflected in the staging.*

STEFAN *and* ANTON *move to the back of the stage. When* TANYA *joins them* STEFAN *puts his arm around her shoulders. They should be a couple, and indeed a family who – when they are together – are physically close.* VIKTOR *and* NATALIA *move to sit side by side.*

ARTEMIS. Safety. It all began with an experiment to improve safety. Friday 25th April 1986. (*To the audience.*) You should understand – no – you *must* understand that a nuclear reactor consists of fuel rods – big columns of radioactive fuel that react with each other and create energy. There are also control rods. Fewer of them. But enough. If they are inserted between these fuel rods, they damp the whole thing down. Break the chain.

NATALIA (*to* VIKTOR). You shouldn't take any notice of Stefan. He has a bee in his bonnet about the plant. You can hardly blame him.

VIKTOR. But he has nothing to worry about.

ARTEMIS. Besides that the fuel rods have to be kept at a particular temperature. If they overheat – which is of course their natural inclination – they might melt and explode and, believe me, that's no joke. To make sure that this didn't happen, there were pumps which circulated water around the fuel rods. Among other things, to keep them nice and cool.

VIKTOR. I'll be on night shift. I wish I was coming home to you.

NATALIA. Your landlady wouldn't be very pleased if she found me in your bed.

VIKTOR. Old dragon!

NATALIA. She's very fond of you.

Do you think Tanya will be any happier when I come to live here?

ARTEMIS. At Chernobyl, these pumps were worked by electricity from the reactor's own generators. That water had to be kept circulating around the fuel rods at all costs. In case of a sudden emergency – say if these generators failed for whatever reason, and the pumps went off – the reactor had standby diesel generators. But there would be a worrying little gap between loss of power on the one hand and the start-up of those standby diesels.

VIKTOR. Are she and Stefan getting on all right?

NATALIA. Of course they are. But she does worry about him.

VIKTOR. She's bound to. But she must have known what his job would be like when she married him.

NATALIA. It isn't the job. I just don't think she enjoys being here very much.

VIKTOR. Why? It's wonderful. We're bloody privileged to be here . . .

ARTEMIS. A few seconds maybe. But in this industry a few seconds may represent the difference between safety and disaster. Things can get very hot very quickly. So an experiment had been devised with the aim of covering that critical gap.

And that's really all you need to know. For now.

NATALIA. *I* know that. And *you* know that. But . . .

VIKTOR. I suppose Stefan doesn't help. All his daft talk about fires at the plant . . . and stills and . . . overmanning . . . it's bound to unsettle her.

NATALIA. I don't think she's so easily influenced as all that.

VIKTOR. She's bound to be. She lives with the guy.

NATALIA. So she does. What a surprise.

VIKTOR. No I mean – they say married couples start to think like one another.

NATALIA. Should I be worried then?

VIKTOR. What do you mean?

NATALIA. It was a joke Viktor!

VIKTOR. Anyway I thought your Tanya loved her job. She loves working with kids, doesn't she?

NATALIA. She does, but her job has nothing to do with it. It's the plant that frightens her.

VIKTOR. And that *is* Stefan's fault. It's just . . . ignorance.

NATALIA. It's not ignorance. Ignorant is the last thing he is.

VIKTOR. What does he know about it? He's a fireman, not a physicist. He doesn't know what he's talking about. And if she believes him she's as daft as he is.

NATALIA. She knows it's not rational but she has dreams. Bad dreams.

VIKTOR. Oh come on, pull the other one!

NATALIA. I'm serious. She has nightmares. Well, one nightmare in particular . . .

VIKTOR. Don't tell me – it's about the power station.

NATALIA. Actually I think it's much more vague than that.

NATALIA moves back to join ARTEMIS, *as before, and* VIKTOR *also moves to one side, allowing* TANYA *and* STEFAN *to take centre stage.*

TANYA walks forward with STEFAN, *telling him about her dream.*

TANYA. All I know is that you and Anton are in terrible danger. And not just Anton but the wee ones in the school too. The ones I teach. The ones I love. I dream about a door . . .

STEFAN. A door?

TANYA. I'm trying to lock it because there's something dreadful outside, something appalling trying to get in. Something monstrous without shape or form.

STEFAN. But that's the way things are in dreams.

TANYA. Only I can't lock the door. I've lost the key.

STEFAN. That's my Tanya! Always losing your keys!

TANYA. Don't laugh at me Stefan. It isn't funny. I've dropped the key somewhere and then I find that I can't even close the door. It's falling off its hinges. I don't know where you are, but you can't help me. I can't see you. And I'm standing there, trying to hold the door up. Physically hold it up. Trying to keep out . . .

STEFAN. What? What are you trying to keep out?

TANYA. What I can't see or feel.

STEFAN. Then how . . . ?

TANYA. But I can taste it. Does that sound crazy? I can taste it, heavy and metallic on my tongue. So heavy that I can't speak any more. I'm dumb with it. With the taste of it. And the door is so heavy. It isn't an ordinary door at all. It's thick and dense like . . . lead. And I know that there's something or somebody just outside. But the door is no good. It won't help. It won't keep anything out . . .

STEFAN *embraces her, very tenderly.*

STEFAN. I know.

TANYA. But you don't. How can you know?

STEFAN. Because . . . I see your face when you wake up. I see the panic on your face.

TANYA. But there's nothing you can do about it. Can you? It isn't your nightmare.

STEFAN. Well. I've been thinking about that.

TANYA. Nobody takes me seriously. Not even you Stefan.

STEFAN. Oh but I do. I do take you seriously.

TANYA. I don't know if I can carry on like this. It's wearing me down.

STEFAN. You have to go and see the doctor.

TANYA. I've already been.

STEFAN. You never told me.

TANYA. Yes. I went to the doctor. A couple of weeks ago.

STEFAN. And?

TANYA. He prescribed sleeping pills.

STEFAN. He would. Wouldn't he?

TANYA. He didn't even look at my face. I saw him in the town a few days ago and he never even recognised me. Anyway I didn't tell him everything. I was afraid of what he might think.

STEFAN. Have you taken the pills?

TANYA. For a few nights. And I slept. But the dreams went on. They still do.

STEFAN. I know. I do know. I think it's catching.

TANYA. What?

STEFAN. I can't say I'm very happy at the moment either.

TANYA. Oh but that's my fault. Isn't it?

They should be physically very close at this point.

STEFAN. It isn't your fault. Listen. We'll go if you like.

TANYA. Go? Go where?

STEFAN. I've been thinking. I could apply for a transfer. To Kiev if you want.

TANYA (*she is very surprised by this suggestion*). Would that be possible?

STEFAN. More than possible. This is a popular posting.

TANYA. They'd think you were crazy.

STEFAN. So?

TANYA. Would you really? Would you do that for me?

STEFAN. I'd do it for all of us. You, Anton. And for myself.

TANYA (*she wants this so much that she feels the need to argue against it*). But – you wouldn't like the city. I was born to it but you . . . you'd hate it.

STEFAN. I wouldn't mind. I'd get used to it.

TANYA. And what about Anton? All his friends are here. He wouldn't want to move.

STEFAN. Oh I don't know so much. He'd have to go to Kiev in a few years time anyway if he wants to study. He's bright.

TANYA. That's true.

STEFAN. Am I persuading you? Can you think of any more arguments against?

TANYA. It isn't that. I just have to be sure. I have to be sure about you.

STEFAN. I wouldn't mind. Honestly. To tell you the truth I've been thinking about it for a while now . . .

TANYA. Have I done this to you? Is it my fault?

STEFAN. No. I don't think it is you. Or your nightmares.

I'm . . . just not comfortable here any more. That's the truth.

TANYA. Natalia wouldn't be very pleased. She's just moving out here and we . . .

STEFAN. It's the way *you* feel that matters. And Natalia will be fine. After all she's got Viktor. (*He pulls a face.*)

TANYA. Don't.

STEFAN. Fine chap. Or he will be when he grows up a bit.

TANYA. She won't like it. She was counting on us being here. Oh God, and your mother. She'd hate it if you went away.

STEFAN. Will you stop conjuring up obstacles Tanya!

My mother will be all right. She can have sightseeing trips to Kiev. She'll like that.

TANYA. True enough.

STEFAN. Christ, I didn't think I'd have to persuade *you*.

TANYA. You don't. I'm just so relieved that it makes me feel guilty!

STEFAN. Tanya, I have to go to work. You do want me to ask about a transfer then? Get things moving . . .

TANYA. I do. More than anything. Listen, I'll walk with you. I'll walk to the end of the street with you.

They move off to one side, but not offstage. ARTEMIS *and* NATALIA *are still together. During the following exchange,* VIKTOR *should come forward as though irresistibly drawn to* ARTEMIS. *As though he too wants to know what happened.*

NATALIA. Why did it happen?

ARTEMIS. Are you asking me?

NATALIA. I ask everybody. One day somebody may be able to give me a sensible answer.

ARTEMIS. Is that why you volunteered to go inside? Is that why you're here?

NATALIA. Maybe. But then it's a question a scientist must ask all the time, isn't it. Why?

ARTEMIS (*after a pause*). Not just why. But what will happen if . . .

NATALIA. So why didn't they ask it then? They weren't fools. Viktor was no fool.

ARTEMIS. Wasn't he?

NATALIA. An idealist maybe, but no fool. So why didn't he ask it? What will happen if we . . .

ARTEMIS. I'll tell you why. They committed a scientific error and one which – if you're truthful with yourself – is far more common than you scientists would have us believe.

NATALIA. What was this error?

ARTEMIS. Simply that they refused to believe the evidence. They're still refusing to believe the evidence to the point of folly. They demand impossible certainties and so they will always find a way of manipulating the truth.

You know, I visited a little hospital on the outskirts of Kiev once. Not long after the accident. Even then they had already treated thousands of children.

NATALIA. I know the place you mean.

ARTEMIS. It was mostly disorders of the blood: everything from leukaemia to chronic anaemia. Thyroid cancers too. Lots of those.

NATALIA. I know.

ARTEMIS. But there were many illnesses that you don't usually find in children: a great wave of sickness and disability among those who are generally most healthy.

NATALIA. I do know . . .

ARTEMIS. Well do you know how many of those illnesses were due to radiation from the . . . accident?

NATALIA. None of them. At least that's what they told the parents.

ARTEMIS. Exactly. They were all the result of natural causes. Defective genes. Stress and worry and poverty and sometimes even parental paranoia.

NATALIA. The parents didn't believe it.

ARTEMIS. Did the doctors believe it?

NATALIA. Yes and no. We're very practised at believing impossible things here.

ARTEMIS. So you see if they can turn a blind eye to that sort of thing, what can they not bring themselves to ignore? Natural human optimism. The desire to think that everything will be fine. Or perhaps just the exploitation of it.

VIKTOR. You know my mum and dad were really proud of me when I got the job here.

NATALIA. I remember. You don't know how lucky you are. That was what your mum kept saying.

VIKTOR. Nobody else in the family had ever done so well.

NATALIA. It was going to be wonderful. For both of us.

VIKTOR. There were so many safeguards in place. We would never ever compromise on safety. We had high ideals.

NATALIA. I believe you did.

ARTEMIS. But can I explain something to you?

VIKTOR. Go on then . . . since you seem to know so much about it . . .

ARTEMIS. The nuclear industry is like so many others that we have become persuaded are necessary for our welfare . . .

NATALIA. Well maybe they are necessary . . .

ARTEMIS. Maybe. But that isn't the point. What I'm talking about is the dangerous concept of unlikeliness.

VIKTOR. Unlikeliness? What do you mean? There's nothing scientific about that.

ARTEMIS. It's very simple really. You work with potentially dangerous substances. Nuclear power. Poisonous chemicals. Lethal viruses. So how do you handle them?

VIKTOR. It is simple. You follow certain safety procedures . . .

ARTEMIS. Yes. And you are extremely conscientious. And then you assume that certain unfortunate eventualities are unlikely ever to happen.

VIKTOR. But that's true. That's nothing less than the truth.

NATALIA. And perhaps that's what you must do. Otherwise nothing could function, could it?

ARTEMIS. Yes. But what if you then go on to suppose that – given all the safety procedures – these errors are so unlikely to happen that they can safely be ignored.

VIKTOR. This is all speculation. This has nothing to do with what happened.

ARTEMIS. You are, for argument's sake, the director of a nuclear power plant like Chernobyl.

VIKTOR. You'd have a lot on your plate.

ARTEMIS. You would. And safety would be just one of many interlinked factors.

An important one, but nevertheless there would be many other considerations. Wouldn't there, Viktor? Economic. Political. To name but two.

VIKTOR. And sometimes they conflict with one another. That's true.

ARTEMIS. So how do you sleep at nights?

NATALIA. I'll tell you what you do. You have to be realistic. You make sure everything is as safe as it possibly can be.

ARTEMIS. Yes, of course you do. Within certain parameters. (*To* VIKTOR.) You even conduct experiments to increase the safety margins. And you feel very pleased with yourself. But then, you decide that some things are so very unlikely to happen that they can safely be ignored. It makes you a bit uneasy, but you can live with it. Besides, you have to get on with the economics and the politics and all the other things you're expected to handle . . .

VIKTOR. As you said.

ARTEMIS. First you persuade yourself of this unlikeliness. Then you can set about persuading other people. And because you genuinely believe it, you are very persuasive indeed. You have covered all eventualities, the unthinkable can't possibly happen now, and so you realise that it would be a waste of time and resources to plan for it happening. So you don't.

VIKTOR. That's nonsense.

ARTEMIS. Is it? Are you absolutely sure Viktor?

NATALIA. And if it should happen? What then? If you haven't even planned for it . . .

ARTEMIS. Ah, you've got it exactly. The fatal flaw in the argument. Because you see, if it should happen, not only will you not know what to do. You will not even know what to think. And worse than that, much worse, if it should even *begin* to happen, neither you, nor your colleagues, will notice until it is much too late to do anything about it.

NATALIA. And you think that's what happened here?

ARTEMIS. Here and other places too. Many other places. I know it. I was here. I saw . . .

NATALIA *stares at* ARTEMIS *in horrified surprise.*

ARTEMIS *tells this smartly, matter of factly, as a report. But also as though interrogating* VIKTOR. VIKTOR, *by contrast, is obviously remembering, confused and moved by his own words. This should be very much a first hand account.* VIKTOR *is living it in his own mind, and we live it with him. There should be a sense of reportage, of 'interview' about it. If anything it is* ARTEMIS *who moves about, rather than* VIKTOR, *who is perhaps pinned down by lights,* ARTEMIS *who demonstrates,* VIKTOR *who remembers and recalls and relives and* NATALIA *relives this with him, increasingly horrified.*

ARTEMIS. Preparations for the experiment began on Friday at 1 a.m. when operators started to reduce the reactor's power output.

VIKTOR. It would take twelve hours to reach half power safely. Safety was paramount. I've told you. But I wasn't on that shift.

ARTEMIS. You weren't on that shift. So by 2 p.m. on Friday it was at half power and the operators then on duty were ready to start their experiment.

VIKTOR. But they didn't.

ARTEMIS. Why not?

NATALIA. He wasn't on duty. He wouldn't know!

VIKTOR. I wasn't on duty. But there had been a phonecall from the controller in Kiev. I heard about it when I came on shift later that evening. He was in a bit of a flap . . . but that was nothing unusual.

ARTEMIS. What did Kiev want?

VIKTOR. They wanted number four reactor to keep on feeding the national grid. The city needed power. It wasn't unusual. Things like that were always happening.

ARTEMIS. *Always* happening?

VIKTOR. I mean the system was under pressure like that. All the time. You didn't argue. You just gave them what they wanted. They had priority. It was no big deal.

ARTEMIS. So the experiment was postponed.

VIKTOR. Until later that night. When I came on shift they were already reducing power again. There was an automatic control. It should have maintained the reactor at a safe power level. But . . .

ARTEMIS. But . . . ?

VIKTOR. They had switched it off.

ARTEMIS. Which was, was it not, a safety violation.

VIKTOR. I'm afraid it was, yes.

ARTEMIS. It was a major safety violation.

VIKTOR. You see if the power falls too low, the reactor can become very unstable.

NATALIA. But you were a new shift . . .

VIKTOR. Nobody noticed. Nobody noticed that the previous shift had switched the control off. I suppose they wanted to hurry things along a bit. What with the delay and all that. You know?

ARTEMIS. So what happened next was due to that oversight?

NATALIA. What did happen next?

VIKTOR. At about midnight the power in the reactor took a sudden dive. Too far too fast.

ARTEMIS. And?

VIKTOR. Well it wasn't serious you know.

ARTEMIS. No big deal either?

VIKTOR. There was no panic or anything. We could control it. But it meant that we couldn't carry on with the experiment. Not then.

NATALIA. Of course not. You would have to try to push the power up again. Wouldn't you?

VIKTOR. Mm.

ARTEMIS. So what did you do?

VIKTOR. Withdrew more control rods. It was a recognised procedure for stabilising the reactor.

NATALIA (to ARTEMIS). It was, you know.

ARTEMIS. Yes, of course. But how many control rods did that leave in the reactor?

VIKTOR. I should say, well, fewer than thirty.

ARTEMIS. Which was less than the minimum number required to keep it stable. A lot less.

VIKTOR. I suppose so. But we thought we were doing the right thing. Our minds were all on the experiment.

ARTEMIS. Ah yes. The safety experiment. So what did you do next? Well?

VIKTOR. We tried to increase steam pressure. That ought to have forced the power up a bit more.

ARTEMIS. And did it?

VIKTOR. Not really. Actually, there was a sudden surge of water and that – well in fact – that *cooled* the reactor.

NATALIA. But that would mean that even more of the control rods were withdrawn!

VIKTOR. Yes. That happened automatically. We couldn't stop it.

NATALIA. Oh dear God, dear God!

ARTEMIS. Tell me Viktor. Had any of you remembered just what you were dealing with here?

VIKTOR. I don't understand you.

ARTEMIS. Were you panicking at this point?

VIKTOR. We were – worried. We were still worried about the experiment. You see we didn't have much time.

ARTEMIS. That's true.

VIKTOR. No. No, I mean in the early morning there would be a great demand for power.

NATALIA. From Kiev.

VIKTOR. The reactor must be back on an even keel by then. But I admit, I was a bit alarmed to see how few control rods were left in the core.

ARTEMIS. A bit alarmed?

VIKTOR. We reduced the supply of water to the reactor again. I remember doing that. And then as a result of that some of the control rods fell back into the core. Which was what we wanted.

ARTEMIS. Tell us – How many control rods were actually in the core at this time Viktor?

VIKTOR. Fewer than fifteen.

ARTEMIS. How many exactly? You must have a good idea.

VIKTOR. Er . . .

ARTEMIS. Speak up!

VIKTOR. Maybe . . . er . . . eight?

ARTEMIS. Maybe as few as six?

VIKTOR. Maybe. I didn't count them. There wasn't time.

NATALIA. Jesus Christ! Fewer than six.

ARTEMIS. That was at 1.21 a.m. precisely I think.

VIKTOR. I suppose so.

ARTEMIS. At 1.22 the computer in the control room went berserk. It printed out a great mass of data. Did nobody see this happening?

VIKTOR. But it happened quite often.

ARTEMIS. So nobody took much notice of it?

VIKTOR. We ignored it. There was too much going on. And not everybody . . .

ARTEMIS. I said speak up!

VIKTOR. Not everybody in the control room could have interpreted it anyway.

NATALIA. Why not? Why on earth not? Even then you could have stopped it.

VIKTOR. Not everybody had the necessary skills.

ARTEMIS. But if someone had. Someone like you for instance?

VIKTOR. Yes. I had those skills. But I was otherwise occupied.

ARTEMIS. If you had not been otherwise occupied, it would have shown you that the reactor must be shut down immediately. That was what the computer was trying to tell you. The computer itself was panicking, even if you weren't.

VIKTOR. But it was unthinkable . . .

ARTEMIS. Ah yes. But the unthinkable was about to happen. You couldn't comprehend that. Could you?

VIKTOR. Nobody had ever . . . there were so many safe-guards . . . it couldn't happen. We knew it couldn't happen. We had been told . . .

ARTEMIS. You all thought the reactor had stabilised.

VIKTOR. It did. We thought we had everything under control. It definitely stabilised. I'd swear to it.

ARTEMIS. For perhaps thirty seconds.

VIKTOR. Yes.

ARTEMIS. You gave it thirty seconds.

NATALIA. You weren't prepared to wait? Why couldn't you wait?

VIKTOR. But we had to begin the safety experiment.

ARTEMIS. So that was what you did.

VIKTOR. Yes. We began the experiment.

ARTEMIS. So what exactly did you do?

VIKTOR. We decreased the flow of cooling water to the reactor.

ARTEMIS. You decreased the flow of cooling water. And what happened then Viktor?

VIKTOR. The temperature at the core rose. Very suddenly.

ARTEMIS. It certainly did. In one second it went to 100 times full power. Then 440 times full power. You did panic then, didn't you?

VIKTOR. We all panicked. Somebody pressed the emergency button.

ARTEMIS. He was trying to drop all the control rods into the core at once. All 205 of them. He was trying to shut down the reactor.

VIKTOR. Yes.

ARTEMIS. At last.

VIKTOR. Yes. But . . .

ARTEMIS. But . . .

VIKTOR. They stuck. But it was too late anyway. There was no time . . .

There is a pause, as though they are frozen in that moment.

Then STEFAN *comes forward slowly.* ARTEMIS *turns to him.*

STEFAN. What will happen if . . . what will happen if . . .

ARTEMIS. The radioactive fuel rods were now red hot. They began to disintegrate into powder and fragments and broke through the outer channels where they encountered . . .

STEFAN. Water.

ARTEMIS. Exactly. You would know. Wouldn't you? Water.

STEFAN *turns to his wife.*

STEFAN. I never saw it. Tanya saw it. But she didn't know what she was seeing.

TANYA. Like fireworks. Catherine wheels made out of stars that rose in the night sky and fell . . .

STEFAN. You could have poured a whole lake on to it and it wouldn't have been enough . . .

ARTEMIS. The explosion lifted the lid off the reactor core. When I say lid, I mean a one thousand tonne steel lid, seventeen metres across and three metres thick. It fell into the vault below and ruptured all the fuel rod channels at once.

VIKTOR. I don't remember.

ARTEMIS. No. Of course you don't remember. There was an explosion that broke through the floor, walls, roof of the building. The radioactive core was exposed to the air and a second explosion followed. A fireball burst over the reactor core. Nine tonnes of radioactive material shot up into the night sky like so many missiles.

The safety experiment was at an end.

End of Act One.

ACT TWO

The playpark as before, but darker. There are shadows from which the characters emerge, weaving the story as in a kind of pattern.

NATALIA *and* ARTEMIS *are sitting or standing to one side.* ANTON *and* STEFAN *to the other.* VIKTOR *is to the rear.* TANYA *is seated.* STEFAN *comes towards her, buttoning up the jacket of his fireman's uniform. He has been changing for work.* TANYA *looks up. She gestures to* STEFAN *who comes closer. She straightens his jacket. It is an intimate and yet habitual gesture.*

TANYA. You'd better get a move on.

STEFAN. Is Anton asleep yet?

TANYA. I think so.

STEFAN. I said I'd try and help him with his project and I never did.

TANYA. It'll just have to wait. There's plenty of time. It doesn't have to be in till next week.

STEFAN. All the same . . .

TANYA. Don't go in please. You know what a light sleeper he is . . .

STEFAN. All right. I'll see him tomorrow. Have you mentioned Kiev to him yet?

TANYA. Sort of.

STEFAN. What do you mean, sort of?

TANYA. I told him it was a possibility. It wasn't certain yet. Just that we were thinking about it.

STEFAN. And?

TANYA. He was quite grown up. Surprised me. Said he didn't think *you'd* like the city much, but he would.

STEFAN. I told you so.

TANYA. Then he said what about Sooty, and I said we'd take her with us of course. But we'd have to butter her paws.

STEFAN. Butter her paws?

TANYA. It's what you're supposed to do.

STEFAN. Why for God's sake?

TANYA. I think they lick it off and get the scent of the new place with it or something.

STEFAN. Doesn't everything get covered in butter?

TANYA. I don't know. Maybe. Maybe she'd be better off here. We could leave her with your mother.

STEFAN. That's the least of our worries.

TANYA. Anton hasn't asked me why yet. But he will. Stefan, are you sure?

STEFAN. Sure I'm sure. Why? Are you beginning to have doubts?

TANYA. No. None at all.

STEFAN. So what will you say to him? When he does ask why, it'll be you he asks. He talks more to you than he ever does to me.

TANYA. I'll tell him the truth.

STEFAN. And what is the truth?

TANYA. That we don't feel . . . comfortable here any more.

STEFAN. Unsettled. That's what I feel like. A cat with buttered paws. Is there any coffee for the morning?

TANYA. A bit. I'll save it for you. It'll only keep me awake. Mind you, I've got more marking to do . . .

STEFAN. You have it. I don't mind.

TANYA. No. It gives me nightmares.

STEFAN *kisses her affectionately. She responds to him, beginning to unbutton the jacket again.*

STEFAN. You and your nightmares. Oh Christ don't. I have to go to work Tanya.

TANYA. We never seem to get any time together these days.

STEFAN. Listen. Don't you stay up too late. Take a tablet if you have to.

TANYA. I can't. I put them in the bin.

STEFAN. Did you?

TANYA. I don't need them. I don't have any trouble *sleeping*.

STEFAN. Well it won't be for much longer.

TANYA. Thank God.

STEFAN. Natalia asleep too?

TANYA. She wanted an early night. Anyway, Viktor's on night shift.

STEFAN. Have you told her yet?

TANYA. I will. I had to tell Anton first.

STEFAN. She'll think we're mad.

TANYA. I know.

STEFAN. And as for Viktor . . .

TANYA. You can cope with Viktor's disapproval can't you!

STEFAN. I should hope so. (*He kisses her again.*) I'm only sorry I'm not coming to bed.

TANYA. Can't you just . . . ?

STEFAN. No. I can't just. I'll be late for my shift. Not that it would make much difference . . . We're so quiet.

TANYA. Touch wood. Take care now.

STEFAN. Don't worry.

Let's go down to the lake tomorrow afternoon? You and me and Anton.

TANYA. All right. Will I see if Natalia and Viktor want to come?

STEFAN. No. Just us eh?

TANYA. All right.

STEFAN. And we can talk. Make some plans.

TANYA. Just us then! See you tomorrow. Take care.

STEFAN. I will.

He exits. TANYA *moves across the stage to* ARTEMIS *and* NATALIA, *taking up the story.* ANTON *and* VIKTOR *are in the shadows.*

TANYA. I saw it. I saw it happening, but I didn't know what I was seeing. The marking took longer than I thought. I was drawing the curtains before I went to bed when I noticed a strange light in the sky. Like the lume of some great city. Except that it came and went. They said afterwards there were explosions. I didn't hear them but then I had been listening to music and I think the music was still playing, a counterpoint to what I found myself watching.

What I saw was very beautiful. It was like some celestial fireworks display. Catherine wheels made out of great big stars that rose in the night sky and fell. I thought it was a natural phenomenon. I even thought Anton and Natalia ought to see it.

NATALIA *and* ANTON *come forward to join her.*

TANYA. Something's happening. Come and see.

ANTON. Wow. What do you think it could be?

TANYA (*to her sister*). Do you know?

NATALIA. I haven't got the faintest idea.

ANTON. You're the scientist Talia. You should know.

NATALIA. I'm not an astronomer.

ANTON. It's like fireworks, isn't it?

TANYA. It's very bright. I suppose it could be the aurora. Or a comet.

NATALIA. I don't think so.

ANTON. Or a meteor shower.

TANYA. No. I've seen those before. Your dad and I stayed up for a whole night once, watching a meteor shower.

ANTON. When?

TANYA. It was before you were born. Anyway, it was nothing like this.

ANTON. UFO's maybe!

TANYA. Don't be daft.

NATALIA. Look. It's dying down.

ANTON. Just a wee trail of smoke in the sky.

TANYA (*suddenly uneasy*). Smoke?

ANTON. Over there.

TANYA. Come on Anton. You should be back in bed. School tomorrow.

ANTON. It's too hot in there. I'll never get back to sleep.

TANYA. Open the window then. Off you go.

He moves back to one of the benches and sits down.

NATALIA. I wonder what it was.

TANYA. I don't know. I wish I hadn't woken him up now. He'll be ages getting back to sleep.

NATALIA. So will I. Do you want some tea?

TANYA. No thanks.

NATALIA. Are you alright?

TANYA. I think so. At first I thought it was beautiful but now . . .

NATALIA. You always did have a vivid imagination . . .

TANYA. So did you. Do you remember, I used to make up stories for you at bedtime and mum used to go mad because you could never get to sleep afterwards!

NATALIA. I remember! I'll bet you used to do the same thing to Anton.

TANYA. No. It was me he kept awake if he was frightened. I think I'll go and close his window.

NATALIA. Leave it . . . You fuss over him too much.

TANYA. Do I?

NATALIA. You're always worrying about something. You've lost weight.

TANYA. I know I have.

NATALIA. You let things get you down. Never mind. You'll be better when I'm living here. I won't let you worry.

TANYA. Talia . . .

NATALIA. What?

TANYA. There's something I have to tell you.

NATALIA. What's the matter?

TANYA. I've been trying to tell you for a few days now . . .

NATALIA. Tell me what? What's wrong? Are you really ill?

TANYA. No. I'm not ill. Nothing's wrong. It's just that we may not be living here for too much longer.

NATALIA. You may not . . . You're not splitting up are you?

TANYA. No, nothing like that. But Stefan's applied for a posting in Kiev. We'll be leaving as soon as we can.

NATALIA. Leaving? Has he gone mad?

TANYA. No. He hasn't gone mad.

NATALIA. But nobody leaves here. Nobody in their right mind leaves here!

TANYA. Then maybe we are mad. But we're leaving all the same.

NATALIA. I don't know what to say.

TANYA. You could wish us luck.

NATALIA (*on the verge of tears*). How can I? I don't. I don't want you to go.

You did this didn't you Tanya? You persuaded him to leave.

TANYA. It was entirely his idea . . .

NATALIA. Naturally he'd say it was. But he'd only do it because he was so worried about you. I can't believe you'd be so selfish. I can't believe you'd do this to him! And to me!

TANYA. Oh Natalia! Don't be like this . . .

NATALIA. Like what? I had it all planned out. Me and Viktor, you and Stefan and Anton . . . It was going to be so . . . so nice. Oh you don't really have to go do you? He could change his mind. It isn't too late!

TANYA. We're not going to change our minds.

NATALIA. But what will I do?

TANYA. You'll have Viktor. You won't need me.

NATALIA. Yes I will. I will need you. More than ever.

TANYA. You'll be married. You'll have your own flat. Your own life to lead. Maybe your own children . . .

NATALIA. Yes but . . . why? Why must you go? It won't do Stefan's career any good at all. Or yours for that matter.

TANYA. Living here isn't doing me any good at all.

NATALIA. Oh it's all nonsense. Can't you see you're worrying about nothing. Nothing! It's so foolish. And to uproot yourselves, all because of . . .

TANYA. Dreams. Nightmares . . . But when they begin to take over your life then perhaps it's time to make a change . . .

NATALIA. How do you know it won't be the same in Kiev?

TANYA. It won't. (*Embracing her.*) I know you're disappointed. But you'll get used to it.

NATALIA. No I won't. And Anton will hate it. He'll be leaving all his friends.

TANYA. Anton's already looking forward to it. We all are. And you can visit us.

NATALIA. But that's not the point . . .

TANYA. Then what is?

NATALIA. It was the whole thing . . . I wanted the whole thing . . . I wanted all of us here together . . . a family.

TANYA. I know. I do know.

NATALIA. You don't. And I can't explain. It just won't be the same. It won't be the same without you . . . you won't be there when I need you.

TANYA. Of course I will. Kiev isn't that far away.

NATALIA. You won't be there when I need you.

TANYA. We're both tired. Let's talk about it in the morning.

NATALIA. All right. Let's talk about it in the morning.

They move to either side of the stage, TANYA *to join* ANTON. NATALIA *comes face to face with* ARTEMIS *but finds it hard to look at him.*

ARTEMIS. Why would it not have been the same without Tanya?

NATALIA (*preoccupied*). She was my sister. We were close . . .

ARTEMIS. You were going to be married. Most people are quite glad to get away from their families.

NATALIA. I know. But don't you see? I'd pictured us all together. Suddenly it was going to be just me and Viktor. I hadn't allowed for that. I hadn't planned for it at all . . . I was stunned and I think I was . . . afraid. You see all my plans had included Tanya and Stefan.

ARTEMIS. So what *did* you do?

NATALIA. I went to bed. But I couldn't sleep for a long time. I kept seeing me and Viktor, with our nice flat and our car and our summer cottage. Just the two of us . . .

Anyway, the next day was Saturday. Tanya was working in the morning. Anton would be going to school too. But I knew that I could sleep in. Stefan wouldn't be home till later.

ARTEMIS. Ah yes. Stefan. He would have been there in the middle of it all, wouldn't he?

But you didn't know it. Not then.

STEFAN *walks to the centre of the stage. He is still dressed in his fireman's uniform but it looks more shabby and dishevelled and his face is grimy. He turns and talks to* ARTEMIS, *gradually becoming more distressed and more lost in what he is describing. Again this is reportage, again, like* VIKTOR, STEFAN *is transfixed by the light, lost in his own past. During the following,* VIKTOR *also comes forward, listening, fascinated and at last driven to comment.*

ARTEMIS. Tell us what happened on the morning of Saturday 26th April 1986.

STEFAN. We arrived at the reactor at 1.35 a.m. We were on night shift in the town. There was a crew stationed at the power plant. They had heard the explosion and were already on the scene.

ARTEMIS. But you were there very soon after.

STEFAN. We were there very quickly. Our lieutenant took a search team into the building. I was one of them. We were told that the reactor core was burning. But we could see that for ourselves.

I mean there was this weird kind of luminous light, coming from the central hall. I've never seen anything like it in my life. It wasn't like an ordinary fire at all. We didn't need to be told. We could see it for ourselves. We knew that the only thing that could be burning like that – with that crazy light – was the reactor core itself.

Our commanding officer was on leave from the station. He could have stayed away but he came back immediately. He was a brave man.

ARTEMIS. Not just a fool?

STEFAN. No. No more than any of us. He stood by us. That has to count for something. There were only twenty-eight of us at that point. It was all an unknown quantity.

ARTEMIS. There had been fires at the plant before.

STEFAN. Fires yes. But nothing like this. Never anything like this.

ARTEMIS. So how did you tackle it? There was no point in pouring water on to the core was there?

STEFAN. Water? It would just have vaporised.

You could have poured a whole bloody lake on to it and it wouldn't have been enough. But the structures above the core were blazing too and there were three other reactors on site. The blaze could have spread to them. So we knew we had to control those fires first. Forget the reactor for the moment. Except that you couldn't forget it. It was there. It filled your mind. Like some monster. Like a dragon. And you know what? It was so fucking beautiful! You couldn't keep your eyes off it!

ARTEMIS. So how did you control the fire in the building?

STEFAN. Some men tried to work from the ground. Only they were being showered with radioactive graphite all the time. Some of us went up on the roof of the turbine building. I was one of them. There were clouds of poisonous gas up there as well as radioactive dust. And the heat was shocking. (*He pauses, remembering.*) We realised after a while that the roof was made of fucking bitumen.

ARTEMIS. Another safety oversight.

STEFAN (*until now he has been almost matter of fact in his description, but now he is angry*). The roof . . . as we were walking . . . the fucking roof was melting under our feet.

ARTEMIS. Did you have any real idea of the danger you were in?

STEFAN. Of course we fucking knew. I'm sorry. I'm sorry. Well, at first, for a moment or two after we got there, we thought it might just be a fire. Like any other fire. But we had a radiation meter with us. And that told us all we needed to know. I saw the operator's face. I saw what he was seeing. It had gone right off the end of the fucking scale. You've no idea what it was like. No idea.

ARTEMIS. And you? Did you stay?

STEFAN. I stayed.

ARTEMIS. That was very heroic of you.

STEFAN. Heroic? It was bloody stupid I know that.

ARTEMIS. Somebody had to do it.

STEFAN. Aye. Somebody had to do it. Some poor sod. You know I thought I was all right at first. Your mind can't really take it in. You think, I'll be fine. I can handle it. That wee optimistic bit of you that thinks it's indestructible. I stayed on for a long time. We were replaced at 4 a.m. The roof and building fires were almost under control by then. So there was no danger of it spreading to the other reactors.

ARTEMIS. And what did they do with those other reactors, Stefan?

STEFAN. The other building? I don't know. I was too busy to find out.

VIKTOR. I know. I know what they would do. I know what they did.

ARTEMIS. Of course you do Viktor.

VIKTOR. They would have to keep Reactors One and Two in operation. Different building. Same site.

ARTEMIS. And how would they do that Viktor? How would they manage to staff the building, in the circumstances?

VIKTOR. They would have to switch off the radiation meters and let the workers come in.

STEFAN. The bastards.

VIKTOR. It's what they would have to do.

ARTEMIS. The workers weren't fools. Somebody would demand an explanation, surely. A reason why the meters were switched off.

VIKTOR. The management would just tell them the meters weren't working. They would say that the explosion had affected them. That's what they would have to do.

STEFAN. The fucking bastards.

VIKTOR. You see they needed the power. They still need the power.

ARTEMIS. In Kiev.

STEFAN (*wearily*). In Kiev. Yes. I suppose they did. I suppose they do.

He and VIKTOR *move back together, leaving centre stage free for* TANYA *who comes forward.*

TANYA. The next morning we had to be in school. Saturday mornings are school mornings. We always left before Stefan was due home from the fire station. When he'd been on Friday nightshift I mean. He would get his own breakfast – just bread – and coffee if we had any – and then he'd sleep. If Natalia was staying with us he'd make her a cup of tea or coffee and take it in to her. I hadn't slept well and I woke up very early.

I went downstairs and outside with the rubbish. It was going to be a lovely day. Blossom on the trees. Spring flowers in the gardens. I thought I might pick some and leave them on the table for Stefan to see when he came in. The sun was up and it was quite warm. But there was a strange heavy feeling in the air. It's hard to explain. At first I thought there had been a frost in the night but it was too warm for frost. There was a little garden outside the block of flats and they had planted roses. The new glossy leaves had this fine white powder on them. Like ash. I touched it. Something else. No birds were singing. None at all.

And then as I was standing by the bins I felt my face beginning to tingle. As though it was raining. You know when you're out in winter and the rain is almost snow, but not quite, and it hurts your skin? It felt like that. There was no smell. But my eyes began to water. And the taste . . . I could taste metal on my tongue, and it brought all those dreams back to me. Dreams about trying to keep something out. Except that this was just an ordinary spring day.

I was afraid. Like an animal. I had this sudden terrible fear. I put my rubbish in the bin and then I went back inside and as I went, I found myself running. Faster and faster up the stairs. And when I slammed the door of the apartment behind me, my heart was pounding.

She is now back beside the bench.

I didn't know what to do. I calmed down enough to phone the fire station. I thought if there was anything wrong, Stefan would know. But Stefan wasn't there. I spoke to one of his colleagues. A woman who works in the office. I knew her. Not well, but we'd met a couple of times.

She said there had been an accident at the power station, but that she didn't think it was too serious. Only I should listen to the radio. That would give me more information. I turned the radio on and they were playing music. Soft soothing music. So I said to the woman, I said was it anything to do with what we had seen the night before. The fireworks and all that. And there was this long pause and then she said no. She didn't think so. But perhaps I ought not to go out that morning. Perhaps we shouldn't go to the school. Just in case. She wouldn't be sending her own children to school. And then she said, you have relatives in Kiev, don't you? Just that, nothing more. And the tone of her voice – I don't know – it worried me.

I thought about Viktor. He'd be able to tell me. So I phoned the plant. But I couldn't get through there. All the lines seemed to be engaged. And I didn't want to call my mother in Kiev. I didn't want to worry her. And then Natalia woke up and came through.

NATALIA *comes forward to join* TANYA. TANYA *is torn between real worry and the desire not to alarm* NATALIA *too much.*

NATALIA. What's the matter? Who have you been phoning?

TANYA. I was trying to speak to Stefan.

NATALIA. Why? He'll be home soon.

TANYA. I couldn't get through to him. He isn't there.

NATALIA. Maybe he's out on a call.

TANYA. They won't say. I think something's happened at the plant. An accident of some sort.

NATALIA. An accident?

TANYA. Nothing serious. They say it's nothing serious.

NATALIA. Another fire in a paint store maybe.

TANYA. Maybe.

NATALIA. I'll phone Viktor. He'll still be there. He'll be able to tell us.

TANYA. I've tried Viktor as well. I can't get through there either.

NATALIA. Can't you?

TANYA. It's always engaged. I did get somebody at the fire station though. She sounded strange. She said we shouldn't go to school today.

NATALIA. Why not?

TANYA. I don't know. She wouldn't say. I don't know what to do!

NATALIA. It can't be anything too bad or we'd have heard.

TANYA. Would we?

NATALIA. Of course we would. Have you tried the radio?

TANYA. There's nothing on. Just music.

I went out to the dustbin a while ago and it didn't . . . it didn't feel right.

NATALIA. What do you mean it didn't feel right?

TANYA. I don't know. I could feel something. I could taste something. I was so frightened . . .

NATALIA. Calm down. You're getting all worked up about nothing.

TANYA. I ought to go to work, you know. Ought to be in school. I should warn the other kids. And their parents.

NATALIA. Warn them about what?

TANYA. I don't know. I'm going out again . . . I have to find out . . .

NATALIA. Where? It's too early for school . . .

TANYA. Just for a walk. Just for a look around.

NATALIA. I'll come with you.

TANYA. No. I'll go. If Anton wakes up tell him I've gone to the early market for bread. Maybe Stefan will be home by the time I come back.

ARTEMIS. Stefan? You didn't go home that morning, did you?

STEFAN (*coming forward into the light, but separate from* TANYA). Home? I wasn't in any condition to go home. I didn't know it but I didn't have a home to go to. Not any more. Oh it was there all right. It's still there. But it's contaminated. Everything from the furniture to the kid's toys, poisoned.

And we weren't allowed to telephone. I was going frantic about Tanya and Anton. Until that moment I'd been too busy to think about them.

We were taken to hospital. But we couldn't rest. We knew it wasn't finished. We knew something had to be done. They were afraid of a meltdown. We all were. We talked about it all the time. What to do. But we didn't know. We were so afraid of a meltdown.

TANYA (*their voices overlapping with each other, like a chorus, while they remain separated*). I went outside and I walked in the direction of the power station. I couldn't go by the normal road because I saw that there were soldiers, blocking the way. So I went down a little side road I knew. And then suddenly I was right in front of Number Four Reactor. Or where the building used to be. I mean it was some distance away – a few hundred metres perhaps. And what was left of it was on fire. Only it wasn't like any fire I'd ever seen before.

STEFAN. It wasn't like an ordinary fire at all. It was a monster. A dragon . . . But it was fucking beautiful. I know that . . .

TANYA. The flames were very beautiful: red, green, yellow, blue. So many colours. Colours I had neither seen nor imagined. They were swaying and moving quite slowly and I stood there, transfixed, watching them. I don't know how long I stood there. And it seemed as it had the night before. It seemed like a natural phenomenon. Totally normal and natural. As if this was exactly what it should be doing. It was me that was wrong. Intrusive.

STEFAN. As if this was exactly what it should be doing. And we shouldn't be there. We didn't belong any more. We had absolutely no resources to deal with this. We were like little kids, playing with matches.

TANYA. There was something sensual, something wholly enticing about it.

STEFAN. It obliterated everything else. It changed everything. You knew that after this, nothing would ever be the same again. And yet you couldn't keep your eyes away from it.

TANYA. I watched and watched. Captivated, enraptured by it. And then I thought 'It's on fire'. I mean I knew that. I could see it. But until then the enormity of it had filled my mind. I couldn't think of anything else. And then I thought 'It's on fire' and I remembered Stefan. I realised that Stefan must be there too. Trying to deal with this. Doing his job.

STEFAN. How could we deal with this dragon? How could anybody deal with it? Why hadn't they told us what it would be like?

TANYA. And the thought of Stefan in there was so awful and there was so little I could do about it, that I just pushed it away. My mind slipped into gear again and I remembered Anton and my sister. I had to get my son and my sister out. Away from this monster.

She has moved back towards NATALIA *and* ANTON.

ANTON. Where have you been? We were worried about you mum. What's wrong?

NATALIA. Tanya . . .

TANYA. We have to go. We have to go to Kiev. Now.

ANTON. But what about school?

TANYA. We're not going to school. Neither of us. Listen. Natalia, can you help him to pack. Get a holdall and pack some clothes . . . not too much. We can't carry too much. I'll have to write a note for Stefan . . . tell him where we've gone . . .

NATALIA. Tanya . . . what is all this? What's happened?

TANYA. There's been an accident at the plant. What we saw last night was . . . we have to go now.

NATALIA. But what about Stefan . . . and Viktor . . . ? Oh Lord, I should go to the plant. I can't just leave. I have to speak to him . . .

TANYA. They won't let you anywhere near it. The streets are full of soldiers.

NATALIA. But how can we just leave?

TANYA. We have to. We're going to Kiev and you have to come with us. We'll be safe there. Safer. I'll leave a note for Stefan . . .

Oh God why can't I ever find a pen or a pencil in this house?

ANTON. But I don't understand. Why can't you just phone him mum?

TANYA. Because I can't. Because he isn't there. Look, will you go and pack!

NATALIA. Come on. You won't need much. Just a holdall.

ANTON. What about Sooty? We can't leave her. She hasn't come home yet.

TANYA (*controlling her distress with a visible effort*). Your dad will be home soon. Sooty'll be fine. He'll look after her. Now go! Go!

NATALIA *and* ANTON *move to one side.*

TANYA. The cat had been out all night. She never came home that morning. And Anton would keep going on about her.

I left a note for Stefan . . . he always went into the kitchen first when he came off night shift. So I left it in there. I suppose it's still there. In the kitchen, propped up beside the coffee pot. I can't remember what I wrote. Love Tanya. I know I put 'love Tanya'.

TANYA *and* ANTON *move together.* NATALIA *resumes the narrative, remembering what happened, telling* ARTEMIS.

ARTEMIS. So you left this place. You tried to get away.

NATALIA. We packed a couple of bags and went to the railway station. Tanya's fear was infectious. But in a way, I knew more than she did. Even then I think I was aware of the awful possibilities.

ARTEMIS. And you were afraid.

NATALIA. I was terrified. But trying not to panic for their sake. And I think they were doing the same for mine. We were trying to protect each other. And we didn't want to think about Viktor and Stefan at all. We walked to the station and the bags seemed very heavy. There were a lot of other people, all heading in the same direction. The station was full of people milling about and there was an empty train on the platform.

ANTON. I'll bet we'll have to stand all the way.

TANYA. Never mind. At least we're here . . .

NATALIA. At last they let us on. But it got very crowded, very quickly, and the three of us were all squashed up together.

She moves over and sits beside ANTON *and* TANYA.

STEFAN. Nobody would tell us what was happening. We kept asking what was going to happen? Would they evacuate people? What about our families? Our children? What had they been told? Nobody seemed to know. Or if they did they weren't telling *us*. I managed to get to a phone. Tried to phone Tanya. But there was no reply. I hoped they hadn't gone to school. I had been willing her to take Anton and Natalia and just leave. I hoped they were all on their way to Kiev. At least they had somewhere to go.

TANYA. Oh God. Why have we stopped?

NATALIA. It's the reactor, isn't it? Is this what you looked at? Is this it?

ANTON. That's some fire!

TANYA. Don't look at it.

ANTON. But I want to see it.

TANYA. You mustn't.

ANTON. Do you think Dad's there? Trying to fight that.

TANYA. Do as I say. Close your eyes. Get under the seat and don't even look at it!

ANTON. Oh mum!

NATALIA. She's right Anton. You mustn't look at it. You stay there until we move again.

TANYA. Don't move! Do you hear me now! Don't you dare move!

ARTEMIS. And it came to pass that he said escape for thy life. Look not behind thee, nor stay thou in all the plain. Escape to the mountain lest thou be consumed . . .

NATALIA *stands up and moves back towards* ARTEMIS.

NATALIA. . . . But Lot's wife looked back from behind him and she became a pillar of salt.

We were there beside the burning reactor for perhaps five minutes.

My mouth was very dry, I remember that. I badly wanted a drink: tea, water, anything. We had nothing. I had to keep moistening my lips with my tongue. I tried hard not to look out of the window but it drew your gaze. There was this impetus to see. To become part of it. Absorbed in it.

Then suddenly the train jerked and moved on again and after that it picked up a bit of speed. But it took a long time to get to Kiev all the same.

STEFAN. Nobody would tell us anything. Nobody seemed to *know* anything . . .

NATALIA. Outside the station we queued for a taxi – there was a long queue and we had to wait. There were some boys just hanging about. They began to jeer at us, laughing and pointing. And that was when I looked at Tanya and saw . . . Anton and I both saw . . .

TANYA. Why are they laughing at us? What's wrong with us?

ARTEMIS *begins to laugh, quietly, but gradually growing louder.*

ANTON. Nothing. There's nothing the matter mum.

TANYA. Are you sure?

NATALIA. It's all right. Let's just get home.

ANTON. Where will dad be now? Will he have got our note do you think?

TANYA. I'm sure he will.

I wish they wouldn't do that. It's so rude.

NATALIA. They're just stupid . . . ignore them.

TANYA. There's nothing wrong with us, is there?

NATALIA. No. We just look a bit scruffy with travelling. Come on. The queue's moving. Soon be home.

ANTON. Will Dad come to Kiev tonight do you think?

TANYA. I expect he'll come as soon as he can. But he'll be busy. You've seen what it was like. He can't just leave can he? He'll have to make sure the fire's out, have to make sure it's safe for everyone to go back . . .

ANTON (*interrupting*). Mum . . .

TANYA. What?

ANTON. It won't be safe will it?

TANYA. Of course it will. Later . . .

ANTON. I'm not stupid.

NATALIA. Anton . . .

ANTON. It won't ever be safe there again . . .

And Dad . . . I mean what does it do to you? A fire like that?

STEFAN. I felt so ill. It got worse and worse as the day wore on.
I even began to wonder if I was in the middle of a dream . . .
a bad dream . . .

It was as though I was standing outside myself. Watching.
I had this strange feeling in the pit of my stomach, and in my
head. When I closed my eyes it was as though I was in the
middle of a whirlpool. Being dragged down.

NATALIA. When we got to the flat Mother was out, visiting a
neighbour. I'd forgotten. They always used to play cards on
Saturday nights. But it didn't matter because I had a key. I
ran a bath for Anton, and made up a bed. Tanya just sat in the
little kitchen drinking glass after glass of water. We were all
so thirsty.We couldn't believe how thirsty we all were.

She moves over to TANYA.

TANYA. Is he all right?

NATALIA. He keeps making little jokes . . . He's half asleep
already . . .

TANYA. But he knows. Doesn't he? He knows how bad it really
is.

NATALIA. Of course he does. He's not daft. I've made him lie
down. I'll wake him up for some supper later. Are you
hungry?

TANYA. No. Not at all.

NATALIA (*looking her full in the face*). Oh dear God Tanya.

TANYA. What's wrong?

NATALIA. I just think you ought to have a bath now. Before
me. Before mother comes in.

TANYA. Yes. I should, shouldn't I? I wish we had a shower
here.

NATALIA. There's a wee shower you can fit on to the bath taps.
I told Anton to use it after his bath. Rinse yourself well. All
over. And make sure you scrub your nails. Fingernails and
toenails. Use fresh water.

TANYA. I know how to have a bath Natalia . . .

NATALIA. Use plenty of fresh water. Lots of it. Do you understand me?

TANYA. It'll contaminate the drains . . .

NATALIA. Sod the drains.

TANYA. Yes. All right. I'll use plenty of water.

NATALIA. I wonder if I could get . . .

TANYA. What?

NATALIA. Iodine tablets from somewhere.

TANYA. I think it's too late. For us anyway.

NATALIA. I'll make us some supper.

TANYA. I don't want anything.

NATALIA. You should eat.

TANYA. I just need water. Nice clean water.

TANYA moves to the front of the stage where she sits on the bench there to take up the story. NATALIA goes to stand by ARTEMIS again. STEFAN stands a little apart from them with VIKTOR behind him.

TANYA. I got into the bath and just lay there. There was steam on the mirror. I soaped myself and rinsed myself and lay there for ages. I heard our mother come in and thought I'd better get out and go and speak to her. Now that we were safe, I kept thinking about Stefan. Funny, I hardly thought about Viktor. Poor Viktor. Only Stefan. He filled my mind. I kept seeing him trying to fight that fire. That strange other-worldly fire. I knew as well as Anton that you didn't just put out a fire like that. But what do you do with it? How could you ever contain it, once it was set alight.

Then I sat up and fitted the little rubber shower attachment to the taps and began to wash my hair. It felt funny. Brittle. (*She rubs at her hair.*) I rubbed it with shampoo and it began to come out, in tufts. I was holding a big piece of my own hair in my fingers. My scalp was very sore. And then I became aware that the skin on my face was sore too. Like when you've fallen asleep in the sun.

She stands up.

TANYA. I got out of the bath and went over to the mirror. I looked down at my body. It was just ordinary. The ordinary body of a youngish woman who has had a child. And then I rubbed away the steam from the mirror and looked at my face. And I knew why those boys had laughed and jeered. My face was a horrible sight: all red and brown, all lined and burned and pitted. The skin was peeling off it in layers.

Natalia and my mother put me to bed and called the doctor. He seemed very alarmed. He gave me some cream to put on the burns and some painkillers. I couldn't get Stefan out of my head. If this had happened to me, who had only looked at the reactor for minutes, what would have happened to my husband?

STEFAN. I was in Moscow. They had moved us to a hospital in Moscow. There I was, still worrying about a meltdown. And then we heard that they had almost caused one.

ARTEMIS. How did that happen?

STEFAN. They tried to cool the reactor with water at first but that was no good. So they sent helicopters on bombing runs over the burning core to try to plug the crater with . . . oh, you name it. Lead, sand, clay, dolomite, boron carbide. It took them a whole week to fill it.

ARTEMIS. Desperate measures. Did they work?

STEFAN. They didn't really know what they were doing. They should have asked us. Firemen. We'd have told them . . .

ARTEMIS. It was an experiment conducted under the least favourable conditions.

STEFAN. Aye. Panic and desperation.

Anyway the only result was this hellish brew in the core. And it began to come to the boil because of the heat building up in the radioactive material underneath it. Which created just the right conditions for . . .

ARTEMIS. Exactly. What might have happened? Viktor?

VIKTOR. The problem was nobody knew how much fuel was left in there. But if the casing of all the remaining fuel rods had melted at once then the fuel itself would concentrate into one huge mass and there would be a chain reaction leading to . . .

ARTEMIS. The ultimate nuclear nightmare: meltdown.

STEFAN. Aye. With the stress on down . . .

ARTEMIS. Because in this case, what goes down also comes up.

VIKTOR. Right below the core there was something called a bubbler pool. And below that again, a basement . . .

STEFAN. . . . which was already flooded.

VIKTOR. So if a meltdown occurred, this mass of radioactive fuel would break through into the bubbler pool and then on to the flooded basement beneath.

ARTEMIS. And then?

VIKTOR. When it came into contact with both these bodies of water there would be another gigantic explosion.

It was a design fault. There should have been no water beneath, no possibility of water beneath . . .

ARTEMIS. What then?

VIKTOR. It would have blown the entire complex sky high. All three remaining reactors included.

ARTEMIS. But that isn't all, is it?

VIKTOR. No.

ARTEMIS. So tell us what it might have done next . . .

VIKTOR. It would carry on moving downwards. The ground beneath couldn't contain it. Nobody knows when it would stop moving down.

ARTEMIS. If at all. But eventually . . .

VIKTOR. Eventually it would come into contact with the water table. And then . . .

STEFAN. Who knows?

VIKTOR. That's one experiment we haven't carried out yet.

STEFAN. So they sent firemen in to drain the bubbler pool and the flooded basement. Not us. But there were others. Volunteers. I knew some of them. The lads practised setting up a pumping operation. They could do it in fourteen minutes. Doctors told them that they only had seven minutes. So they did it in five. Just to be on the safe side. Amazing what fear can do for you.

And then they built a concrete sarcophagus over the core. They made it into a permanent tomb.

ARTEMIS. But how permanent? It's already full of holes. The birds fly in and out. And there's so much dust in there. Plutonium dust. But there's no money to make it safe, is there? Even if anyone really knew how.

STEFAN *begins to take off his outer protective clothing and lies down.*

NATALIA. Viktor was killed in the explosion. You know, for so long I kept thinking maybe he wasn't on that shift after all. Maybe he'd come walking in the door. And he'd be fine. Only he never did. I could never come to terms with how completely he . . . And Stefan. Dear Stefan . . .

TANYA. You never do come to terms with it. No matter how they die, they disappear suddenly and completely. After the fire Stefan was taken to Moscow. They all were. It took me a long time to find out what had become of him. They didn't want to release any information. Not even to wives and families. I saw him once and even then the doctors didn't want to let me in. I had to insist. You see he was radioactive. There was radiation coming out of his body all the time.

STEFAN *is very ill. His voice is hoarse. But he does not let her touch him.*

STEFAN. You shouldn't be here.

TANYA. I know. Does it matter?

STEFAN. Promise me you won't bring Anton.

TANYA. He wanted to come. He was so angry. I told him it wasn't allowed. But I've brought some photographs. I'll put them up for you. And he's sent you a letter. And his football scarf.

STEFAN. Is he well?

TANYA. He's all right.

STEFAN. You're sure he's well.

TANYA (*weeping*). Missing you. And he keeps wondering about Sooty. We both do. It makes me cry.

STEFAN. Oh don't, don't Tanya. (*He begins to cry too.*) Look at me. I'm as daft as you are.

TANYA. Are you in pain?

STEFAN. It's not too bad. Just a bit uncomfortable that's all.

TANYA. Me too.

STEFAN. Your poor face.

TANYA. I'm such a fool. Crying about a cat. I keep thinking of her. Wondering where everybody's gone. Only perhaps she's dead by now. Do you think she's dead?

STEFAN. Maybe she's gone off into the forest. Cats can usually look after themselves. How's Natalia?

TANYA. She's fine. She wanted to come too. Only I wouldn't let her.

STEFAN. Better not.

TANYA. No. Listen. I'm going to start Anton at school in Kiev. I'm looking for a job too.

STEFAN. Are you well enough?

TANYA. I'm all right. Just very tired . . .

STEFAN. What does the doctor . . . ?

TANYA. He says it's the trauma. I'll get over it. We all will. No great harm done.

STEFAN. I get tired too.

TANYA. Do you?

STEFAN. Sometimes I feel as if I can't even raise a spoon to my mouth. And as for a knife and fork . . . well . . . it's a bloody good job they give us a lot of soup. (*He laughs, then is suddenly sad again.*) Sometimes it's too much of an effort to breathe.

TANYA. I'll stay here with you. I'm not going back to Kiev till you're better.

STEFAN. You can't do that. What about Anton?

TANYA. Natalia will take care of him. I'll stay here.

STEFAN. You mustn't. I won't let you.

TANYA. You can't stop me.

STEFAN. Listen to me. Why do you think they keep us in all the time?

TANYA. You're not well. They want you to rest.

STEFAN. Christ Tanya! It isn't for the good of *our* health. It's because we're walking hot spots. How could they ever let us out?

TANYA. Don't say such things.

STEFAN. If I don't say them now I never will. I should never have laughed at your nightmares.

TANYA. You didn't laugh.

STEFAN. We could have left sooner.

TANYA. Don't.

STEFAN. When I'm better I'll come straight to Kiev. I'm sure I'll be posted straight there. We might even get a flat.

TANYA (*in tears*). Yes. They owe us that at least.

STEFAN. Don't cry any more. You'll set me off.

TANYA. I'm sorry. It's just that . . . we don't have anything Stefan. All our things . . . we don't even have a stick of furniture.

STEFAN. Then we'll just have to start again, won't we? Look, I'll be here for a few months and then I'll be well. By the autumn I'll be well. I feel stronger every day.

TANYA *looks at him.*

STEFAN. They say my voice will come back properly soon.

TANYA. Will it?

STEFAN. God, I can't wait to get home and see Anton. Tell him he'd better start kicking that ball about. Get in some practice.

TANYA. He gets tired. Doesn't play much football now. They've given him vitamin pills.

They say it's . . .

STEFAN. The trauma. I know. You should go. You've been here long enough.

TANYA. How can I leave you.

She tries to kiss him but he pushes her away gently.

STEFAN. The doctors don't come near us. They treat us like lepers. As if it's some sort of plague.

TANYA. How can I leave you alone?

STEFAN. I won't be alone. The rest of the lads are here. We keep each other's spirits up.

TANYA. I don't care. I have to be able to remember . . . Please.

STEFAN *resists and then capitulates, suddenly.*

They kiss, passionately. And then he very deliberately puts her away from him.

TANYA. He survived for twenty-one days after the explosion. When they buried him it was in a lead lined coffin.

NATALIA. My sister had longer. She just seemed to go downhill slowly and then she got pneumonia and . . . Just about that time we found out Anton had thyroid cancer. I took him for treatment but a year later he died.

ARTEMIS. And you? What about you?

NATALIA. I'm fine. Fit and well. But then, I never really looked at it, did I? There was some kind of magic in it, and I only glimpsed it briefly through the window of a train.

ARTEMIS. So did Anton.

NATALIA. Yes. But he slept with his window open that night. Tanya wanted to go and close it and I told her not to fuss. And now they're both dead. And I'm all right.

ARTEMIS. Why must you assign reasons all the time?

NATALIA. Because it makes me feel . . .

ARTEMIS. Safe? As though there are rules? Maybe there are. Maybe . . .

NATALIA. I used to be quite religious you know. Now I just think it's a lottery.

ARTEMIS. Isn't it time you were going in?

NATALIA. I'm so frightened.

ARTEMIS. It is frightening.

So why are you going in? Why put yourself at risk?

NATALIA. I've lost so much that I loved. All these years I've thought about the manner of their dying. I still lie awake and imagine horrors. It's like an aching tooth that your tongue goes back to again and again . . . I thought I might exorcise those feelings. Somehow.

ARTEMIS. Is that all they are? All they ever were? The way in which they died?

NATALIA. No. Of course not. They're so much more than that. But I can't stop myself from thinking about it can I?

ARTEMIS. You could. If you really wanted to.

NATALIA. But I feel guilty?

ARTEMIS. Because you're alive and they're dead.

NATALIA. Yes.

ARTEMIS. And yet it's probably the least important thing about them. The manner of their dying, as you call it.

NATALIA. Then what *does* matter?

ARTEMIS. The manner of their living? The way they died doesn't change what they were to you. What they are to you still.

NATALIA. But it shouldn't have happened. Not like this.

ARTEMIS. No. So maybe those are the reasons you have to look for. Why did it happen at all and can you prevent it from happening again?

NATALIA. How can I prevent anything from happening? What do you want me to do?

ARTEMIS. I *want* nothing. I have no axes to grind. It's all one to me. I just tell you the truth. Or try to make you see it.

NATALIA. I think I will join the others and go in. It's what I can do. I can find out more.

ARTEMIS. And then?

NATALIA. Oh then . . . One step at a time please.

ARTEMIS. I must be going too.

NATALIA. Where?

ARTEMIS. I can't tell you. I hardly know myself.

NATALIA. Who are you?

ARTEMIS. Don't you know me yet? I was always here. Right from the start.

NATALIA. Do you have a name?

ARTEMIS. My name could be Artemis.

TANYA. What I saw was very beautiful. Catherine wheels made out of great big stars that rose in the night sky and fell.

NATALIA. Artemis?

ARTEMIS. Any of the various plants of the genus Artemisia. Sometimes called absinthe. Now there's a jolly name. And a fragrant one. A strong green drink.

NATALIA. Gives you hallucinations. So I'm told.

ARTEMIS. Dreams and revelations. Or perhaps in the English, Wormwood.

NATALIA. Wormwood?

ARTEMIS. Also something that embitters, such as a painful experience.

VIKTOR. There were so many safeguards. It couldn't happen. We knew it couldn't happen. We had been told.

ARTEMIS. Do people learn from their painful experiences?

NATALIA. Sometimes.

VIKTOR. They needed the power. They still do.

STEFAN. It was so beautiful. I'd never seen anything like it in my life. And I've been a fireman for fifteen years.

TANYA. It seemed totally normal and natural. As if this was exactly what it should be doing.

STEFAN. It wasn't like an ordinary fire at all. It was a monster … a dragon … but it was beautiful. I knew that.

ARTEMIS. Wormwood. In the Russian, Chernobyl.

And the third angel sounded
And there fell a great star from heaven
Burning as it were a lamp.
And it fell upon a third part of the rivers
And upon the fountains of waters.

And the name of the star is called Wormwood.
And the third part of the waters became Wormwood
And many men died of the waters
Because they were made bitter.

You must go now Natalia. But be careful. They pretend to know so much. Even scientists speak in metaphors and call them facts. We all do.

NATALIA. And afterwards? What do I do then?

ARTEMIS. Start thinking the unthinkable? What will happen if . . .

You might even find that you begin to assume the worst and plan for it.

NATALIA. How? How can you possibly plan for something so unpredictable . . .

ARTEMIS. If you find that to be the truth, then maybe you have to think very carefully about whether you can continue to subscribe to the whole bargain.

NATALIA. And then? What then?

ARTEMIS. Oh, there would be consequences of course. There are always consequences.

NATALIA. But what? And how would we cope with them?

ARTEMIS. Nobody knows. Perhaps you have to find out. Know your enemy. If he is your enemy. Enjoy your visit Natalia. But take care . . . won't you?

NATALIA *moves slowly across the stage leaving* ARTEMIS *alone.*

NATALIA. Good bye.

ARTEMIS. Oh I'll be seeing you again.

NATALIA. Will you?

ARTEMIS. Somewhere or other . . . for sure.

ANTON *comes forward. He is kicking, or bouncing a football. 'Keepie-uppies' that gradually wind down.*
ARTEMIS *and* NATALIA *watch as* ANTON *sits down, and then lies down, holding the football. As the stage darkens the football is seen in light, luminous, spinning.*

End.

Note

When the Chernobyl disaster occurred in April 1986 I was three months pregnant. The feeling of helplessness as the radioactive cloud drifted towards Scotland has remained with me over the years, as it has with friends who were in a similar situation. And yet it seems to me that the magnitude of the accident and the chain of human errors which caused it have always been played down in the West. I knew then that I wanted to write about Chernobyl, but wasn't quite sure what form the writing would take. In the meantime I read about the subject and the more I read, the more troubled I became.

The play began, some three years ago, with a voice in my head, a hesitant voice, someone trying to describe the events of that warm April night in the Ukraine, in terms that would not only be comprehensible to the lay person, myself included, but which would convey some of the horror, and the sense of inevitability which seemed to lie at the heart of it. With that voice came a clear vision of an abandoned place, a place where time – and normality – had stood still; a place where human lives had been destroyed, and so many potential futures ruined. As I found out more about those real lives, the idea of *Wormwood* began to take shape. I did not want this to be a play about some remote disaster that 'couldn't happen here'. Because the more I explored, the more convinced I became that, given a particular set of demands upon human fallibility anything can happen anywhere.

Albert Einstein said 'The splitting of the atom has changed everything except our way of thinking and thus we drift towards unparalleled catastrophe.' *Wormwood* is about the effects of one such catastrophe on a group of people most closely involved. But I think that all of us are involved, and many of us are still feeling those disastrous effects even now.

Catherine Czerkawska

BROTHERS OF THUNDER

Ann Marie Di Mambro

Ann Marie Di Mambro was born in 1950 and studied at Glasgow University, Girton College, Cambridge, and Bolton College of Education, before becoming a teacher. Her stage plays include *Hocus Pocus* and *Joe* (Annexe Theatre Company); *Visible Differences* (TAG Theatre Company); *Sheila*, *Tally's Blood* and *Brothers of Thunder* (Traverse); *The Letter-Box* (part of *Long Story Short*, toured by 7:84 Scotland, published by Nick Hern Books in *Scot-Free*).

Her television work includes extensive script editing and writing for *Take the High Road*, *Dr Finlay* and *Machair*; also *Drama-rama* and *Winners and Losers* (STV).

From 1989 to 1990 she was Thames Television Resident Playwright at the Traverse Theatre.

Brothers Of Thunder was first performed at the Traverse
Theatre, Edinburgh, on 22 March 1994, with the following cast:

JAMES, *a priest, around forty*   Finlay Welsh
JOHN, *early twenties*   Tom Smith
SIMON, *American, late twenties*   Stuart Bowman

Directed by   Philip Howard
Designed by   Mark Leese
Lighting designed by   Jeanine Davies
Sound designed   by John Irvine

Setting: in and around James's chapel house.

Time: present day

Scene One

Lights up. JAMES *at altar, with a list of parish announcements. He does it on automatic pilot.*

JAMES. The winners of this month's 200 Club draw will be announced in the church hall after this mass. So if you're a member, please go along. This could be your lucky day. Now, Mrs. Morgan is still looking for new members of the choir. Choir practice is at half seven on Thursday. If you'd like to join, just turn up then, that all right Mr. Morgan? Just turn up? Right. Just turn up. Thursdays. Half past seven.

As he talks, lights up on JOHN *at other side of the stage. He dumps his bags, bored, edgy.*

The trip to St. Bernadette's Grotto. There's one or two places left on the bus, according to Mrs. Dolan. So, if you'd like to go, there's still time to get your name down. And finally, as I'm sure you all know, Father Allan is leaving us. Today's his last day. Mrs. Ross has organised a presentation for him and she's asked me to thank you for your generosity. Now please stand for the final blessing.

He makes the sign of the cross.

The mass is ended. Go in peace to love and serve the lord. Amen. Oh, on your way out, will you please make sure you return your hymn books.

He removes his surplice and looks round, surprised to see JOHN, *goes over to him.*

Lights down on altar.

John?

JOHN. Yes.

JAMES. I'm James. (*He shakes* JOHN's *hand with a warmth that is not returned.*) I wasn't expecting you till later on this afternoon. Were you at that mass?

JOHN. No.

JAMES. That all you've got?

JOHN. Yes.

JAMES. Here, let me help you with them.

Before JAMES *can help,* JOHN *picks them up.*

Come on, I'll show you up.

They go offstage. Lights up on room as they come in.
JAMES*'s attitude is warm, anxious to please.* JOHN *is*
withdrawn, wanting to be alone. The bed is bare with sheets
folded, ready on the bed.

Here it is. All right for you?

JOHN *glances round but shows no reaction.*

I'm sorry it's not more welcoming. Look at it. The fire's not
lit. The bed's not made. I was going to spend the afternoon
getting it ready for you. I don't have a housekeeper you see.
I look after everything myself. (*Smiles.*) Explains why it's
never done right. Come on, I'll give you a hand to make
the bed.

JOHN. It's all right.

JAMES. Two minutes.

JAMES *starts to make the bed.* JOHN *helps reluctantly.*

I did iron these sheets for you, which is a rare honour I can
tell you. I love watching the nurses making beds. Don't mind
watching the nurses at any time, come to that. The way they
just fling the sheets in the air and let them flutter down
without so much as a crease, and then they sort of karate
chop the corners in and voilà! Perfection. You hungry?

JOHN. I'll manage from here (*i.e. the bed*).

JAMES *carries on making the bed.* JOHN *abandons it.*

JAMES. Have you eaten?

JOHN. I'm not hungry.

JAMES. We're having a farewell lunch for Father Allan
downstairs. It would be nice if you joined us.

JOHN. No thank you.

JAMES. You'd be very welcome.

JOHN *shakes his head.*

You sure?

JOHN. Yes.

JAMES. There's more than enough to go round.

JOHN. I said no thank you.

JAMES. Fine.

JAMES a bit taken aback by the tone.

Anyway, the kitchen's downstairs. You can use it whenever you like. All the time if you like. But look over here. This used to be the housekeeper's flat so it's got this kitchen area here. Look – dishes in here. Space for your foodstuff. Wee fridge over here. (*He smiles as he pats the microwave.*) Let me tell you a story about this microwave. One of the local shops donated it last year as first prize in the raffle at the school's Christmas panto. They asked me to draw the tickets and guess what. I won, didn't I. Brought the house down. I wanted to give it back, of course, raffle it again, but the headmistress insisted I keep it. Said I'd find a good use for it. So here it is. But you can use the downstairs kitchen whenever you like.

JOHN. This'll do fine.

JAMES. Just you suit yourself.

A lull. It bothers JAMES but does not bother JOHN.

Anyway, there's various groups use downstairs during the day. Making tea and what have you. So feel free to mix in. Any time you fancy some company just wander down.

A lull.

JAMES rubs his hands together, smiles at JOHN expectantly.

So?

JOHN wanders away from kitchen area, goes to the window, looks out, unhappily (at the hospital across the road).
JAMES watches him, them goes over, stands behind him, follows his gaze.

JAMES. Not a bad view from here, eh?

No reply.

JAMES. You're nice and handy anyway.

No reply.

I said you're nice and handy.

No reply.

So . . . Gordon was telling me you're a Catholic.

JOHN. What?

JAMES. Gordon. The social worker across the road. He was saying –

JOHN *cuts him off, vicious.*

JOHN. And what else did Gordon tell you? That I'm a homosexual? That I got AIDS because I fucked one guy. Just one guy.

JAMES. Don't be shy, son. Just come right out and say what you mean.

JOHN. I don't like him talking about me.

JAMES. He wasn't talking about you.

JOHN. Yes he does. He tells me about other people. So he must talk about me.

JAMES. He doesn't mean anything.

JOHN. I don't like it. I know he does it and I don't like it.

JAMES. He told me very little.

JOHN. The tragic story of the brilliant young student, his whole career ahead of him, infected by the only partner he ever had. Is that how he told it?

JAMES. No.

JOHN. Anyway, he's got it all wrong. I was a stunningly mediocre student and degrees in Modern Languages aren't worth that. (*Snaps his fingers.*)

JAMES. He only mentioned it.

JOHN. Mentioned what?

JAMES. You being a Catholic.

JOHN. Well I'm not. Let's get that clear straight off. I don't believe any of that stuff any more. If I ever did. That's not why I'm here.

JAMES *backs off.*

JAMES. Right. Fine. That's my understanding of it too.

JOHN. Then why bring it up?

JAMES. Look, John, it makes no difference to me what your religion is. Or if you don't have a religion. That's not why I agreed to this. So you can relax, I'll not be trying to convert you.

JOHN *gives him a look as if to say 'you'd better not'.*

Look, this arrangement's got nothing to do with the Church. All right? Nothing to do with me being a priest. I've not even told the Bishop you were coming here. Never asked him. Why should I? It doesn't concern him. It's between me and the hospital. O.K?

He waits for a reply. None comes.

O.K?

JOHN. O.K.

JAMES. You come and go as you please. Nobody will bother you here. Now Father Allan's going there's only me here. I don't even have a housekeeper.

JOHN. You told me.

JAMES. I never asked the Bishop about that either. It was my decision to run this place without one.

JAMES *dries for a moment, but the silence is too much so he prattles on.*

JAMES. Apart from anything else, how can I begin to understand ordinary people unless I live like one. It's not right I should be waited on hand and foot, is it? Somebody cooking my meals, cleaning up after me. Washing my clothes. (*Beat.*) Mind you, I'm not much good at it. I mean look at me today. I've got on two odd socks.

He lifts his trousers legs and looks down at his feet.

JOHN. Don't worry. I *did* notice.

JAMES *slightly put down. He opens the door of the room and looks out into the hall and points.*

JAMES. Here, let me show you. That's my bedroom along at the other end. That's Father Allan's room 'Was' Father Allan's room. That's my bathroom. Here's your bathroom here. (*Suddenly embarrassed.*) Not that you have to use a separate bathroom. I've no . . . I mean it wouldn't worry me if . . . I wouldn't like you to think it's got anything . . . It's just the

way the house is built, this bathroom is next to your room.
The other bathroom's up there next to my room. It makes
more sense. But by all means, use any bathroom. Feel free.

JOHN. I'll just use this one, thanks.

JAMES. You do whatever you feel like doing, John. I don't want
you thinking of this place as a chapel house. This is where
I live. It just happens to be next to the chapel.

*JOHN sneers at the patness of this. JAMES hovers, not sure
what to say next. Eventually –*

So . . . how are you feeling then?

JOHN gives him a look. JAMES feels stupid for asking.

Is there anything I can get you? Anything you need?

JOHN. I'm fine.

JAMES. Anything? A cup of tea? A glass of wine?

JOHN shakes his head.

If there's anything, just give me a call. I'm just along in my
room . . . or in the kitchen. You'll find me.

JOHN. Thanks.

Lull. JAMES looks out the window.

JAMES. At least you're nice and handy for the hospital.

JOHN groans silently.

They're really great across the road, aren't they?

No reply.

Only time I've been in hospital was a few years ago. I was
rushed in to get my appendix out. Pretty scary at the time.

JOHN. I better start unpacking.

JOHN picks up a bag.

JAMES. You want a hand?

JOHN. No.

JAMES. You sure you won't join us for lunch?

JOHN. Quite sure.

JAMES. I'll save some for you. You can have it later.

JOHN. Don't bother.

JAMES. Oh I'm sorry . . . I never thought. Do you have a special diet or something?

JOHN. Look. I'm feeling pretty tired.

JAMES. Of course. You must be. I'm sorry. I rattle on sometimes. (*Laughs to himself, a bit nervously.*) I found out recently the kids at the school call me Father Talkalot. I love kids. Don't you? Father Talkalot. Good that, isn't it?

JAMES is straining JOHN's patience.

JOHN. Actually . . . Father . . .

JAMES. James.

JOHN. Father James, I . . .

JAMES. No, James. Just James. We're equals here. You're John. I'm James, O.K?

JOHN. Fine.

JAMES. James and John. That's good. I like that. 'Boanarges'.

JOHN. I'm sorry?

JAMES. 'Boanarges.' The sons of thunder.

JOHN looks blank.

JAMES. The apostles James and John were two brothers, sons of Zebedee. But they loved Jesus with such a passion that he called them the sons of thunder. He was a great one for
  . giving people nicknames. Jesus. If anyone was giving Jesus a hard time, James and John wanted to get right in there, sort them out . . . (*Realising JOHN not listening.*) Anyway, you're tired. I'll leave you to it.

He goes leaving JOHN alone. JOHN looks round place, obviously desperately low. He starts to unpack. Door opens, JAMES comes in with scuttle of coal and sticks, etc. And heads straight for the fire.

JAMES. Sorry to bother you again, John, but we better get this fire lit. Heat this place up. I'll do it if you like.

JOHN. I'll do it later.

JAMES. No. I'm good at lighting fires. I used to love watching my mother. She could light a fire with anything.

JAMES *stocks the fire. As he talks* JOHN's *annoyance grows.*

We're supposed to be getting central heating in one of these days, but it's not a priority with me. The money's always needed for other things. Last year we were given two thousand pounds to get it installed and I used the money instead to take away the altar rails. And I'm glad I did it. A few folk didn't like it, but they're the kind of folk who still want the Latin mass.

JOHN. You know what your nightmare must be? Running out of things to talk about.

JAMES *tries to laugh but is a bit hurt.*

JAMES. The thing is, I'm just trying to get a word in edgeways, with you blabbering all the time.

JOHN *not amused.*

JAMES. Look, I'm sorry. I know I go on.

JOHN *says nothing.*

I know this can't be easy for you.

JOHN *gives him a look of incredulity.*

And I want you to feel welcome. It's important to me that you . . . 'enjoy' is not the right word . . . that you're comfortable here. That you feel at home.

JOHN. If you'd leave that, I'll get it (*i.e. the fire*).

JAMES. Not at all. It's the least I can do. Then I'll give you peace. It'll soon heat up in here, once it gets going.

JOHN. Will you please leave it?

JAMES *looks round.*

I'll manage it. Please.

JAMES. You sure?

JOHN. Yes.

JAMES *gets up.*

JAMES. Remember to screw the paper up really tightly. That's the secret. A few sticks of wood on top, criss-crossed to let the air through –

JOHN. I'll manage.

JAMES. There's plenty of coal. It's in the bunker outside the back door. Just help yourself. You got matches?

JOHN. No.

JAMES takes some from his pocket.

JAMES. Here, take these.

He puts box on mantlepiece.

Now you're sure you're all right?

JOHN. Yes.

JAMES. Right, I better get downstairs for this lunch thing. I'll see you later.

JAMES goes. JOHN kneels in front of the fire, starts scrunching up the papers. JAMES in again.

Look at this. I nearly forgot. Your keys. That's the key to the front door, the storm door, the back door and your room. Obviously you come and go as you please.

JOHN looks round but does not get up.

I'll put them down here.

He puts them on table. He goes, pulling door behind him but not quite. JOHN puts some sticks on the fire. Drained, he leans his head against the fire surround. He does not see JAMES open the door a fraction and look in. JAMES's expression saddens as he takes in the scene and gently closes the door.

Scene Two

*JOHN comes into his room from outside, his jacket on.
He stands and looks around with rising suspicion and anger.
He turns round sharply, opens the door and goes out to the hall, his voice raised.*

JOHN. Hey . . . You there? James . . . Father . . . whatever they call you . . . Can you come in here a minute. In here . . . In here.

JOHN into room, followed by JAMES.

JAMES. What's up?

JOHN. You've been in my room?

JAMES *looks caught.*

JOHN. You have. You've been in my room.

JAMES. I was but –

JOHN. You've no right to come into my room.

JAMES. Look, I'm –

JOHN. You've no right to come into my room. Make my bed. Touch my things. Why did you come into my room?

JAMES. I'm sorry, I didn't mean –

JOHN. Why did you come into my room?

JAMES. I don't usually . . .

JOHN. Why?

JAMES. Look, it won't . . .

JOHN. Answer me.

JAMES. I was . . . showing someone round.

JOHN. You what?

JAMES. I'd a visitor and I was showing her round the house –

JOHN. You showed someone my room?

JAMES *looks sheepish.*

You actually showed someone my room?

JAMES. Look –

JOHN. You showed a stranger into my room?

JAMES. She's not a stranger. She works at the –

JOHN. Why did you let her into my room?

JAMES*'s discomfort is rising.*

JAMES. I didn't mean any harm.

JOHN. I said why did you let her into my room?

JAMES. Look, John –

JOHN. Why?

JAMES. I was just showing her the house and I wanted to give her an idea of the kinds of things I'm trying to do here.

JOHN. And just what kind of things are you trying to do here?

JAMES (*squirming*). Let her see that I'm trying, among other things, to raise awareness – you know – to open up this house – this parish – to wider social issues.

JOHN. I'm not a wider social issue.

JAMES. I know, I –

JOHN. I am not a 'thing' that you do.

JAMES. Look, I'm sorry.

JOHN. I am not here so everyone can see what a great guy you are. 'Hey, look at me, I care about AIDS'.

JAMES. All right, John, I get your point.

JOHN. No, you don't. I've told you but you talk so much you don't know how to listen. I am here for one reason only. Because I need treatment and you've got a room right across from the hospital. That's it. End of story.

JAMES. I really am sorry.

JOHN. The DSS pays you for the room, don't they?

JAMES. That's not the point.

JOHN. That is exactly the point. I'm not your little charity number.

JAMES. I said I'm sorry, John. It was an invasion of your privacy. I realise that now and, I assure you, it won't happen again.

JOHN *scoffs*.

I give you my word.

Silence. JOHN *expects* JAMES *to go, but he hovers.*

JOHN. What?

JAMES. I said it won't happen again.

JOHN. Fine.

JAMES. I won't come in your room again when you're not here. That's a promise.

JOHN. Right. So you said.

JAMES. But that doesn't mean I'm going to stop caring about you.

JOHN. Oh give it a rest.

JAMES. I can't.

JOHN *groans, puts on the kettle.* JAMES *hangs around, watching him, trying to think of something to say.*

Everything going all right at the hospital?

JOHN *doesn't answer.*

Hey, I knew there was something I meant to tell you. I was over at the school yesterday. We got talking in the staffroom. And one of the teachers was saying she's doing a unit on AIDS with her R.E. class –

JOHN. The answer's no.

JAMES (*puzzled*). No what?

JOHN. To what you're going to ask me.

JAMES. What? What am I going to ask you?

JOHN. You know.

JAMES. I don't.

JOHN. I am not coming to the school and giving a talk about AIDS.

JAMES. I wasn't going to ask you that.

JOHN. You were. You were leading up to it.

JAMES. I wasn't.

JOHN. In your wee sleekit priesty way.

JAMES. I was not.

JOHN. It's the kind of thing Gordon tried to rope me into. Once this team from the radio visited the Unit. Some discussion programme or other. They wanted me to answer questions, talk about myself. This illness! They think it makes you public property.

JAMES. Any chance of a cup?

JOHN *gestures to cups, etc. And walks away and sits down.* JAMES *makes himself a cup.*

I was on the radio once. Five one-minute talks. I did them all in one session and then they played one a day through the week. (*Beat.*) I don't suppose you heard any of them?

No reply from JOHN.

The theme was 'Finding God in Unusual Places'. I told the one about the priest telling the class 'God is Everywhere' and the wee boy pipes up, 'I hope he's not up my jumper eating my crisps'.

JAMES *laughs,* JOHN *doesn't.*

'Up my jumper eating my crisps.'

JOHN. How did you get on to it?

JAMES. The Catholic Press Office phoned. Someone had pulled out at the last minute and –

JOHN. I meant talking about AIDS in the staffroom?

JAMES (*uncomfortable*). Oh it just came up.

JOHN. It just came up?

JAMES. Yes.

JOHN. How?

JAMES. How what?

JOHN. How did it come up?

JAMES. I don't know.

JOHN. You don't know?

JAMES. I don't know. It just came up.

JOHN *sighs, gives up. Lull.* JAMES *finishes making his cup of coffee, changes subject quite deliberately.*

Did I ever tell you, John, how I came to be here?

JOHN. No.

JAMES. If you've got a few minutes I'd quite like to tell you about it.

No encouragement from JOHN.

You realise I am fairly young to be a parish priest.

JOHN. I wouldn't know.

JAMES. Well I am. My only regret is my parents not being alive to see it.

While JAMES *talks* JOHN *slumps in his chair, not listening.*

It was quite a surprising appointment, I can tell you, and there was nobody more surprised than me. You see, I always was a bit of a rebel. Got a kick out of flouting authority. Right from the moment I was ordained. It's embarrassing, looking back. The long hair – I had more hair then, of course – the denim jeans, open-neck shirts, no dog collar, guitars on the altar. I got into trouble once for singing 'The Times They Are A-Changing' as an entrance hymn. But it was the seventies. We were all singing Dylan. There was a wee group of us then, out to change the Church. Change the world. We'd tell people it didn't matter if they missed mass, or made up their own minds about contraception. Jesus broke all the rules, didn't he. We were always being called before the bishop, told off, reminded where our duties lay . . .

He breaks off, realising JOHN*'s dozed off, his cup falling out of his hand.* JAMES *crouches in front of him and starts to ease the mug out of his grip.* JOHN *jumps, wakes up suddenly, disoriented, unguarded. He lets out a cry, full of fear. It distresses* JAMES.

Hey, hey, it's O.K.

JOHN (*disoriented*). What? What?

JAMES. I didn't mean to scare you.

JOHN. It's O.K. I'm O.K.

JAMES. Can I get you anything?

JOHN. I'm all right.

JAMES. You're shivering.

JAMES *gets blanket from the bed, puts it round* JOHN *who does not resist.* JAMES *stays crouched in front of him.*

JAMES. What about your family, John?

JOHN. What about them?

JAMES. A young man like you, you must have a family. Surely?

No reply.

Where are your parents, John?

JOHN *turns his head away.*

Do they know about you?

No reply.

Have you told your parents, John?

No reply.

You have told them?

JOHN. There's only my mother.

JAMES. And does she know?

JOHN *reacts.*

You have told her?

JOHN (*very quietly*). Yes.

JAMES. And?

JOHN. She didn't take it very well.

A wry smile at his own understatement.

JAMES. Did she know before . . . about . . . (*i.e. John's sexuality*).

JOHN. She found out on the same day her boy was gay and he had AIDS.

JAMES *closes his eyes.*

JAMES. God help her.

JOHN. God help *her*?

JAMES. How is she now?

JOHN. I wouldn't know. I've not been back.

JAMES. But she knows where you are?

JOHN. No.

JAMES. Oh John.

JOHN (*snaps*). Look! What is it to you?

JAMES. John. John. She's your mother. She'll be out of her mind with worry.

JOHN. No, let me tell you what's worrying her. What is she going to tell people is wrong with me. She actually said that.

JAMES. And that's why you've never been back?

JOHN. That's not all she said, believe me.

JAMES. John, people say things when they're upset. You threw this at your mother. You shouldn't judge her on that one reaction.

JOHN. One *honest* reaction.

JAMES. John, listen to me, please. However she reacted, whatever she said, there won't be a day that she doesn't regret it.

JOHN. Tough.

JAMES. Doesn't she deserve the chance to make it up to you?

JOHN. Why? Nobody gave me a second chance, did they?

JOHN *huddles into his blanket.* JAMES *tries to control his frustration.*

JAMES. I know you're bitter.

JOHN *scoffs.*

But I wish I could make you see that what's happened to you affects her too.

JOHN. Don't.

JAMES. It does, John. Whether you're prepared to admit it or not, AIDS affects all of us. It affects me when I'm called over to the hospital and I see people suffering. There's a young man I'm seeing now. Matthew. (*He shakes his head.*) He affects me. It affects me, you living here.

JOHN. I never asked you to be affected.

JAMES. No, but you can't stop it. Like you can't stop your mother loving you. Like you can't stop me praying for you.

JOHN. Oh God. That's all I need. Nobody asked you to pray for me. I don't want you praying for me.

JAMES. But I do. All the time.

JOHN. And what do you pray for, eh? A miracle cure? A death-bed conversion? A quick and painless death?

JAMES. For none of these, my brother of thunder.

JOHN *looks away, slightly affected by the sadness in* JAMES*'s tone.*

JAMES. The wife of Zebedee . . .

JOHN *groans but* JAMES *carries on.*

JAMES. . . . The mother of James and John, one day asked Jesus, 'When you are in heaven, will you see to it, please, that my sons sit beside you. One on one side. And one on the other'. Don't you see. That's what every mother wants for her son. The best there is. On heaven and on earth. That's what your mother wants for you, John.

Lull.

You could write to her.

JOHN. No.

JAMES. Just a note. Just to let her know –

JOHN. 'Dear Mum, The AIDS is going very nicely. Blood count's down of course. The pneumonia was a bit unpleasant but mustn't complain. I'll let you know when the first KS lesion comes along. Kiss, kiss, kiss.

JAMES. Do you know the story of Jonah?

JOHN. Oh why don't you give it a rest?

JAMES. I think it's important, John. God wanted Jonah to go and preach in Nineveh. Jonah said, 'No way. What's the point? They're heathens, they won't even listen.' And so he boarded a ship, heading in the completely opposite direction. But on his way he was swallowed by a whale and it kept him in its belly till it swam to Nineveh where it spat him out. He realised he'd no choice. He had to go.

Waits for reaction from JOHN. *Gets none.*

The point is, John, some things you can't turn your back on. Even if you don't want to, the day will come when you have to deal with them, so why not deal with it now?

JOHN. Have you finished?

A lull: JAMES *hovers, embarrassed, searching for the right words.*

JAMES. It's not a problem for me you know.

JOHN. What isn't?

JAMES. You . . . the way you . . . are . . . your . . . the way you've chosen . . . Oh you probably think I'm shocked but I could tell you things. About me. I've been lonely. I've done things I . . . So if you want to talk . . . about anything . . . anything at all . . .

JOHN. I don't.

JAMES. I mean just talk. I don't want to hear your confession.

JOHN. Yes you do.

> JAMES *smiles.*

JAMES. I suppose your idea of confession is a dark box, priest on one side, you on the other, whispering your guilty secrets through a grille and a curtain. I'm right, amn't I?

> *No reply.*

> We've moved on from there, John. We don't see it as doing penance for your sins. It's more about unburdening your soul. Healing. Healing the whole person.

> JOHN *gets to his feet.*

JOHN. That's it. Out.

JAMES. What?

JOHN. I said out. I've had enough. I knew this would happen.

JAMES. What?

JOHN. I knew I'd have some priest hounding me.

JAMES. I'm not.

JOHN. Yes you are! You just can't leave it alone, can you? It's as big an intrusion as coming into my room when I'm not here. Worse. I want you out. Now.

> JAMES *laughs, disbelieving, embarrassed.*

> Now!

JAMES. Look, I'm sorry. I'll shut up.

JOHN. You can't. You don't know how to. I'm surprised you can shut up long enough to hear a confession. Now go – please.

JAMES. Look, there's no need.

JOHN. I want you out.

> JOHN *goes to the door, holds it open, without looking at* JAMES. JAMES *goes to the door, turns back as if to say something.*

> Go!

> JAMES *goes.* JOHN *shuts the door decisively after him.*

Scene Three

JAMES *at the altar, deep in thought for a moment. Then he starts to speak. At first it seems like he is giving a sermon. By the end there is a rising desperation in his voice and we realise he is on his own.*

JAMES. Prayer is the raising up of the mind and heart to God. It is an awareness of his presence in all that we do. In prayer, God speaks to us, in the stillness and silence of our souls. When shutting out all else, we abandon ourselves completely to the thought of Him alone. When we pray we talk to God, who is always present, closer than the beating of our own hearts. We pray to God for our sins to be forgiven, to thank Him for His blessings, to place before him the needs of the world. And through prayer we find grace and peace.

Lord, God, you are my first thought when I wake up. My last thought as I go to sleep. Every waking moment is filled with love for you. I have dedicated my life to you . . . So why then can't I pray? Why can't I pray?

He turns away.

Scene Four

JOHN *standing at the window, looking out. Still in his coat. He looks spent. Knock on door. He sighs. Knock again, door opens a crack and JAMES comes in, carrying a tray with some food.*

JAMES. Hi.

JOHN. Hello.

JAMES. I heard you come in.

JOHN. I'm just back.

JAMES. Have you eaten yet?

JOHN *looks at the tray, he's hungry.* JAMES *holds it out to him.*

JAMES. Minestrone.

JOHN. Smells good.

JAMES. Please, don't let it get cold.

JAMES *turns to go.*

JOHN. Wait.

JAMES *stops.*

I met Gordon at the hospital. You've to get in touch with him.

JAMES. Will do.

He makes to go again.

JOHN. Something about Matthew.

This stops JAMES. *He turns round.*

JAMES. Is he worse?

JOHN. He didn't say.

JAMES. Right . . . I'll phone him just now.

He's at the door now.

JOHN. Is Matthew quite tall? With sort of reddish hair? And freckles?

JAMES. Why?

JOHN. I think I've seen him, being wheeled down the corridor.

JAMES. Maybe you have.

JOHN. How old would he be?

JAMES. He's only young. (*He sighs.*) I've known Matthew's family for years. They used to be parishioners of mine. A lovely family. Good, good people.

JOHN. This is good (*i.e. soup*).

JAMES. There's plenty more.

JOHN. This is fine.

JAMES. Monday night I make a couple of big pots and on the Tuesday I say mass at midday for the pensioners. Then they come over to the house for a plate of soup and a glass of wine.

JOHN. That would be it. The noise I heard downstairs.

JAMES. I'm sorry. Did it disturb you?

JOHN. No.

JAMES. You could have come down.

JOHN. I was going out.

JAMES. Were you?

JOHN. To the hospital.

JAMES. You never go anywhere else, John?

No reply.

You never go out? You sit in this room, night after night. No-one ever comes to see you.

No reply.

What about your friends?

Before JOHN *gets annoyed* JAMES *gets in.*

I know. It's none of my business. I know.

JOHN *hands him back the tray and turns away.*

JOHN. Thanks.

JAMES *puts the tray down on the edge of the table.*

JAMES. Look, I got this today. (*He takes letter from his pocket, hands it to* JOHN *who glances at it.*)

'I thought your sermon on Sunday was a disgrace to the church and an insult to the Bishop. Why don't you cut the theological gymnastics and bring Christ back on to the altar.' Whatever that's supposed to mean.

JOHN. There's no signature.

JAMES. It's amazing how many Catholics are prepared to stand up and be counted so long as nobody knows who they are.

JOHN *manages a wee half smile.*

The sermon was a bit outrageous I suppose but I wanted it to be. It's good to jolt people at mass now and again. Make them think.

JOHN. You don't want them to think, surely? They might realise what a farce it is.

JAMES *laughs.*

JAMES. No disrespect, but when were *you* last at mass?

JOHN. My father's funeral.

JAMES *had not expected an answer, is taken aback.*

JAMES. I'm sorry.

JOHN. It was a mockery.

JAMES. Now hold on, John, I can't let you say that –

JOHN. I'd been to confession the night before. So I could go to communion at his funeral mass.

JAMES. Go on.

JOHN. Because you can't go to communion if you've been lying in confession and . . . I had been lying in confession, compounding my sin by not speaking its name. So I would have to go confession and this time tell the priest everything . . . Everything . . .

His voices fades off. He lifts it.

Anyway, I went to a church where no-one would know me. I knelt outside that confessional for over an hour, letting everyone in before me. I watched them. In and out. In and out. A couple of minutes and it's over. When I finally did go in I told the priest I wasn't attracted to women but to men, owned up to a few exploratory gropes . . .

His voice trails off.

JAMES. And?

JOHN. He told me to stop it. Cut it out. I said I didn't think I could . . . The upshot was he refused me absolution and told me to stay away from communion.

JAMES. Oh for God's sake!

JOHN. The next day I went to communion anyway. I couldn't not go. Everyone was going.

He looks at JAMES *directly.*

That's how I made a mockery of my father's funeral.

JAMES. No, you didn't John. If you wanted to go to communion –

JOHN. It doesn't matter any more.

JAMES. You can't let one priest . . . some died-in-the-wool old fogey like Father Allan –

JOHN. A few months later this young priest came to visit my mum. Trendy, upfront, 'call me Bob'. My mum was out but I asked him in, got him talking, and he was brilliant. Turns out Bob's totally sympathetic to gay people. Hey – God made them and God made them gay. That's cool! Liberating stuff! There was no sin or state of shame attached to being gay, says Bob. Unless, of course, there's sex involved. In which case it's a mortal sin.

JAMES *groans*.

JOHN. Punishable in hell's fires for all eternity.

JAMES. Oh for God's sake, John, a mortal sin is when you murder somebody or –

JOHN. Not according to Bob.

JAMES. Oh come on.

JOHN. He said it was Church doctrine.

JAMES. You've got to see beyond doctrine.

JOHN. How? What would you have said? It's O.K. *S*crew who you like?

JAMES. Hey, listen, I'm hopeless at putting church doctrine into practice. In fact, I failed my Pastoral Examinations. Twice. Quite proud of that, actually. The first time the examiner asked me what would you do if a woman came to you in confession because she'd allowed her fifteen year old daughter to go on the pill. I said I'd give her absolution, seeing that's the whole point of confession.

He smiles.

I just wish it had been me you'd come to then.

JOHN. I don't see it would have made any difference. Deep down, you're all the same.

JAMES *tries to sound light.*

JAMES. You can try me now if you like.

JAMES *is dead serious.* JOHN *meets his eye, for a moment, hands him back the letter.*

JOHN. Here.

JAMES *sighs, puts the letter into his jacket, takes out a card.*

JAMES. Oh for goodness sake, I put this in my pocket this morning and I meant to give it to you. It's a card. From Spain.

JOHN *freezes.*

I'm sorry, but you can't help but look can you.

No reaction from JOHN. JAMES *holds it out.*

JOHN. I don't want it.

JAMES *looks at it.* JOHN's *discomfort is mounting.*

JAMES. The Costa del Sol. It looks lovely. I can't make out the writing. I think it's . . . Simon, that's it. Simon.

JOHN. I don't want it.

JAMES. You might as well take it.

JOHN (*shouts*). I said I don't want the fucking card.

JOHN turns away, visibly shaken. JAMES *glances at it again then reacts, as realisation dawns.*

JAMES. John I'm so sorry. He was the one that you . . . ?

JOHN turns on him.

JOHN. That's none of your fucking business.

Pause. JAMES *strokes his garments.*

JAMES. O.K. O.K. But could we at least have some respect for the cloth.

It defuses it slightly.

JOHN. I'm sorry.

JAMES. No. I'm sorry.

Lull. JAMES *puts the card on the mantelpiece. Thinks carefully about what he is going to say.*

You probably think that a priest is the last person to understand anything about sex. About sexuality. And you'd be right. But I do understand, John, more than you realise.

No encouragement from JOHN. JAMES *takes a deep breath. This is not a story that trips off the tongue. As it progresses it gets more difficult for him.*

When I was first ordained it never bothered me, the lack of sex in my life. I was busy. I believe they now tell the young priests that their sexuality is an energy that can be channelled into their work. Maybe there's some truth in that, but even so, it wears off. I know a few guys that have left because of it.

Others that have stayed and . . . let's say . . . made their own arrangements. Anyway, when I was at St. Rock's I got involved in a voluntary group that was setting up a drugs unit for young people. In fact, that's when I first met Matthew. *He halts, looking for some courage, he sees* JOHN*'s glass of wine, half drunk, lifts it up.*

Here, give's a swig. There was a woman, one of the volunteers. She was great with the kids, strong, loving . . . We spent a lot of time together, me and . . . this woman. We shared some late night shifts and I'd run her home in the wee small hours . . . What I'm trying to say is, we had opportunities to be together . . . for seclusion. And it was tough work, you know. The kids took it out of you. You needed to look out for each other, care for each other. And we were growing closer and closer . . . I suppose I should have realised . . . but . . . the thing is . . . the time came when . . .

JOHN. I really should lie down for a couple of hours when I get back from the hospital.

JAMES *is wounded, embarrassed.*

JAMES. Yes of course.

JOHN. So, if you don't mind . . .

JAMES. Of course not. I'll get out of your way. Do you want me to light the fire for you?

JOHN. No thanks, I'll do it.

JAMES. I'll see you later then.

For once he's actually quite glad to go. JOHN *picks up the card from the mantelpiece. He stands still, holding the card.*

Lights up on SIMON. *He is fixing his water ski.*

SIMON. O.K, my little choirboy – you've done them all, haven't you. Every Cathedral from Santiago to Seville. And now you've reached me. You've got Fodor, I've got Spartacus. Not so hot on the Cathedrals, great on the bars. Hey, what's wrong with that? My Cathedrals are filled with people who see the world the same way I do – people who don't judge me, who accept me, people like us . . . yeah, like us. They're your people too, John. What are you so afraid of?

Lights down on SIMON, *up on* JOHN *as he rips the card into pieces and throws them on the fire.*

Scene Five

A candle lights up on the altar. JAMES *on his own, in a quiet moment, praying.*

JAMES. How long must I wait for you, O God. Come back and make peace with me.

He pauses. Prays to himself.

JOHN *into room from outside, jacket on. He looks drained, a bit shocked looking. He has had bad news. He takes off his jacket, throws it on bed.*

JAMES. Give me an answer God when I call you. Lord our God, how powerful is your name everywhere on earth.

JOHN *goes to door, looks out, comes back in, leaving the door slightly ajar. He is restless. He looks out the window, sighs, turns away, sits down, picks up a book, tries to read it then abandons it.*

JAMES. I came back, Lord, like the single leper. I am your shepherd, Lord, let me bring back the sheep that is lost.

JOHN *wanders back to the window, stands staring out.*

JAMES. In your love I would be so secure. As in a mother's womb, with you, my highest Good, my God, in your love I would be so secure . . . and so would he.

JOHN *closes the curtains as lights down on* JAMES.

Stay on JOHN. *He gets up from the bed, wanders over to the fire, which is out, pokers it, gives up. He hears noises off of* JAMES *arriving. He waits, looks at the door expectantly. No-one comes. He hears footsteps moving away. He wanders over to the door, looks out.*

JOHN. Hi there.

JAMES. Hi.

They wander in together.

I thought you'd be in bed.

JOHN. No. (*Scoffs.*) I'm tired all day but when the night comes I can't sleep.

JAMES. I'm bushed tonight. See you in the morning.

He turns to go.

JOHN. The hospital phoned.

JAMES. They want me to go over?

JOHN. They said they'd ring back.

JAMES. Right. (*On his way out.*) I was going to make a cup of tea then go to bed, but there's no milk. So I'll turn in.

JOHN. I've got milk.

JAMES. I wouldn't want to leave you short.

JOHN. I've got enough for two cups.

He puts on the kettle. JAMES *a bit surprised at the hospitality.*

JAMES. Everything O.K?

JOHN. It's been pretty quiet here today.

JAMES. I've been away all day. Visiting. You know . . . Doing the rounds. How was your day?

JOHN. Same as usual. Hospital then back here. Slept mostly. Read a bit. I hope you don't mind, I went into your room for some matches to light the fire.

JAMES looks at the unlit fire.

JAMES. Not very successful were you?

JOHN. No . . . well . . . I gave up eventually.

JAMES. It's chilly in here.

Takes off his jacket, starts to role up his sleeves.

You make the tea.

JAMES starts to work on the fire, JOHN *starts to make the tea. They work in silence. For a moment or two. then* JOHN *tries to sound casual, keeping his back to* JAMES.

JOHN. I saw the consultant today.

JAMES. Did you?

JOHN. Yes. He says the course of treatment I'm on, they're stopping it.

JAMES. Oh?

JOHN. Apparently it's not working any more.

JAMES. I see.

JOHN. The way it goes.

JAMES. So what do they do now?

JOHN. Oh he said they'd start me on another one by the end of the week.

JAMES. You'll still be a day patient?

JOHN. For a while, yes . . . Till I end up over the road.

JAMES picks up the fear in his voice, takes a step towards him.

You take sugar?

JAMES sighs.

Two please.

JOHN. You hungry?

JAMES. Not really. I'd something to eat at – (*Cuts off.*) I've already had something.

JOHN. Because I've got some soup. I could heat it up in the microwave.

JAMES. Now you mention it . . .

JOHN. And I've got some cheese, some bread, some ham . . .

JAMES. Tell you what. Cancel the tea. I've got some wine in my room. You want to go get it?

JOHN. All right.

JOHN goes, JAMES calls after him.

JOHN. It's on my desk.

JAMES carries on with the fire. No sign of JOHN.

JAMES (*shouts*). Or maybe it's on the shelf.

No sign of JOHN.

JAMES. The shelf above the fire.

No sign for a moment then JOHN reappears. No bottle. He looks stunned.

JAMES. Don't tell me you couldn't find it.

JOHN just stands.

Don't tell me I've scoffed it.

JOHN. No, it's still there.

JAMES. What's wrong?

JOHN. I found this in your desk.

JAMES. What?

JOHN *thrusts piece of paper at him. It is a list of telephone numbers.* JAMES *horrified.*

Look, I can explain.

JOHN. It's quite a list.

JAMES. Please, John – let me –

JOHN. How did you do it. Phone them all up and say 'Sorry to bother you, Madame, but do you have a son called John who suffers from AIDS?

JAMES. I thought it was for the best.

JOHN. Who are you to make that decision?

JAMES. I had to do something.

JOHN. And what makes you think you've got the right?

JAMES. Look, I know you said . . . I just thought . . .

JOHN. God! I hate this! You think you've got the right to decide for me. Decide that I don't mean what I say. That I don't know what I want.

JAMES. I just thought your mother had the right to –

JOHN (*anger rising*). You're doing it again. Now you're deciding what my mother should know. Now you listen to me. I forbid you. I absolutely forbid you to go and see my mother . . . (*Realisation dawning.*) Oh no . . . oh no . . . you've been, haven't you?

JAMES *squirms.*

That's where you were today.

JAMES*'s looks says it's true.*

And when were you going to tell me?

JAMES. I was going to decide . . . (*He catches* JOHN*'s look and stops.*) I can't say I'm sorry, John, because I'm not. I'm glad I saw your mother. I liked her. I liked her a lot. She's a nice woman. A good woman.

JOHN. I never said she wasn't.

JAMES. And she was glad of news of you, I can tell you. Glad
you were getting treatment. Glad you were –

JOHN. – living with a priest?

JAMES. So what? If it gives her comfort.

JOHN shakes his head.

But don't worry. I didn't give her this number. She knows
you don't want to see her or anyone just yet. (*Beat.*) But I did
say I'd get in touch again.

JOHN scoffs.

JAMES. She told me your father was very proud of you. She
said he never told you himself, but he was.

JOHN has to struggle not to react to this. JAMES sees it.

He knew you'd got a place at university and it meant
everything to him.

No reply.

And she told me how you went to teach in Spain for a year.
And she showed me the cards you sent her and the terracotta
pots you brought her back.

JOHN weakening.

She said you'd changed when you came back. You were
secretive and moody.

JOHN sneers.

Your mother loves you, John. If you knew how much then
you'd know what she's suffering now.

JOHN takes refuge in anger.

JOHN. Oh God that's all I need. Don't you think I've got
enough to carry, on my own, without 'what my mother's
going through'?

JAMES. At least she's got your sister. (*Beat.*) Actually, she's
asked me to go and see your sister. Have a talk with her.
Apparently she's taken this really badly.

*JOHN scoffs quite openly. JAMES allows himself to get
annoyed.*

I don't know what you want people to do? Cut themselves off. Stop feeling because you have. Why can't you accept that people love you? What is it that's eating away at you?

JOHN. It's called AIDS, Father.

JAMES. No, son. I see AIDS all the time and I don't know anyone as screwed up as you. Nobody's to help you. Nobody's to feel any compassion for you. Every act of love gets thrown back. And God forbid that anything should ever touch you. You might break down and start believing in something.

JOHN. You think I haven't tried? Don't you think if I could have found something to believe in, I would've held on with both hands and never let it go?

JAMES reaches out to him.

JAMES. John . . . John . . . let me help you.

JOHN shoves up his hands to ward him off.

JOHN. No. Leave me.

JAMES. John, please, listen to me . . .

JOHN. No . . . No . . . I don't want to listen. I don't want sucked in.

JAMES. John . . . please . . .

The anger and the passion rise in JOHN.

JOHN. You think I don't need solace? You think I haven't begged for help? From the depths of my soul I have called his name. I've been on my knees! I have hammered my fists against the floor until my knuckles bled. Jesus Christ, I AM DYING! I am dying, God. Help me. Please God, help me. God give me the strength to bear what's happening to me . . . Show me there's . . . Something . . . Anything . . . just show me . . .

He quietens.

But there's no-one there. Nothing there.

He is now back in control. His voice becomes quiet again. He looks at JAMES coldly.

So? You still want a shot at convincing me? Go ahead, I'm listening.

He folds his arms expectantly.

JOHN. On you go.

JAMES *uncomfortable.* JOHN*'s tone is goading.*

Oh? You not even going to try?

JAMES. No.

JOHN. Oh come on.

JAMES. No.

JOHN. You disappoint me, Father. Come on. Have a go.

JAMES. Not like this.

JOHN. Oh why not. It's what you've been after from the word go.

JAMES. John, please, stop this.

JOHN. Stop what? Isn't it what you want? To bring me back to the fold? Save my immortal soul? Well it's what I want too now. And my time's nearly up so you better get cracking.

JAMES. This is a mockery.

JOHN. That is what you want, isn't it?

JAMES. Enough, John.

JOHN. You wouldn't deny me, Father. It's what I want.

JAMES. No. I'll tell you what you want. You want a life-time's faith in two minutes. Snap your fingers and hey – there's God. The minute you want Him, He's there. Come! Heel! Stay! It doesn't work that way.

JOHN *laughs.*

JOHN. You guys make up the rules as you go along.

JAMES. I don't know about you, John, but I'm ready to call it a day here. You win. But you're right. I have been hoping, and praying, that I could help you find peace in your soul. But I'm ready to give up trying.

JOHN. Suits me.

JAMES. Maybe if you let go of whatever it is. Those nails that have been driven through your heart . . . But, I'll not be bothering you any more. I promise.

JOHN. Alleluia!

JAMES. I'll leave you to it.

He turns to go, turns back.

Oh by the way, your mother gave me some money.

JOHN. I don't want her money.

JAMES. She didn't give it to you. She gave it to me.

JOHN *looks hurt but tries to hide it.*

JAMES. Said if I knew of any needy causes . . .

JAMES *takes out a letter.*

But she gave me this for you. I suppose you better have it now.

The phone rings in the hall. JAMES *hands* JOHN *the letter and nods and leaves, without saying anything else.*

JOHN *stands, trying not to look at the letter in his hand.*

He hears JAMES*'s voice off. It is full of concern.*

JAMES. Hello . . . Yes, speaking . . . Oh no . . . Yes of course . . . Are his parents with him? . . . I'll come right over.

JOHN *looks at the door, takes a step towards it, expecting* JAMES *to come back in. He doesn't. He feels desperately alone. He opens the letter from his mother and starts to read it, he hears the outside door slam. He looks at the letter again.*

Lights slowly down on JOHN, *to blackout.*

Scene Six

Lights up on JAMES, *behind the altar, saying mass. He looks tired and worn and his voice is full of sadness.*

JAMES. I would like to offer this morning's mass for the repose of the soul of a young man called Matthew who died of AIDS in the early hours of this morning. He put up a brave fight against the disease right up till the end. He was nineteen. In particular I'd ask you to pray for his parents, that their faith will give them strength in their sorrow and their confusion. Eternal rest grant unto him, O Lord.

A moment's pause.

And let perpetual light shine upon him. May he rest in peace.

JOHN (*quietly, reverently*). Amen.

JAMES looks up in disbelief. Sees JOHN standing there, on the periphery of the light, his head bowed, his hands clasped. JAMES stares at him a moment, then looks back to face the congregation.

JAMES. May his soul and the souls of all the faithful departed through the mercy of God rest in peace.

He looks over to JOHN, anticipating 'Amen' – but JOHN is no longer there.

Amen.

JAMES looks round, wondering if he imagined seeing him there. He starts the prayer, but cannot concentrate.

Out of the depths have I cried to thee, O Lord, Lord hear my voice. Let thine ears consider well the voice of my supplication . . .

Lights down on JAMES, up on JOHN.

Scene Seven

Immediately following. JOHN is standing in his room, shaken. JAMES knocks on door, lets self in. There is a sense of urgency about him as he comes in. He is still wearing surplice, has come straight from the altar. But when he's there, in the presence of JOHN, he is very still. In contrast to all his incessant chatter of previous scenes, he is bereft of words, aware something vital could happen here. But the moment is bigger than JAMES and he is humbled by it, feels some sense of awe. Maybe even fear. Also, it is important, that JAMES does not lead JOHN in this scene. It must come from JOHN.

JAMES stands still, looking at JOHN. JOHN does not look at him.

JAMES. You were there?

JOHN. Yes.

JAMES opens his mouth to speak, and pulls back, afraid to say the wrong thing. So he waits for JOHN. JOHN is also struggling with the moment. Eventually –

James . . . I need some help here.

JAMES does not jump in. This is the moment he's hoped for – and he's tiny compared to it. It is greater than all his gab can cope with. He is not calculating how best to play it. He genuinely does not yet know what is expected of him. There is a long pause. Eventually –

JAMES. Can I do anything?

JOHN does not even look at JAMES. He finally speaks.

JOHN. I know what it is.

JAMES. Can I do anything?

He waits. JOHN holds the moment, then speaks.

JOHN. What you said last night. I know what it is. It's not the anger. It's not the bitterness. Not the fear of dying. God it's all of those, but the one thing . . . The one thing I can't . . . I need help . . .

He looks directly at JAMES.

JOHN. I need help to forgive someone.

JOHN slumps down on his knees, exhausted. JAMES looks at him. He now knows what the moment is asking of him. He goes over to JOHN. Stands in front of him, holding his right hand above JOHN's head.

JAMES. As we forgive those who trespass against us, so God our Father forgives us. I absolve you from your sins.

He signs the cross over JOHN's head with his right hand.

In the name of the Father and of the Son and of the Holy Spirit.

He places his two hands on JOHN's head.

May the peace of God be with you all the days of your life.

He holds his two hands there for a moment, then removes them and puts his hand gently on JOHN's shoulder. JOHN holds on to JAMES's arm with both his hands and clings to it. JAMES puts his other arm round JOHN's shoulder and holds him.

Scene Eight

Lights up JOHN *lying on his bed then lights up on* SIMON *as before in* JOHN*'s mind's eye, though now sitting much closer to him.*

SIMON. O.K, it was good, John – but that doesn't make it right. I'm telling you now, it won't happen again – not ever. A couple of years I've been playing safe – maybe longer. But not long enough to be certain. Oh, I pray I haven't got the virus. There you go, one thing even I pray for. But even if I have, I'm not making a present of it to you – no way José. Last night was a mistake and it's not happening again. O.K? (*Pause.*) Shit, John. You know how I feel about this stuff. 'Safe'? You bet. But that doesn't mean we have to be 'Celibate'. For me the party goes on till I drop. You get me? Stick around kid and you get to party too.

Lights go down on SIMON *and then down on* JOHN.

Scene Nine

Lights up on JAMES, *in* JOHN*'s room on his own. He looks out of the window, looks at his watch, goes to tend to the fire. He is relieved when he hears noises off of* JOHN *coming in.* JOHN *in from outside. He is carrying a paper bag.*

JAMES. There you are.

JOHN. Hi.

JAMES. I was wondering when you'd be back.

JOHN. Oh you've lit the fire.

JAMES. I thought it would be nice to come home to.

JOHN. It is. Thanks, James.

JOHN *takes off his jacket and sits down. He looks spent.* JAMES *hovers, anxious to know more.*

JAMES. How did it go?

No reply. JOHN *tired.*

You did go?

JOHN. Don't worry.

JAMES. I've thought about you all day. About both of you.

JOHN. She's aged, James.

JAMES (*quietly*). She will have.

JOHN. But it was good.

JAMES. What did I tell you.

JOHN. God, James. When she opened the door and she saw me standing there, she just held out her arms. And she shooshed me, like I was a wee boy again. 'There, there, it's all right. It's all right.'

He gives himself a shake.

All this emotional stuff lately. It was easier being a pain in the arse.

He hands JAMES *the paper bag.*

Here.

JAMES. What's this?

JAMES takes out a bottle of whisky.

JOHN. It's for you.

JAMES. What for?

JOHN. I didn't know what else to get you.

JAMES. You didn't have to get me anything.

JOHN. My mum gave me some money.

JAMES. But you shouldn't spend it on me.

JOHN. Wheesht. Now get yourself a glass.

JAMES gets two glasses.

She was incredible, James. Really strong. Much more under-standing than I imagined. Than I ever gave her credit for.

JAMES. It's often the way. The number of times I've advised young people to talk to their parents and they freak out. 'They'll kill me.' 'They'd die if they knew.'

JAMES pours. Holds up the bottle to JOHN.

JOHN. Not for me. I better not.

JAMES. Then the parents bail them out and their peers dump them. Who rallies round the pregnant teenagers, eh? The mammies and the aunties? And who was there for Matthew at the end? Not the pals that shared his needles.

A moment. JAMES *catches* JOHN'*s eye and looks away, wishing he hadn't just said what he did. He looks to his glass for a change of subject.*

This is good stuff. You can't beat a fine malt.

JOHN. I might take the tiniest bit, with lots of water. It might help me sleep.

JAMES *gets him some.*

My mum wanted me to stay tonight, but I couldn't. Not with the hospital. But she's coming here on Sunday, if that's O.K?

JAMES. Tell you what. Phone her. Tell her to come for lunch and she can go to twelve o'clock mass.

JOHN (*smiles*). Mass with my mother?

JAMES. She'll love it. What'll we make her? Let's think. Something nice.

JOHN. You don't need to go to any bother.

JAMES. But I want to. I want it to be special. Just the three of us.

JOHN. We-ell . . .

JAMES. I'll show her round the place. It'll be nothing like she expects.

JOHN. She thinks the world of you, you know.

JAMES *makes a dismissive gesture.*

She does. I think she gets a lot of comfort knowing I'm here with you.

JAMES. I'm pleased.

JOHN. And it's important to me too. It gives me comfort . . . Knowing you'll be there for her . . . After . . .

JAMES. Don't John.

JOHN. But you will be won't you?

JAMES. Hey come on.

JOHN. You'll be there for her?

JAMES. It might be years.

JOHN. Say you will be.

JAMES. You know I will be.

> JOHN *relaxes.* JAMES *wants change of subject. He pours another whisky, he takes a letter out of his pocket.*

What do you make of this.

JOHN. Not another one?

JAMES. Read it.

JOHN. From the same person?

JAMES. Just read it.

> JOHN *reads it to himself.*

JAMES (*as if reciting*). They don't like the way I run the house. The place is like a free for all and I'm spending too much time on things that don't concern the parish.

JOHN (*looks up, concerned*). Does that mean me?

JAMES. No.

JOHN. But they're writing to complain to the Bishop!

JAMES. He knew the kind of guy I was when he put me in here.

JOHN. Even so . . . ?

JAMES. It's not a problem, honest. I've got a meeting with him next month anyway, and I'm looking forward to it. (*Beat.*) It'll be a riot. He talks like translated Latin. Never use a small word if a big one will suffice adequately for the occasion. That's him. I remember once he said mass at the opening service of a new church in the diocese and at the dinner afterwards he proposed a toast to 'Father Matheson's magnificent erection'.

> JOHN *and* JAMES *share a smile. Then, in the lightness of the moment.*

JOHN. What was her name?

JAMES. Who?

JOHN. The woman. The one you told me about.

> *Moment tenses.* JAMES *silenced.*

Remember you started telling me.

JAMES. Yes I remember.

JOHN waits for JAMES to go on. He doesn't.

JOHN. I'm sorry.

Eventually –

JAMES. Veronica. Beautiful name, isn't it?

JOHN. It is.

JAMES (*pensive, more to himself*). Veronica. She's been in my mind a lot lately. Something to do with you being here.

Shakes himself out of it.

Anyway, what can I tell you about Veronica?

Thinks for a second or two.

Do you remember, when you made your First Communion, you had to stick out your tongue? The old pillar box routine?

JOHN. I remember.

JAMES. Most people nowadays take communion in their hands. But in my early days, the pre-Vatican Two days, it went straight into the mouth. These two fingers of the priest's right hand were blessed, because a priest, and no-one but a priest, could touch the sacred host. At college we were taught that the one and only exception was if the priest accidentally drops it down the front of a woman's blouse. In which case the woman has to fish it out herself. 'Oh, excuse me, Father.' Sadly, it's never actually happened to me.

JOHN laughs.

JAMES. It's not funny, John. That was the understanding and experience of women I took into my relationship with Veronica.

He pauses.

I did start telling you about her, didn't I. But did I tell you I was ready to leave the priesthood for her.

JOHN takes note.

No, I didn't. Because I've never told anyone. Oh I've made references to 'being tempted' and 'breaking my vows' but never . . . Anyway, Veronica. Do you know who Veronica was? When Jesus was carrying his cross to Calvary she was the woman who stepped out from the crowd to wipe the blood and sweat from his face . . . Anyway, we planned to go away together. I had seven hundred pounds my father had left me and Veronica had some money of her own. We were going to start a new life somewhere else. I was going to tell the Bishop in the morning and meet Veronica in a hotel in Cumbria that afternoon. Then we were going to write to our respective families.

He is not proud of the plan.

We thought, that way, it would cause less stress all round.

He sighs, needs courage to go on.

Anyway, the morning I was due to see the Bishop I took ill. Saying eight o'clock mass I suddenly doubled over with this incredible pain in my stomach. I'd to be taken off the altar and someone sent for an ambulance.

JOHN. What about Veronica?

JAMES. I'd a whole lot of tests and finally they rushed me to surgery and took out my appendix. I was in such pain I've actually no memory of it.

JOHN. But what happened to Veronica?

JAMES. What I do remember is them giving me the anaesthetic and me struggling, trying to say 'I've got to phone, I've got to phone' and them thinking I was delirious.

In answer to JOHN's *question.*

Veronica went to the hotel and she waited. If only she'd phoned the chapel house . . . Anyway, even the next day I still couldn't get to a phone. I was very weak and I had this drip in. When I finally did get in contact with the hotel she was gone. I was told she'd stayed two nights then checked out. But she didn't go home. I found out later, indirectly, that she went on to her brother's in Kent.

JOHN. Couldn't you get in touch with her there?

JAMES. And open all those wounds again? (*Beat.*) No, John, some things are better left in God's hands.

JOHN *silenced by this.*

I did love her, John. And I know she deserved better.

While JAMES *speaks* JOHN *is feeling increasingly unwell.*

When I got out I went to see the Bishop. I told him I'd had a lot of personal problems and that I was struggling. He didn't ask any questions. Just said I needed a rest and sent me on a retreat for two months. Then this place came up.

The strange thing is, my appendix, when they took it out, do you know there was nothing wrong with it. They never did find out what I had. It was as if the whale had swallowed me up and was holding me in its belly for something else.

He looks at JOHN *lovingly, smiles.*

You, maybe.

He looks into his glass.

And I can honestly say that I believe I am a better priest for understanding the reality of physical love.

JOHN *tries to get out of his chair and falls.*

JAMES. John!

JOHN. Got up too quickly, that's all. I'm fine.

He's not. JAMES *supports him.*

JAMES. Come on.

JOHN. Just tired.

He leans heavily on JAMES.

So tired these days.

JAMES. Come on. Lie down.

He leads JOHN *to the bed. Takes off his shoes, covers him.*

You've overdone it today. Packed a lot in. And here's me rattling on about myself as usual. You should have stopped me.

JOHN. No. No.

JAMES. It was probably the whisky. That's all. Just you lie there.

JOHN. I'm sorry.

JAMES. That's what it would be. The whisky. Can I get you something?

JOHN. No. Just stay.

JOHN *goes quiet.* JAMES *sits for a few seconds then makes to move.* JOHN *grabs his wrist.*

JOHN. Don't go.

JAMES. Just going to shut the curtains.

He does so.

JOHN. James?

JAMES *comes back and sits on the bed.*

JAMES. I'm here.

JOHN. What was Matthew like, at the end?

JAMES *feels pain at this.* JOHN *gets increasingly agitated.*

JAMES. You don't need to think of that yet, John.

JOHN. Some days I think I do.

JAMES. You've got plenty days, John. Plenty days.

JOHN. It's not the days, James. It's the nights. The darkness and the quiet of the night. The fear, it grips me and it won't let go.

JAMES. Shhh . . .

JOHN. I start wondering what it will be like going to sleep, knowing I might not be there to see the morning.

JAMES. John, don't.

JOHN. What was Matthew like?

JAMES. Don't distress yourself.

JOHN. You were there, weren't you?

JAMES. John, please.

JOHN *grabs* JAMES*'s hand.*

JOHN. Tell me what was he like?

JAMES. John. John.

JOHN. Was he scared?

JAMES. No. He wasn't scared.

JOHN. How was he?

JAMES *does not reply at once.*

JOHN (*voice raised*). How was he, James?

JAMES. He was . . . well, he was ready.

JOHN. He was ready?

JAMES. Yes.

JOHN. Will I be ready?

JAMES. Yes, you'll be ready. You'll be ready, John.

JOHN. What will it be like?

JAMES. Please John.

JOHN. I want you to tell me.

JAMES. How can I know. I'm not a doctor?

JOHN. That's not . . .

His distress rises.

JAMES. All right. All right . . . When the time comes, you'll be ready. You will. You'll be at peace. And you'll be surrounded by love. The love of your family and the love of God. The fear will lose its grip and you'll feel safe. It'll be like . . . like going home. Like it was today with your mother. God the Father will be waiting for you. He'll take you in his arms and he'll bring you home. Now, sleep, John. Sleep. For it won't be tonight and it won't be tomorrow and I won't leave you.

JAMES strokes JOHN's arm and looks at him sadly till JOHN drifts into an exhausted sleep.

Lights down.

Scene Ten

Lights up as SIMON in. Top half naked, his hair wet, a towel round his neck. He is carrying a rucksack and washbag which he dumps on the floor. He kneels in front of the fire and starts to dry his hair with the towel.

JAMES in, carrying some clean towels and sheets. He glances at SIMON in passing, takes him for JOHN.

JAMES. Oh good. You're up. You had me worried last night.

He heads for the bed, SIMON *looks round but* JAMES *has his back to him, making the bed.*

JAMES. Our friend's been at it again.

He takes a letter out his pocket and puts it on JOHN*'s bedside table.*

You can read it later. I thought I might put it on the notice board at the back of the chapel. See if that puts a stop to it. But I'd hate your mother to see it.

SIMON *is about to speak but* JAMES *carries on.*

It even crossed my mind that it could be Father Allan. You get a lot of jealousy in the clergy you know.

SIMON. I think you've got the wrong guy.

JAMES is startled. He gets up.

JAMES. Oh . . . I'm sorry, I thought –

SIMON. You're looking for John?

JAMES. Eh . . . yes.

SIMON. He's just gone out. He'll be right back.

JAMES. Oh you're a friend of his?

SIMON. Yeh . . .

He sees the inquisitive way JAMES *is looking at him, the towel etc. He smiles.*

I got soaked through, walking from the station. Does it always rain as much here?

JAMES. You're an American?

SIMON. West Coast born and bred.

JAMES. Really? I was in America once. Part of an exchange. New Mexico. For six weeks. Place called Jemee Springs. Don't suppose you know it.

SIMON. It is a pretty big country.

JAMES. Stupid question, I know.

SIMON. You must be James . . . No . . . wait a minute . . . it's 'Father', isn't it? 'Father James'? Isn't that right? That's what you say? Father?

JAMES. Yes . . . well . . . it doesn't bother me.

SIMON. No, I like it. 'Father'. It's good.

JAMES. How long you here for?

> JOHN *in, carrying a bag of groceries. Takes in the sight of* JAMES *and* SIMON *together.*

JOHN. Oh good. James. I was coming to find you.

JAMES. You're a dark horse. You might have said your friend was coming.

JOHN. I didn't know. He just turned up. You've still not told me how you managed to find me?

SIMON. It wasn't easy. (*To* JAMES.) A difficult guy to catch hold of, this.

> JAMES *smiles.*

JAMES. I know.

SIMON (*to* JOHN). I don't suppose you've been trying to find me?

JOHN. No.

SIMON. Didn't think so. Just as well, really. I've been on the road most of this year.

JAMES. Really? You've been travelling? Doing your American tourist bit? 'Doing Europe' as they say.

SIMON. Been all over Europe.

JAMES. Good for you.

SIMON. South of France, Italy, Greece, Denmark, Portugal. But Spain mostly. I settled in Spain for a while. That's where I met John.

> *Realisation dawning on* JAMES *of who* SIMON *is. He looks from* SIMON *to* JOHN *and back again.*

JAMES. In Spain?

SIMON. Yeh. South Coast. Run speedboat rides from the shore.

JAMES (*uncomfortable*). I see.

SIMON. Spent the last couple of months in London. Rains all the time there too. Now what've you got there, John?

> JOHN *delves into the bag.* SIMON *over to him.* JAMES *takes in their apparent closeness and ease with each other which makes him increasingly uncomfortable.*

JOHN. Ohhh . . . pizzas, garlic mushrooms, Italian bread . . .

SIMON. Something smells good.

JOHN. It's the bread. It's still warm. Try some, Simon?

>JAMES *reacts to 'SIMON'.*

>JOHN *breaks off some bread and puts it to* SIMON's *lips.*

SIMON (*appreciatively*). Mmmm . . .

>*Hold the moment. It is private but not overtly sexual, but seen through* JAMES's *eyes, it has all kinds of overtones.*

JOHN. Good?

SIMON. Mmmm . . . yeh . . .

>JAMES, *embarrassed, makes a slight noise as he picks the towel up from where* SIMON *has left it, on the floor by the fire. He drapes it over the back of the chair. They remember him.*

JOHN. You hungry James?

JAMES. Not particularly.

>SIMON *sits on the edge of the bed, one foot up on it. His ease irks* JAMES.

SIMON. So, who all live here?

JOHN. Just us.

SIMON. What? Just the two of you? You share this place?

JOHN. Yes.

SIMON. Like 'The Odd Couple'.

JOHN. Who?

>SIMON *smiles.*

SIMON. You know the American sit-com. Oscar and Felix.

>*He hums the theme tune –*

>Doo de doo de doo, doo de doo dooo.

JOHN. Yes. Yes. I'm with you now. That's good, isn't it, James? That's us.

>JOHN *amused.* JAMES *not.* SIMON *lies back on the bed, hands behind his head, still humming 'The Odd Couple' to himself.* JOHN *takes wine from the bag and opens it.*

JAMES. I'd better leave you to it then.

JOHN. James? You're not going?

JAMES. I have to.

JOHN. Oh no, stay, please.

JAMES looks unsure, uncomfortable.

JOHN. I want you to stay.

JAMES pulls him aside, out of SIMON's hearing.

JAMES. Everything all right here?

JOHN. Everything's fine.

JAMES. You sure?

JOHN. Yes.

JAMES. How'd he get here?

JOHN. He just turned up.

JAMES. He just turned up?

JOHN. Yes. He just turned up. But it's O.K. I'm O.K. about it.

JAMES. Come on.

JOHN. No, I am. I'm O.K. Honest. Hey Simon, did I tell you James and I were Brothers of Thunder.

SIMON. Brothers of what?

JOHN. Brothers of Thunder. We've got it all worked out. When we go to heaven, James will sit on one side of God and I'll sit on the other.

SIMON. Sounds cool. So long as I get to sit on his knee.

JOHN laughs. JAMES tenses.

JOHN. What does 'Simon' mean, James?

JAMES. I don't know.

JOHN. Isn't there a story about a Simon in the Bible?

JAMES. I can't think off hand.

JOHN. Oh come on. Even I know there was a Simon.

JAMES sighs, barely concealing his reluctance.

JAMES. There was Simon the disciple. Yes.

JOHN. I knew it. Did he have a nickname. (*To* SIMON.) Jesus was great at giving people nicknames. (*To* JAMES.) What did he call Simon?

JAMES. He called him Peter.

JOHN. Peter?

JAMES. He wanted him to be head of the church so he called him Peter.

SIMON. Sounds reasonable.

JAMES. Peter as in 'petros' as in rock. As in 'You are Peter and on this rock I will build my church'.

SIMON. Hey, that's great. I'm a rock. You can call me Rocky.

JOHN. I like it.

SIMON. Have you been to St. Peter's in Rome, Father?

JAMES. I think I'll push off now.

JOHN. You're not going to eat with us?

JAMES. I don't think so.

JOHN. I wish you would.

SIMON. Yes, please stay, Father. We've got plenty.

This rankles JAMES. *Makes him decide to go.*

JAMES. I can't possibly. I've got things to do tonight. I'm sorry.

JOHN. Well at least have a glass of wine.

JAMES hovers.

Just a glass.

JOHN goes to the kitchen area to get glasses, leaving JAMES and SIMON alone. SIMON smiles at JAMES. JAMES moves closer, lowers his voice, but tries to sound casual.

JAMES. There is a legend that by the time he died St. Peter's face was lined with scars, from the tears he wept every day of his life for betraying Jesus.

SIMON unsure what to make of this, smiles awkwardly.

SIMON. Right.

Uncomfortable under JAMES's glare, he backs off in the direction of the kitchen. He comes back with JOHN and a glass of wine. JOHN gives a glass to JAMES.

JOHN. Here's to . . . what are we drinking to?

JAMES. I don't know. Whatever you like.

JOHN. Here's to . . . Happy Days.

SIMON. Happy Days.

> JOHN *and* SIMON *exchange the briefest of sad looks then look away.* SIMON *glaces at* JAMES.

SIMON. You sure you won't eat with us, Father?

> JAMES *shakes his head.*

JOHN. What have you got on tonight, anyway?

JAMES. I'm seeing some people after Benediction.

SIMON. What's Benediction?

JOHN. You could look in later.

JAMES. No, it's people from the Liturgy Group. It'll probably go on. Benediction, Simon, is a church service, for the adoration of Jesus, who is eucharistically present, in the form of bread exposed on the altar.

> SIMON *knows it is a put-down but smiles through it.*

SIMON. Right. Right. I'm with you now. You know, I love your church, Father. It's a wonderfully imposing building.

JAMES. Handy too, for John. It's right across from the Hospital.

> *He puts down his glass.*

Enjoy your meal.

> JAMES *goes.* JOHN *watches him go.*

SIMON. Look, John, if it's a problem, me being here.

JOHN. I told you. It's not.

> JOHN *looks at him and looks away, busies himself with the table. Without* JAMES, *they are aware of being alone together. A few seconds of glancing at each other, wondering who will be the first to speak.*

SIMON. John . . .

JOHN. What did you do with the boat?

SIMON. Sold it.

> SIMON *wanders over to the fire, tries to warm himself.*

God it's cold.

JOHN *watches him.* SIMON *uncomfortable.*

JOHN. Why didn't you tell me you were coming?

SIMON. I did. I sent you a card.

JOHN *takes this in, turns away.*

I guess I'm about the last person you ever wanted to see.

JOHN. No. No. I wouldn't say that.

SIMON. What would you say then?

Lull.

JOHN. Why did you come, Simon?

SIMON. To see you.

JOHN. So, you've seen me.

SIMON. Yeh, I've seen you.

SIMON *looks at him sadly, aware of his illness.*

You want me to go away again or what?

JOHN. I don't think so. I . . . Look . . . I still can hardly take this in. I didn't expect I'd ever see you again, and yet here you are. Right here. In my room. In front of my fire. You really are here. (*Smiles nervously.*) Even though you look so different without your trunks.

SIMON. Well, maybe if I'd kept my trunks on . . .

They manage to share a smile. It blends into sadness.

I swear to God I didn't know.

JOHN. You told me.

SIMON. You have to believe me.

JOHN. I do. I believe you. What else do you want me to say?

SIMON. I don't know.

JOHN. It's all right. I'm all right about it.

SIMON. Oh come on. How can you say that? You must hate me?

JOHN. No. Simon, I don't hate you. I did at first and for a long time. But a lot has happened to me since then.

Pause, SIMON *takes this in.*

SIMON. How are you?

JOHN. Worse than you.

This registers with SIMON.

SIMON. It didn't take long with you, did it, kid?

JOHN *shrugs, looks away.*

Don't know how long I've had it. Could be years. It's not fair, is it. You're like this and so far I'm still O.K? I can't tell you how bad that makes me feel.

JOHN. Not me. I'm glad for you. (*Beat.*) And I am glad to see you.

SIMON. I can't handle this.

SIMON *turns away.*

JOHN. I can. I can now. But if you knew the state I was in when I first came here . . .

SIMON *looks round, they share a look, he looks away.*

I've dumped it, Simon – it's all out there – and in the time I've left I don't want to pick it all up again. Just believe it, Simon. Whatever I'm feeling right now, I don't feel bitter.

SIMON. Christ I do. If I could get my hands on the bastard that gave me this! (*Smiles.*) Fat chance. I'd need to line up all the beach boys on the Costa del Sol.

JOHN. Oh thanks. That makes me feel really special.

SIMON. You were special, John. (*Beat.*) Why did you leave so suddenly?

JOHN *looks away.*

SIMON. You just upped and left.

JOHN. I don't know. I couldn't cope.

SIMON. Cope with me? Cope with us? What?

JOHN. Couldn't cope with you looking at other guys.

SIMON. Hey! I always look at guys. Guys look at me, I look at them. It's no great shakes.

JOHN. But you didn't just look.

SIMON. Well maybe if you'd looked a bit more, loosened up. got into the scene a bit –

JOHN. What does it matter now?

SIMON. You and me, John. You and me. It was special. I thought we . . . had something.

Catches glimpse in JOHN*'s eye.*

Don't even think it . . . What I'm trying to say, John . . . No way could I go back to the States without finding you.

JOHN *nods.*

JOHN. I appreciate that.

SIMON. And what I want . . . (*Takes deep breath.*) I want you to come back with me. To the States.

JOHN. What?

SIMON. Come back to the States with me. There you have it. It's out now.

JOHN. You want me to . . . ?

SIMON. Come back with me, John. Please.

JOHN. I don't see . . .

SIMON. Please. I've still got some money from the boat. Enough to get us there, and more . . .

JOHN. Hang on. Hang on.

SIMON. You'll be better off there, John. It's a better place to . . . It's just better. There's more awareness, a deeper understanding. You'd be better off there. And it's warm. It's beautiful, it's near the ocean. Go on, John. Say you'll come.

JOHN. Si. You can't throw this at me.

SIMON. I met some Americans in Paris, at the clinic. Really great people. They've got this place in San Raphael. Up from the coast. A terrific place. Truly. For about fifteen guys or so, they live together, support each other. They've got counselling, they've got medical care . . .

JOHN. You mean a hospice?

SIMON *hates the word.*

SIMON. Thomas and Eve – they run it. You'll love them.

JOHN. And how would I pay for all this?

SIMON. I told you. The money I got from the boat.

Pause.

JOHN. You don't have to do this.

SIMON. I want to.

JOHN. You don't have to feel responsible for me.

SIMON. But I am responsible for you. Jesus Christ, I know that. Before you, I was never into picking up guys with no experience. As scruples go it's no great shakes, but there you go, it's one I've got.

JOHN *sighs.*

Say you'll think about it.

JOHN. I can't, Simon.

SIMON. Don't answer me now. Just think about it. We can talk it through. Remember Spain. It'll be like Spain.

JOHN. I don't think so.

SIMON. But at least I'll be near. I'll be able to see you.

JOHN. You don't have to do this.

SIMON. Yes I do. I think I do.

JOHN. The answer's no, Simon.

SIMON. No?

JOHN *shakes his head.*

Just 'No'?

JOHN. It's really too late.

SIMON *takes this in.*

SIMON. So? Where will you go?

JOHN. Here.

SIMON. Here?

JOHN. Yes.

SIMON. In this place?

JOHN. Yes.

SIMON. This church place?

JOHN. Look! It's not where I expected to end up, O.K. But then again . . .

He shrugs.

SIMON *backs off.*

SIMON. O.K.

JOHN. And when the time comes, Simon . . . I'll want my family round me.

SIMON. You don't want to be with your own kind?

JOHN. People have been good to me.

SIMON. You want to think about it for a few days? Play around with it?

JOHN *shakes his head.*

I'm sad.

JOHN. Don't be.

SIMON. Is there anything you need? Anything?

JOHN. Simon, you've carried this long enough. You can let go now.

SIMON *can't speak. He nods.*

Let it go.

SIMON *is quite overcome.*

SIMON. God, John!

Puts his head on JOHN's *shoulder, an arm round his neck.* JOHN *pats him on the back.*

JOHN. It's all right.

SIMON. Can I stay in touch?

JOHN. I'll write.

SIMON. I'd like that.

JOHN. I'll make sure you find out . . . what happens.

SIMON *nods. Then he pulls back, changes tone.*

SIMON. Hey, what happened to that food?

JOHN *smiles and gets up to see to the food.*

JOHN. How long you staying?

SIMON. I've not thought about it.

JOHN. You got a place for tonight?

The question hangs in the air.

SIMON. Eh . . .

JOHN. You can stay here.

SIMON. I hadn't . . . is that all right with you?

JOHN. Yes. I'd like you to stay.

He smiles.

JOHN. You're looking good.

SIMON. So far I'm O.K.

JOHN. You're not scared?

SIMON. Me? No. Not really. Not as scared as I would be of growing old.

JOHN smiles.

SIMON. I mean it. I never wanted to get old. Who wants to get old? Imagine being thirty. Or thirty-five. Or forty-five. Or fifty! Jesus! Different if you've got kids, grandkids. But what is there for an old queen? . . . It's the saddest thing. You see a bunch of young guys on the beach, laughing and playing ball in the sand. And there'll be some old queen, looking at them, smiling at them. 'Hey, I was young once. Brings it all back'. But inside he's screaming with loneliness. At least we won't end up like that, John.

JOHN. No, we won't.

SIMON. The way I see it. I've had a ball, I've surfed, I've sailed, I've lain in the sun.

JOHN. That's not all there is, Simon.

SIMON. I think it is, John. Life's just one long beach.

JOHN smiles.

SIMON. That's all there is. And it's enough. Life's a beach, and then you die.

He strokes JOHN's face gently with his finger.

But do you know what makes me really sad for you. You've had so little fun. You've had so little fun and I was it. I mean, I know I'm good . . .

They share a smile.

SIMON. Are you scared?

JOHN. Only of the nights. The stillness and the quiet of the nights. Sometimes there's a fear . . .

His voice breaks off.

SIMON. Sshhh.

SIMON *holds him, kisses him on the lips, pulls away.*

I'm sorry.

JOHN. No . . . Please.

He kisses SIMON.

SIMON. Are you well enough, John?

JOHN. I'm better than I've been for a long time.

Lights down as they embrace.

Scene Eleven

Lights up on JAMES *at the altar. He is deeply uneasy, avoiding eye contact with the congregation. Lights also up on* SIMON *and* JOHN, *on the bed in each others' arms, asleep.*

JAMES. This is the word of the Lord.

He kisses the book.

Praise to thee, Lord Jesus Christ.

Lights down on SIMON *and* JOHN.

There will be no sermon today.

Pause

The offertory hymn will be number 342. And can I remind you please to make sure you return your hymn books to the back of the chapel?

Now please stay standing for the creed.

Slow cross fade as JAMES *makes his way from the altar down the steps and sits on a stool, which we might think of as being inside a confessional.*

Meanwhile, SIMON *has wandered into the church and stands nearby in his own light – as it were – not too far from the other side of the confessional. (*SIMON *is not really aware of it, but he is seeking some kind of solace.)* JAMES *becomes aware of his presence. He sits in silence for a moment. Finally:*

JAMES. I don't suppose you've come to make your confession.

SIMON. I guess not. Though I sometimes wish that I had learned to pray. (*Smiles.*) But I was never big on kneeling.

Silence from JAMES. *He's missed the moment.*

If you could only have seen him. So thin and frail without his clothes and his skin like paper.

JAMES. He's dying.

SIMON. Someone who's dying – now that's a first.

JAMES can hardly bear to listen. Looks away.

SIMON. But he's not dying yet. Oh I know you want to prepare him. But you can have his death, Father. I want his life. And it's not over yet. Not for me or him. Last night . . . I know I helped him.

JAMES reacts.

I know what you people think about guys like me. But I want to tell you, James, last night . . . what we had . . . It was good. It made him feel alive. For a moment.

JAMES can't listen any more, gets up and wanders away. SIMON, *deep in his own thoughts, doesn't realise.*

And that's all there is. Moments. You can share a moment with another guy, but you can't pick up his cross. You can't share his suffering. If I could take away his pain by taking it upon myself . . . I guess . . . I wouldn't do it. So . . . there, Father . . . you've gotten a confession after all.

A moment's pause.

Right, I've done what I came here to do. So now I can look at myself in the mirror again. (*He smiles.*) I like that. The adoration of everything I worship and . . . revere.

Are you still there? Where the hell are you? God this church is cold. Shit, this is no place for a Californian boy. I need the sun on my back and the sand between my toes. I need life.

And SIMON *goes.*

Scene Twelve

JOHN *is looking out the window, pensive, but not unhappy. Knock on door,* JOHN *does not turn round.*

JOHN. It's open.

Knock again.

It's open.

Nobody there. JOHN *goes over and opens door.* JAMES *is standing there.* JOHN *smiles, surprised (at* JAMES *knocking).*

Hi.

JAMES. You were looking for me earlier?

JOHN. Yes. James, I've got to talk to you. Come on in.

JAMES *hovers at doorway.*

Come in, man.

JAMES *comes in hesitantly. He glances round for signs of* SIMON. *There's none.*

JAMES. On your own?

JOHN. Yes.

JAMES *relaxes slightly, looks round more freely.*

Simon's gone.

JAMES. Oh.

Lull.

JOHN. James, I need to talk to you.

JAMES *uneasy, does not want to hear.*

About what happened yesterday. About last night.

JAMES. Look. What you do is up to you.

JOHN *does not pick up on it. His mood is up.*

JOHN. No, I want to talk about it. That was Simon – (*Smiles.*) – obviously. If you knew – well you do know – the bitterness I felt towards him. It was destroying me. But then he came and I was faced with him and I saw for myself how much I've moved on from there.

JAMES *still can't look at him.*

JAMES. I'm pleased for you.

JOHN. I can't get over it, James. It was good. Uplifting. We talked so many things out. (*He smiles remembering.*) I'd forgotten how droll Simon can be. The thing is, James, even after all that's happened, we still . . .

JAMES. You better watch your time. For getting to the hospital.

JOHN. I've time yet.

JAMES. Well I've not I'm afraid. I've to go out.

JOHN. Where?

JAMES. To the shops.

JOHN. Can't you go later?

JAMES. I'm busy later.

JOHN. What's wrong with you?

JAMES. Nothing's wrong. I'm going to the shops. That's all. Is there anything you want me to get?

JOHN. Something *is* wrong.

JAMES. Look, your mother's coming to dinner tomorrow, remember.

JOHN. Yes, I remember.

JAMES (*more to self*). That's something anyway.

JOHN. I'm sorry?

A lull, JOHN *looks at* JAMES, *wondering about his mood.*

JAMES. Spaghetti bolognese all right with you? She'll like that?

JOHN. Yes. Fine.

JAMES. What about wine? Does she like wine?

JOHN. Sometimes. Yes.

JAMES. What kind?

JOHN. I don't know.

JAMES. You must know that, surely?

JOHN. I don't.

JAMES. Then decide. Red or white?

JOHN. It doesn't matter.

JAMES. It does matter. You've invited your mother over. Now give some thought to the wine.

JOHN. She won't mind.

JAMES. Just decide.

JOHN. I don't know . . . White.

JAMES. All right. White it is. O.K? That's fine by me.

JOHN. Look, have I done something?

JAMES looks away, embarrassed.

What? What have I done?

No reply from JAMES.

Tell me what's bothering you, James.

JAMES heads for the door, tries to cover.

JAMES. I'll see you later.

JOHN stands in front of door.

JOHN. No. You'll see me now.

JOHN determined. JAMES looks away.

JAMES. Look, I don't have time for this.

JOHN's stand becomes more adamant. JAMES's annoyance beginning to show. Trying not to look at JOHN, but JOHN's look is penetrating.

JOHN. Well?

JAMES. You know, maybe if you were the least bit sorry . . .

JOHN. Sorry? For what?

JAMES scoffs.

Look at me, James.

JAMES. Look, I'm no use at this. I don't want to be drawn into any big chat about anything. All right? Anyway, you know what it is.

JOHN. I'm sorry?

JAMES. You know what it is.

JOHN. It's Simon, isn't it?

JAMES looks away.

You didn't know what to make of him, did you?

A flicker of an eyebrow raise from JAMES.

O.K. I know it was a bit of a shock – the way he turned up – but, I mean, if *I* could cope with it . . .

JAMES. Look, I want to go before the town gets mobbed.

JOHN. Did you give yourself a chance to get to know him? He's come all this way to find me. Don't you want to know why?

No reply from JAMES.

He offered to take me back with him. To the States. To look after me . . .

JAMES lets out a little gasp of contempt. JOHN clocks it, is annoyed.

Maybe if you'd stayed last night . . .

JAMES scoffs. JOHN looks hurt.

I wanted you to stay, James. We both did.

JAMES annoyed at this, gives in to it.

JAMES. Don't give me that. I know what went on in here last night.

Embarrassment. JOHN a bit stunned. JAMES looks at him directly.

JAMES (*gentle, irrefutable*). I know what went on in here last night. (*Beat.*) And you're supposed to be sick.

JOHN relaxes. Hint of a smile at what he takes to be JAMES's naivety.

JOHN. Come on, James. What harm can it do? Me and Simon, we can't re-infect each other.

JAMES. I'm not stupid. (*Beat.*) Or deaf.

JOHN. Oh Jesus . . . I'm sorry, James. I really am. I didn't mean to embarrass you.

JAMES. I'm not embarrassed.

JOHN. Well I am. I said I was sorry, now can we leave it at that, please? Can we forget it? (*Beat.*) I hate to say this, but it really isn't your business.

JAMES. I think it is, under the circumstances.

JOHN *unsettled, does not want to hear the rest.*

JOHN. What circumstances?

JAMES. I mean, this is the chapel, for God's sake. Do you think I can turn a blind eye to two guys . . .

JOHN *is totally taken aback as full realisation dawns. He takes a step back, goes very quiet.*

JOHN. So that's it.

He walks away, sits on the edge of the bed, deflated. JAMES *gentler.*

JAMES. Think of the position it puts me in, John. You know the kind of work I'm trying to do here – you see what I'm up against. I'm meeting the Bishop next month. Suppose he got to hear about something like this . . .

JOHN. We certainly can't have you upsetting the Bishop can we?

JAMES *tries to become conciliatory.*

JAMES. Look, John. If it was up to me . . .

JOHN *looks at him.* JAMES *stops.*

JAMES. I do try to understand. Believe me I do. But can you try and see it from my point of view. You're the first person I've taken in from across the road . . . You realise what I'm saying here?

JOHN. Do you?

JAMES *tries another tack.*

JAMES. Look, I'm not blaming you. If anything I blame myself. I should've stayed last night. I shouldn't have left you two alone.

JOHN. Don't say any more, James . . .

JAMES. God knows, what you've been through, how could I blame you. I'm not saying it's right or wrong. But the need for comfort, the refuge of a moment's consolation. I could understand, I could –

JOHN. . . . please . . .

JAMES. – if it was anyone else but him.

JOHN *closes his eyes.*

JAMES. But after what he did to you . . . How could you let him . . . It's a question of dignity, John. Human dignity.

JOHN. Really? I thought it was a question of forgiveness.

Pause. JAMES *hears this, is about to start on another tack, but* JOHN *carries on.*

And the forgiveness was real because I forgave Simon. In fact, it was *you* that taught me to forgive. Or have you forgotten that?

JAMES. No, of course not . . .

JOHN. I blamed him and I hated him and I hated myself. And you lifted that from me.

JAMES. Yes, but don't you see.

JOHN. You told me God loved me.

JAMES. God does love you –

JOHN. 'But . . . ?' Is that what you're saying now? God loves me but – But what?

JAMES *becomes very gentle.*

JAMES. John. John. What pains me most . . . I thought that you had made your peace with God.

JOHN. . . . And to lose God for a fuck, eh? . . .

JAMES (*annoyed*). Oh I'm not getting into this.

JOHN. You are in it. Because of you I let myself believe. I learned to love myself again and to love other people. I didn't feel shame, I didn't feel I was being punished. And now you're trying to take that away from me?

JAMES. No I'm not. I'm not, John. Nobody can take it away from you. Only you can take it away from yourself.

JOHN *gives bitter laugh.*

JOHN. God, you guys are clever. Got all the answers haven't you.

JAMES. It's not me that makes the rules.

JOHN *looks at him hard. No need for an answer (i.e. that the rules are made by the Church). A lull.* JAMES *becomes gentle again.*

JAMES. John, I know it's difficult for you. I've got difficulty with it myself sometimes. But you have to understand the Church's position . . .

JOHN. Oh I do. I do now. I thought I could be part of it, but I can't. I don't fit in. I never did.

JAMES. You can, John, if you'd only . . .

JOHN (*interrupting – angry*). 'If' . . . if . . . if? 'God loves you but . . . ' 'You're one of us if . . . '

He gives a little laugh.

I'm going to die. No 'ifs' about that.

JAMES. John please . . .

JOHN. Hey, it's O.K. I mean, we've all got to die, haven't we? Isn't that what it's all about? Being good in this world so we'll have a place in the next?

JAMES *would interrupt,* JOHN *puts up his hand to carry on.*

So, anyway, I'm going to die and I'm going to come face to face with the Lord. He'll be waiting for me, his arms open. Like you told me. Waiting for me. And he'll put his arms round me and he'll hold me and he'll call me by my name. He'll say, 'John, John I like you a hell of a lot. In fact I love you. In fact, I died for you. But. Well . . . the thing is . . . the Pope says that people like you are intrinsically disordered. I'm sorry, son. I love you and I want you here with me, but what can I do? He *is* the Pope. My hands are tied. I'm only God.

JAMES. That's not funny.

JOHN. I never said it was. But it's the bottom line.

JAMES. It's not as simple as that.

No reply from JOHN.

It's not as simple as that.

JOHN. Then this is where you and me part company.

JOHN looks round, deciding to pull out. He gets up wearily.

From now on I'll manage on my own.

JAMES. You don't know what you're talking about. You think you do, but you don't.

JOHN does not answer at first. He gets a bag, puts it on his bed.

JOHN. Well, when it comes to talk I bow before the master. They named you well, didn't they? 'Father Talkalot'?

JAMES is stung.

Talk about being a rebel, fighting authority, breaking the rules. It was all . . . Talk.

JAMES. You don't know what you're saying . . .

JOHN. Maybe when you were young, with your pals round about you. You rocked the boat a bit. But look at you now! Your own parish, this place to yourself, your own cosy wee scene. Where's it gone, James?

Pause. JAMES deeply uncomfortable.

JAMES. Look, John, I . . .

JOHN. You mean well, I'll give you that. But it's finished for you.

JAMES tries to scoff, but JOHN's remarks are hitting home.

And I can tell you when it happened. The day and the hour. It finished for you the day you let them take out your appendix.

Silence. JAMES is shaken, struggling with the truth of this. He takes a second or two to find his voice.

JAMES. I've made mistakes in my life. I don't deny it.

JOHN is weary.

JOHN. What does it matter now?

JAMES. But whatever else you might think of me, John, ask yourself this. Have I ever shown you anything else but love?

JOHN. No . . . until now.

Lull as this goes home with JAMES.

But then you've done that before haven't you? Giving someone your love and taking it away at the last minute. Still, I suppose I should be glad I'm not waiting for you in some hotel room.

JAMES *stunned by truth of this. He has to sit down or turn away.* JOHN, *looks down at his bags, relents slightly.*

JOHN. That was cruel.

JAMES *can't look at* JOHN.

JAMES. You know, when we were at seminary, we were warned about the dangers of getting close to anyone. Not just women. That was obvious. Other people – parishioners – people that come to us for help – even each other . . .

He sighs, taking in the wisdom of this. He turns to face JOHN, *notices the packing.*

Look . . . What's this?

JOHN. What does it look like.

JAMES. You're not leaving?

JOHN carries on packing.

JAMES. You going back with Simon?

JOHN. Think that if you like.

JOHN relents.

JOHN. No. I'm not.

JAMES. Then why . . . ?

JOHN. Because I can't stay here. Not now.

JAMES. Don't be silly. Where else can you go?

JOHN. It's not on.

He looks at JAMES *directly.*

Not on for either of us really.

This is true. JAMES *looks away.*

JAMES. What about your mother?

JOHN. What about her?

JAMES. She's supposed to be coming tomorrow.

JOHN. I'll ring her.

JAMES. And say what?

JOHN. I don't know. Something.

He carries on packing.

JAMES. Where will you go?

JOHN. I'll see Gordon today. He'll find me a place.

JAMES hovers.

JOHN. A room somewhere. Near the hospital.

JAMES. This is a room near the hospital.

*JAMES is not being pushy or conciliatory. He is being
practical.*

JOHN. Look, James –

JAMES. Be sensible, son. You're sick. You probably don't have
the strength for another move.

*JOHN knows this is true. He sighs, sits on the edge of the
bed, trapped.*

JAMES. So just stay.

JOHN. I can't take back the things I said.

JAMES. Don't worry about it. You certainly said some very
interesting things. Some good points you raised. And I'll
think about them. I will. I'll give them a lot of thought.

JOHN. You do that.

*JAMES goes. JOHN is left, weary, he sits on the edge of the
bed, drained. He does not look round as SIMON comes in.*

SIMON looks at him, smiles. Eventually JOHN looks round.

SIMON. Hi.

JOHN tenses.

I had a chat with your Father James. Well hardly a chat. I
talked and he listened. John, if you won't come back with me
I'd kind of like to stick around. (*Smiles, shrugs.*) Don't know,
thought the clubs might be worth checking out.

JOHN is silent.

What's the matter? Is nobody going to talk to me this
morning? You look tired John. Can I get you anything?

JOHN. No.

SIMON. John I . . .

He reaches out to touch JOHN. JOHN *flinches*.

JOHN. Don't.

SIMON *taken aback by the tone*.

Who the hell do you think you are that you can walk back into my life after what you did to me?

SIMON. John . . . Please . . .

JOHN. Get out of my sight.

SIMON *reaches out to touch him*.

JOHN. Just go.

JOHN *looks at* SIMON *with hatred, then turns away, shutting him out*. SIMON *looks at him in disbelief and sadness, then goes*. JOHN *does not react to his going*.

Throughout next scene, lights stay up on JOHN.

Scene Thirteen

Lights up on JAMES *at the pulpit, surplice on for Sunday mass, as he was at the start of the play, making announcements*.

JAMES. The winners of this month's Two Hundred Club are Brian Ferguson who wins fifty pounds and Mrs. May Bell and Mrs. Eileen Thomson who each win twenty-five pounds.

We've had a letter from Father Allan, thanking us for our generous presentation. Apparently he's used the money to buy himself a new set of golf clubs.

There's a new housekeeper starting at the end of next week. Mrs. Farrell. I'm sure you'll make her very welcome.

Now there's been a disappointing response to Mr. Morgan's appeal for choir members. It's only an hour's practice on a Thursday. (*Accusing*.) One hour on a Thursday!

The anger starts to simmer.

Now about these hymn books. They were new at the start of the year. They cost good money and you leave them lying around, you drop them on the floor. They get dirty. They get stood on. They get lost. I've told you time and time again – will you put them at the back of the chapel at the end of mass. I've got more important things to do than pick up your hymn books.

Now can you stand please, for the final blessing.

JOHN, *at the other end of the stage, has pulled himself into a foetal position on top of his bed, shutting out everything but his own bitterness.*

End.

PASSING PLACES

Stephen Greenhorn

Stephen Greenhorn was born in West Lothian and has been
writing professionally since 1988. His stage plays include
Heart and Bone (Edinburgh Festival Fringe First Award); two
children's plays for *Visible Fiction*s; *The Salt Wound* (7:84
Scotland); a version of Aristophanes' *The Birds* (Gate, London);
co-author of *Sleeping Around* (Paines Plough, 1998); *Passing
Places* (Traverse, 1997, and tour 1998).

His television work includes episodes of *The Bill* and *Where the
Heart Is*. He has written three plays for BBC Radio 4 and a
radio version of *Passing Places* for Radio 3.

He is currently writing the screenplay of *Passing Places* for
BBC Films and is under commission to 7:84 Scotland for
Dissent.

138

Passing Places was first performed at the Traverse Theatre, Edinburgh on 31 January 1997, with the following cast:

ALEX	Paul Thomas Hickey
BRIAN	Colin McCredie
MIRREN	Veronica Leer
BINKS, *Motherwell gangster*	Kenneth Bryans
KID, *Motherwell delinquent*	Stuart Bowman
IONA, *Canadian geologist*	Kathryn Howden
SERGE, *French sculptor*	Iain Macrae
DIESEL, *English traveller*	Iain Macrae
TOM, *Mirren's dad*	Iain Macrae
SHAPER, *mystic surf guru*	Stuart Bowman
MO, *Cornish surfer*	Kathryn Howden
YOUTHS	Iain Macrae
	Kathryn Howden
ALEX'S MUM	Kathryn Howden
LOLLIPOP	Stuart Bowman
GUNN	Stuart Bowman
PUMP HAND	Stuart Bowman
WALKER	Stuart Bowman
BARMAN	Iain Macrae

Directed by   John Tiffany
Designed by   Neil Warmington
Lighting designed by   Ben Ormerod
Music composed and performed by   Mick Slaven
Movement directed by   Marisa Zanotti

1

ALEX *and* BRIAN *enter.*

ALEX. Motherwell!

BRIAN. West central Scotland. Population 27,000.

ALEX. Work base . . .

BRIAN. Traditionally . . . heavy industry . . . predominantly steel . . .

ALEX. And now . . .

BRIAN *shrugs.*

ALEX. Alright . . . Famous for . . .

BRIAN. Winning the Scottish Cup in extra time?

ALEX. And . . . ?

BRIAN. And!

ALEX. Surfing.

BRIAN. Oh. Yeah. Surfing.

ALEX. Motherwell. Surf City. The Bondi Beach of Lanarkshire. Malibu of the North.

BRIAN. Ideally situated.

ALEX. Twenty-five miles from the fucking sea!

2

The shop. Doorbell goes as the KID *enters. Thirteen going on thirty.*

ALEX. What do you want?

KID. Chill man. I've been saving up. I'm looking for a new pair of Air Jordans.

ALEX. How much have you got?

KID. Here.

> KID *slaps a bunch of notes on the counter.*
>
> ALEX *counts them.*

ALEX. Not enough. Unless you're one-legged.

KID. Aw no. What about instalments?

ALEX. Aye. You can buy one shoe now and hop it.

KID. Very funny.

ALEX. Away and mug somebody.

KID. Nobody round here worth mugging.

ALEX. Beat it then.

KID. Cool the beans, pal. I'm going. But I'll be back.

> *He goes to the door.*

KID. Here.

ALEX. What?

> *He waves sarcastically.*

KID. There's a wee wave for your surf-board.

ALEX. Get to fuck!

> KID *exits laughing.* ALEX *regards the surf-board.*

ALEX. Two years that bastard thing's been in the window. Two years! And I've had to dust it every second day. All because he thinks he's the Don-fucking-Jonson of Meikle Earnock!

> BRIAN *interjects from the Library.*

BRIAN. Three hundred and twelve!

ALEX. Eh?

BRIAN. Three times a week for two years not counting holidays.

> ALEX *scowls at him.*

ALEX. The library! Hang out for pensioners who can't pay their gas bills. Ex-steelworkers who can't bring themselves to watch Australian soap-operas. Jakeys who fall asleep over The Independent . . . And Brian!

BRIAN. I was just saying!

3

Shop doorbell interrupts. BINKS *enters.*

ALEX. Mr. Binks, I thought . . .

BINKS. Shut it, arse-face.

He goes behind the counter, rakes for an empty shoe box then takes a hand-gun from his waistband, wraps it and stashes it in the box. He stores the box back under the counter. ALEX is staring.

BINKS. What're you looking at?

ALEX. Nothing.

BINKS. That's right. And don't you . . . Eh? . . . Aye.

ALEX. Sorry?

BINKS. Am I speaking to you?

ALEX. But you . . .

BINKS. Ronnie's saying you have to be deaf, dumb and blind to work here.

ALEX. Dumb anyway.

BINKS. Eh?

ALEX. Nothing.

BINKS. Dinnae mutter son. I cannae stand muttering.

ALEX. Sorry, Mr. Binks.

BINKS *moves to the surf-board. He strokes it.*

BINKS. When was the last time you dusted my wee beauty here?

ALEX. Yesterday.

BINKS. Do it again.

ALEX. But . . .

BINKS. Again, I said!

ALEX. It . . . eh . . . it doesn't have a price on it.

BINKS. That's 'cause it's not for sale, ya retard. Right?

ALEX. So if anyone asks about it . . . ?

BINKS. Are you deaf? It's not for fucking sale. This is my
retirement. My pension plan. In a few years' time me and
Ronnie and this wee beauty'll be jetting off to a beach house
in Hawaii. So long Lanarkshire, hello Honolulu! Wearing
flowery shirts, chasing birds in grass skirts, drinking Buckie
out of half-coconuts. Fucking paradise.

ALEX. Aye.

BINKS. So make sure you run a fucking duster over it before
I come back this afternoon.

Eh? . . . Aye. Right enough, Ronnie . . . Dumb! Dumb as
a . . . doorbell.

He exits.

ALEX. Fucking psycho.

BRIAN. Mr. Binks is subject to a bizarre paranormal
phenomenon whereby he is in constant contact with the spirit
of his twin brother who died at birth.

ALEX. Shite.

BRIAN. Not necessarily.

ALEX. He's barking. Nothing but a mental sports shop owner.
And it's not even a real sports shop. All it sells are trainers
and baseball caps. And bloody shell-suits. The only people
who ever come in are all –

4

Shop doorbell again. Two YOUTHS *enter.*

ALEX. Like Sauchiehall Street in here! Can I help you?

SECOND YOUTH. We're looking for baseball caps.

ALEX. By the window.

FIRST YOUTH. Right.

SECOND YOUTH. Your shop?

ALEX. I just work here.

SECOND YOUTH. Been busy?

ALEX. Not bad.

They pick out a couple of hats.

FIRST YOUTH. We'll take these.

ALEX. Anything else?

FIRST YOUTH. Bats.

ALEX. Bats?

SECOND YOUTH. We're thinking of starting a team.

ALEX. Yeah?

ALEX *places a baseball bat on the counter. One of the youths picks it up.*

FIRST YOUTH. This is good. Nice weight.

SECOND YOUTH. That'll do then.

ALEX. Anything else?

SECOND YOUTH. Yeah.

ALEX. What?

SECOND YOUTH. Everything.

ALEX *is whacked with the bat and thumps to the floor.*

BRIAN. And that's where all the trouble started . . .

5

BINKS *enters the ransacked shop. He checks first that the board is O.K. then that his gun is still there. It is. Only then does he try to revive ALEX.*

BINKS. Wake up ya wee prick.

ALEX *groans.*

BINKS. I don't think he's listening, Ronnie . . . Aye. Good idea.

He hauls a concussed ALEX *to his feet and gives him a shake.*

ALEX. Mr. Binks.

BINKS. Something you want to tell me, son?

ALEX. God. What a mess.

BINKS. That's right. A real mess. In my shop. So maybe you could explain it, before I get angry and Ron gets violent . . . He says he wants your knee-caps for castanets. And I don't like to deny him his little treats.

ALEX. Two guys. Young guys. I've never seen them before. They came in for baseball caps then they wanted to look at a bat . . .

BINKS. And you gave them one?

ALEX. They said they were starting a team.

BINKS. Ron says he can guess what happened next.

ALEX. They clubbed me over the head.

BINKS. Ahh. And does it hurt?

ALEX. Aye. It does.

BINKS. Good! I hope they've fractured your fucking skull! I hope you've got fucking brain damage! Except, I don't think you've got a brain to damage!

ALEX. I tried to stop them but they . . .

BINKS. They had the fucking bat that you gave them ya clown! And while you were in Noddy-land they made a home run with the till and most of my stock.

ALEX. Sorry.

BINKS. You will be.

ALEX. Have you phoned the police?

BINKS. So they can come round and have a good laugh too?

ALEX. Well, what are you going to do then?

BINKS. I'm going to boot your arse out that door . . . Or mibbe the window, Ronnie's suggesting.

ALEX. Are you saying I'm fired?

BINKS. Wasn't I clear enough for you?

ALEX. But what about my money. I'm due wages.

BINKS. They were in the till, weren't they. Looks like you got robbed too.

ALEX. That's not fair.

BINKS. Tough.

6

ALEX *and* BRIAN *are in a pub.* ALEX *is very drunk,* BRIAN *only slightly less so. There is a trivia quiz going on in which* BRIAN *is trying to participate.*

ALEX. See, what gets me . . . what gets me, right, is he really thinks he's a gangster or something.

BRIAN. He is.

ALEX. Well, I know. But he thinks he's Al Pacino. Scarface or something. Michael Corleone.

QUIZ. C'mon now folks get the scores sorted. One round to go.

BRIAN. They've taken a point off 'cause we spelt Azerbaijan wrong. Nine out of ten.

ALEX. Bastard thinks he's in a big movie.

BRIAN. Still third. I think we can win if we have a good last round.

ALEX. Don't you think you've had enough?

QUIZ. Last round, ladies and gentlemen. And it's ten questions on . . . Sport.

BRIAN. Shit. Rangers players and greyhounds!

ALEX *gets up to go.*

ALEX. I've had enough of this. You coming?

BRIAN. O.K. O.K.

They stumble away from the table.

QUIZ. Which former Rangers star now trains greyhounds?

7

In the street. Night. The two lads are weaving their way home through the empty pedestrian precinct.

ALEX. Look at this place. Nothing but shoe shops and burger bars.

BRIAN. I'm starving.

ALEX. IT DOES MY HEAD IN!

BRIAN. You'll have the cops doing your head in if you don't shut up.

ALEX. Huh. They're the same. Too many episodes of Miami Vice. Rush around going 'freeze'. And, 'make my day'! Half of them couldn't even make their beds.

BRIAN. Time to go home, I think.

ALEX. No. Wait. Look. The scene of the crime.

The sports shop. They peer through the window.

BRIAN. They really cleaned it out, didn't they.

ALEX. Took everything.

BRIAN. Except the surf-board.

ALEX. Left that just to piss me off.

BRIAN. Binks' pride and joy.

ALEX. Stupid psychedelic phallic symbol.

BRIAN. Must be worth a wee bit too.

ALEX. Three hundred and twelve. Not counting holidays. Skivvying for that prick. Makes me sick. Wouldn't even give me the money he owes me.

BRIAN. Forget it, Alex. There's nothing you can do.

ALEX. Is there not?

ALEX goes looking for something.

BRIAN. Alex?

ALEX has found a litter bin.

BRIAN. What're you doing?

ALEX grunts with effort as he lifts the bin up.

BRIAN. Alex? Bloody hell!

An enormous crash as the litter-bin flies through the shop window. An alarm bell begins to clatter loudly. ALEX scrunches through the broken glass.

BRIAN. Fucking hell! What're you doing? Let's get out of here. Come on.

ALEX. Hold on.

BRIAN. Oh no. Alex. You can't take that.

ALEX is wrestling with the surf-board.

ALEX. Can I not?

BRIAN. I don't believe this.

ALEX. Grab an end then!

They pick the thing up.

ALEX. Surf's up!

They haphazardly make their escape into the night with the board. ALEX laughing hysterically. The alarm ringing in their ears.

8

Next morning. ALEX's house. The phone rings. ALEX'S MUM enters and answers it.

MUM. Hello . . . Who's calling please? . . . Alright, I'll just get him for you . . .

She switches off her 'telephone' voice.

MUM. ALEX!

ALEX. What?

MUM. Phone.

ALEX. Right.

Pause. ALEX realises he is in bed with the surf-board.

ALEX. Ohmygod!

He is panic stricken.

MUM. Alex!

ALEX. I'm not in.

MUM. It's Mr. Binks.

ALEX. Aaah! I'm not here. Tell him I've gone. Away. The Army. Or dead. Tell him I'm dead.

MUM. Alex . . . ?

ALEX. Just tell him I'm NOT HERE. Please!

MUM. Huh.

She goes back to the phone as ALEX *begins dressing and packing in a frenzy.*

MUM. I'm afraid he's not here Mr. Binks. He must've gone out already . . . Well to his work, I suppose . . . Oh. No, I didn't know that . . . Yes . . . I'll be sure to tell him . . . bye then.

She goes into the bedroom.

MUM. What the hell've you been up to?

ALEX. What did he say?

MUM. He said you got fired yesterday.

ALEX. And?

MUM. And! What d'you mean, 'and'?

ALEX. Did he say anything else?

MUM. Something about castanets.

ALEX. Oh God!

She spies the board.

MUM. Have you been nicking stuff from your work?

ALEX. No.

MUM. What's that then, a leaving present?

ALEX. Look . . .

MUM. Look nothing. I'm not having the polis at my door because of you. If you've got yourself into trouble you can get yourself out of here. I've warned you, you can pack your bags and . . .

She notices that ALEX *has done just that.*

MUM. Where are you going?

ALEX. Eh?

MUM. Oh aye. Spain, is it? Costa del Crime n'that, eh?

ALEX. Spain!

MUM. Castanets.

ALEX. No. Look. I just need to go away for a while. Trust me.

MUM. About as far as I could throw you.

ALEX. It's fine.

MUM. I'm not going through all that business again. D'you hear me?

ALEX. I hear you. I have to go.

ALEX *clatters out with the board.*

MUM. Just like his father. Bastard.

9

BRIAN*'s house.* BRIAN *is trying to dress.* ALEX *is trying to explain his plan.*

BRIAN. But couldn't we just take it back and offer to pay for the window?

ALEX. Are you off your fucking head!

BRIAN. Shut-up. You'll wake my dad.

ALEX. An earthquake couldn't wake your dad before the first race.

BRIAN. So what're we going to do?

ALEX. Get out of the way for a bit. Get rid of the evidence.

BRIAN. Where?

ALEX. North.

BRIAN. D'you think you could be a wee bit more specific?

ALEX. There's a place, I read about it in one of those magazines in the shop. It's full of all those surfing bastards. We could sell this and then use the money to lie low for a while.

BRIAN. What place is this then?

ALEX. Thurso.

BRIAN. Thurso! Do you know where that is?

ALEX. North. On the coast, I presume.

BRIAN. North is right. Next stop Iceland. How are we going to get up there with a surfboard?

ALEX. Aye well. I was thinking about that . . .

10

A car shrouded beneath a dust-sheet. ALEX approaches it confidently. BRIAN is deeply wary. ALEX whips the sheet off to reveal a clapped out Lada Riva.

BRIAN. Our George'll kill me.

ALEX. He'll understand.

BRIAN. He's not the understanding type.

ALEX. It's only a fucking Lada.

    ALEX gets in.

BRIAN. He can do things with his hands, you know. They train them. Cut off oxygen to the brain. Dead in under a minute.

ALEX. Brian. George is in the catering corps. The deadliest thing he can do with his hands is not wash them.

    ALEX tries the engine. It starts reluctantly.

ALEX. We're in business.

11

In the car. ALEX drives, crunching gears occasionally. BRIAN is a nervous passenger.

BRIAN. Are you insured for this?

ALEX. Maybe George's policy covers it.

BRIAN. What if we get stopped?

ALEX. It doesn't matter. It's not taxed either.

BRIAN. Oh god.

12

They stutter to a halt at a traffic light. ALEX revs impatiently.

ALEX. Come on. Change!

    The KID enters and approaches them.

KID. Hey! You that guy that works in the sports shop up the centre?

ALEX. No.

KID. Aye y'ur. You chucked me out of there yesterday.

ALEX. Should you not be at school?

KID. Should you not be at work?

ALEX. I retired. Piss off.

KID. Nice car! D'you know there's stuff dripping underneath at the front? What's on the roof? Skateboard for when you break down?

ALEX. I'm warning you. Beat it.

KID. Where're you going then? Scrappy?

BRIAN. Thurso.

ALEX. No!

KID. Make your minds up.

ALEX. Away and play on the motorway.

KID. I've more chance of getting there than you. Especially with ma new trainers.

ALEX. Where did you get them?

KID. Twenty quid. No questions.

ALEX. They're nicked!

KID. Should've let me join the Christmas club, eh?

KID runs off laughing again.

ALEX. Prick.

Car horn sounds impatiently behind them.

BRIAN. It's green. We can go.

ALEX crunches the gears again and they drive off.

13

The remains of the shop. BINKS *sweeping up broken glass.*

BINKS. I'll kill the wee bastard when I get my hands on him. I will. I'll fucking kill him . . . Of course it was him. Who else would it be?

The KID *enters cautiously.*

KID. Hey mister. You missing a surf-board?

BINKS. What's it to you?

KID. I might know where it is.

The broom drops to the floor and BINKS *suddenly has the* KID *by the throat.*

KID. Aow!

BINKS. Talk or choke, Ron says. Up to you.

KID. I saw that guy who was working here with it. Him and his mate. They were in a car. A Lada. In town. The surf-board was tied to the roof.

BINKS. Bastards. I knew it!

KID. They were leaving. Said they were . . . going to . . .

BINKS. Where? Going where?

KID. My throat! I can't . . .

BINKS *relaxes his grip a little.*

BINKS. Where?

KID. Thurso.

BINKS. Are you sure?

KID. Aye.

BINKS. Bastards!

KID. Do I get a reward?

BINKS *ignores this. He is distracted by the information. His grip tightens on the* KID's *throat. The* KID *starts to choke.*

BINKS. Thurso . . . Aye, Ronnie. Track them down . . . We'll get it back alright . . . Thurso, that's what he said . . . Well, I don't fucking know . . . I'll buy a map or something, alright? . . . What? . . . Eh? . . . Oh. Aye.

He lets go of the KID *who is barely conscious.*

BINKS. Thanks wee man.

KID. S'alright.

14

ALEX *and* BRIAN *in the car.*

BRIAN. It is!

ALEX. I'm not arguing.

BRIAN. Yes you are.

ALEX. I just thought Loch Ness was bigger.

BRIAN. But we're talking area. This is Loch Lomond. The largest area of fresh water.

ALEX. If you say so.

BRIAN. It is.

ALEX. Fine.

Pause.

ALEX. How far is it exactly?

BRIAN. Depends on which way you go.

ALEX. How many can there be?

BRIAN. Two. The obvious and the sneaky.

ALEX. And is the sneaky way very complicated?

BRIAN. Not if I'm navigating.

ALEX. You've got the map.

BRIAN. O.K. Another few miles up the A82, then take a left through to Arrochar on the A83, then . . .

ALEX. That's enough to be going on with.

BRIAN. It's a much more interesting route as well.

ALEX. We're not on holiday, Brian.

BRIAN. Closest I've been to a holiday for years.

ALEX. What about that weekend on Arran?

BRIAN. That was an Outward Bound course.

ALEX. So?

BRIAN. Not a holiday.

15

A lay-by in a mountain pass. The car bonnet is open. Steam rises. ALEX *fumes.*

BRIAN. They're designed for Murmansk not Milngavie. It's meant to be traversing the icy wastes of Siberia. It's out of its natural environment. Give it a chance.

ALEX. Brian, how are we going to get to Thurso if this thing won't do more than forty-five and can't even get us over a fucking hill?

BRIAN. It's not a hill. It's a mountain. Three thousand three hundred and eighteen feet. That makes it a Munro.

ALEX. I don't give a fuck.

A beat.

BRIAN. It's only the radiator. We just have to wait for it to cool down, then top it up with fresh water.

ALEX. From where?

BRIAN. There'll be some around somewhere.

ALEX. How do you know?

BRIAN. It's the Highlands. There's always water.

Pause.

ALEX. Where are we?

BRIAN. It's called 'Rest and be thankful'.

ALEX. Of course.

BRIAN. The top of the pass. It's the route of the old military road. Look, you can see.

ALEX. Where are we going?

BRIAN. Well . . .

ALEX. Doesn't that map tell you?

BRIAN. You've not quite got it yet, have you?

ALEX. Got what?

BRIAN. The whole concept.

ALEX. What concept?

BRIAN. Maps. Imaginary landscapes. Representations of the world. All the information's there. Everything you need to know. But you still have to prescribe your own course of action.

ALEX. What the fuck are you on about?

BRIAN. A map's not for telling you where to go. What it tells you is exactly where you are. It only describes your position. You have to decide your own destination and journey. See?

Pause.

ALEX. This is going to be a very long drive, isn't it?

16

Motherwell. BINKS *prepares to begin his pursuit. He is wearing motorcycle leathers.*

BINKS. Right, Ronnie. North. Time for payback.

He kickstarts a motorcycle and revs it.

What?. . . . Eh? . . . Aye alright. I'll no go too fast.

He lets out the clutch and screeches away.

17

In the car. BRIAN *in guide book mode.*

BRIAN. Inverary. A picturesque township on the shores of Loch Fyne. Notable for its carefully planned layout, its church tower and its historic court-house, now an award-winning museum.

ALEX. White-washed tourist hell-hole.

BRIAN. Excellent sea-fishing opportunities. In season.

ALEX. We're not stopping.

BRIAN. Hard right on to the B819 up and through Glen Aray.

ALEX. More hills.

BRIAN. Then down to the shore of Loch Awe.

ALEX. More water.

BRIAN. Loch Awe is the longest inland loch in Britain if you include the bit that goes off at right-angles. If you don't then Loch Ness is longest.

ALEX. More useless shite.

BRIAN. Left on to the A85 and towards Oban along the Pass of Brander. Past Ben Cruachan. They blasted a huge cavern under it and built a hydro-electric power-station completely underground.

ALEX. Fascinating.

BRIAN. You can go on guided tours.

ALEX. We're not stopping.

BRIAN. It has Britain's longest staircase.

ALEX. For fucks sake! It's like being on the road with Norris McWhirter!

BRIAN. I was just saying . . .

ALEX. We're not tourists, Brian.

BRIAN. I've not been here before.

ALEX. We live here.

BRIAN. Not here.

ALEX. We're only a hundred miles from Glasgow.

BRIAN. Yeah? Look though. See anything familiar?

ALEX. Only you talking shite.

18

A lay-by near Loch Creran. The car is again steaming. ALEX *sighs.*

ALEX. It's your turn to get the water.

BRIAN. I'll go in a minute.

ALEX. This is going to take fucking days.

BRIAN. There's no hurry, is there?

ALEX. Not at this rate there's not.

BRIAN. No point in getting harassed, then.

ALEX. You been reading those Yoga books again?

A pause. A noise outside. ALEX *sits up.*

ALEX. Someone's coming.

BRIAN. Eh?

ALEX. Look. Worzel McGummidge.

BRIAN. What does he want?

ALEX. How should I know?

DIESEL *enters. A new-age traveller carrying a poached rabbit.* ALEX *and* BRIAN *get out of the car.*

DIESEL. Having problems?

ALEX. Just letting it cool down.

DIESEL. Radiator leaking?

ALEX. Aye. A wee bit. We have to top it up now and then.

DIESEL. Where are you headed?

BRIAN. Thurso.

ALEX. Maybe. We don't know.

BRIAN. We're just . . .

ALEX. Driving.

BRIAN. And stopping.

DIESEL. I see.

A beat.

DIESEL. And is that a surf-board?

ALEX. Sort of.

DIESEL. A sort of surf-board?

ALEX. Aye.

DIESEL. Why is it wrapped in bin-liners?

ALEX. Didn't want to get it wet.

DIESEL. Isn't it waterproof?

BRIAN. Acid rain. Damages the . . . the eh . . . thing.

DIESEL. Right.

DIESEL has a look under the bonnet.

DIESEL. Have you been using the headlights on this?

ALEX. Eh aye. Of course. Why?

DIESEL. 'Cause you haven't got any.

ALEX. What!

DIESEL. There's no connections, or bulb mountings, or bulbs.

ALEX. Shit.

DIESEL. I think your battery's leaking as well. It probably won't be holding a charge. Could be your alternator's buggered too.

ALEX. Jesus.

BRIAN. Are you a mechanic?

DIESEL. Not really. I know a bit about engines though.

He comes out from under the bonnet.

DIESEL. The name's Diesel.

BRIAN. I'm Brian. He's Alex.

DIESEL. How you doing?

BRIAN. Not very well, by the sound of it.

ALEX. Will it go?

DIESEL. To Thurso?

ALEX. To anywhere?

DIESEL. Not tonight.

ALEX. Shit.

Pause.

DIESEL. Have you got anywhere to stay?

BRIAN. The back seat.

DIESEL. Could you sleep in a tent?

BRIAN. Yeah.

DIESEL. Well, our camp's just down there. We could probably
find you a blanket or two.

ALEX. You camping?

DIESEL. We're travellers.

ALEX. New age?

DIESEL. All different ages.

BRIAN. Are you sure it's not any trouble . . .

DIESEL. Nah. I can have a look at the car tomorrow if you like.

BRIAN. That'd be great. Eh?

ALEX. Yeah. Great. Thanks.

19

The travellers' camp. BRIAN *and* ALEX *describe.*

ALEX. The camp. A bus, two lorries, a caravan, a proper tent
and a couple of home-made ones . . .

BRIAN. Benders.

ALEX. . . . Lots of facial hair. Two kids . . .

BRIAN. . . . and a baby . . .

ALEX. . . . a dog, two cats and a goat . . .

BRIAN. . . . called Maggie.

ALEX. Woodsmoke. Smells of cooking.

BRIAN. Rabbit stew. It was nice. With bread. They bake their
own.

ALEX. Water from the stream and . . .

BRIAN. And her.

> ALEX *and* BRIAN *are by a campfire.* MIRREN *approaches
> and dumps some blankets beside them.*

MIRREN. These should keep you warm enough. The nights are
fairly mild anyway.

BRIAN. Thanks.

She sits down beside them.

BRIAN. I'm Brian, by the way. This is Alex.

MIRREN. Mirren.

BRIAN. That's a nice name. Is it Gaelic?

MIRREN. No. My dad chose it. He's from Paisley. Big football fan.

Pause.

MIRREN. You're from Glasgow then?

ALEX. Motherwell.

MIRREN. On holiday?

ALEX. Not exactly.

MIRREN. Going to Thurso? For the surfing?

ALEX. No.

MIRREN. You've got a board.

ALEX. We're delivering it.

MIRREN. I didn't realise Motherwell had a big surfing scene.

BRIAN. It doesn't anymore. We've nicked it.

ALEX *gives* BRIAN *a kick.*

MIRREN. You on the run then?

ALEX. We're just taking the board to Thurso.

MIRREN. If you say so.

ALEX. I do.

MIRREN. I don't know what you're worried about. We're hardly likely to turn you in, are we? It's not as if you're the Great Train Robbers, is it?

She laughs. ALEX *sighs.*

ALEX. So he goes and tells her the whole story.

BRIAN. They were nice to us.

ALEX. She thinks it's a great laugh.

BRIAN. Well . . .

ALEX. Thinks we're a right pair of prats.

BRIAN. She doesn't.

ALEX. So much for keeping a low profile.

BRIAN. It wasn't a fucking press conference.

   MIRREN *laughing*. DIESEL *joins them by the fire*.

DIESEL. What are you lot laughing about?

MIRREN. Nothing. How's the car?

DIESEL. Well, I've fished out an old battery and left it to charge off the van. It's not up to much but it's better than what you've got. It'll be ready in the morning. It should fit.

ALEX. Thanks.

DIESEL. You really need to replace some parts. I haven't got any for a Lada.

BRIAN. Are you sure you're not a mechanic?

DIESEL. Not really.

MIRREN. Your Lada's too lightweight for him. He used to fix tanks.

BRIAN. Tanks? Were you in the army?

DIESEL. For a bit.

MIRREN. Nine years.

DIESEL. Quite a bit.

BRIAN. So how did you end up here?

DIESEL. Couldn't settle. Ended up on the road. Met some other folk in the same boat. Moved around a bit. Headed north. Been here five months now. It's nice.

BRIAN. Are you planning to stay?

DIESEL. Till they move us on. They'll get round to it sooner or later. They always do.

   Pause.

BRIAN. How long have you been on the road, Mirren?

MIRREN. Well . . . uhm . . .

DIESEL. Mirren's just visiting.

BRIAN. Oh.

DIESEL. Heading off soon as well. Maybe these guys could give you a lift.

MIRREN. You just said the car won't make it.

DIESEL. I might be wrong.

BRIAN. Where are you going?

DIESEL. Up to Tom's, isn't it? Tongue.

MIRREN. I don't think this . . .

DIESEL. That's on the way to Thurso.

BRIAN. It's right next door.

MIRREN. I was going to Skye first. To see Iona.

DIESEL. Even better idea! Serge might be just the man for
    Ladas.

BRIAN. I thought Iona was by Mull.

DIESEL. This one's a person. Lives on Skye with a weird
    French bloke – Serge. Always doing things with old cars.
    Lots of Ladas and Skodas and stuff. He's got loads of bits.
    He might be able to help you.

BRIAN. That sounds like a good idea.

ALEX. Skye?

MIRREN. It's a bit of a detour.

DIESEL. Rubbish. You go over at Mallaig and back on the
    bridge. No problem.

MIRREN. You've got it all worked out haven't you?

DIESEL. Makes sense. Two birds with one stone.

BRIAN. Go on, Mirren.

MIRREN. I don't want to hold you back.

BRIAN. You'd be doing us a favour, eh Alex?

ALEX. We don't want to put you to any trouble . . .

BRIAN. Please.

    Pause. MIRREN *looks at* DIESEL.

MIRREN. Alright.

BRIAN. Brilliant. A guide. You can't beat local knowledge.

DIESEL. Sorted then.

MIRREN. Yeah. Sorted. Thanks, Diesel.

A beat.

MIRREN. I suppose if I'm going I'd better get my shit together.

She stands.

DIESEL. And I have to sort out some tent space for you two.

He stands too.

MIRREN. See you in the morning.

BRIAN. Night.

MIRREN *and* DIESEL *move away.*

MIRREN. I didn't realise you wanted rid of me.

DIESEL. You know it's not like that.

MIRREN. I thought . . .

DIESEL. I know. It's been good. But you can't stay.

MIRREN. Why not?

DIESEL. Because you're still looking for answers, Mirren. And there's none here for you.

They exit. ALEX *watches them go.*

ALEX. I don't think she wants to come with us.

BRIAN. Rubbish. It'll be great.

ALEX. You think?

20

Next morning. At the car.

MIRREN. Who's driving then?

ALEX. Me.

MIRREN. Will I go in the back?

BRIAN. I'll go. You go in the front.

MIRREN. Are you sure?

BRIAN. You can give directions better from there.

MIRREN. But if you've got a map . . .

BRIAN. No, honestly . . .

MIRREN. I don't want to be in the way.

BRIAN. You won't be.

MIRREN. But if you'd prefer . . .

BRIAN. Really, I don't mind . . .

ALEX. Will you just get in the fucking thing and we'll see if it starts.

They get in.

21

In the car. On the road. Later.

MIRREN. So, what's it like being outlaws then?

BRIAN. It's really interesting. We've never been this far North before.

MIRREN. Maybe you should have turned to crime sooner.

BRIAN. Yeah.

ALEX. It's not a joke. We're only here because we want to keep our knee-caps.

MIRREN. And where would you rather be?

ALEX. Right now, I'd settle for Thurso.

BRIAN. Skye first. What's the best way d'you think?

MIRREN. If you cross Loch Linnhe at the Corran ferry, you can go up to Mallaig without having to go through Fort William.

BRIAN. Sounds good.

ALEX. How far to this ferry then?

BRIAN. On the left just after the bridge at Ballachulish.

ALEX. Ballachulish.

BRIAN. Used to be a centre for quarrying slate. For roofs.

MIRREN. That's right.

BRIAN. They've got a new visitor centre too.

ALEX. We're not stopping.

22

BINKS *is in Fort William. He is by the road trying to attract the attention of a* LOLLIPOP LADY.

BINKS. Excuse me. Oi! Lollipop! Are you deaf?

LADY. Patience dear. We'll get you across in a minute.

BINKS. I don't want to cross the road.

LADY. What are you standing there for then?

BINKS. Are you on duty all day?

LADY. Not all day. Not quite. I have to get home before five for the cat.

BINKS. Have you seen two men in a Lada with a surf-board on the roof?

LADY. Pardon?

BINKS. Have you seen two men in a Lada with a surf-board on the roof?

Pause.

LADY. Ah. I know who you'll be.

BINKS. Eh?

LADY. You'll be from the Sunday Post, won't you? Asking trick questions and seeing if anybody recognises you.

BINKS. No.

LADY. You're supposed to give me some money if I know the right answer. Wait a minute now. It'll come to me. I was reading it just the other day . . .

BINKS. Look, I think you're . . .

LADY. Aw, come on now give me a chance. It's on the tip of my tongue.

BINKS. Will you listen . . . ?

LADY. Now, is it a fiver or a tenner you give me?

BINKS. I'm not the man from the Sunday Post!

LADY. Give us a wee clue, will you? I get it every week but my memory's not what it was. Go on. Tell me what to say.

BINKS. I don't want you to say anything.

LADY. I just get the money for recognising you?

BINKS. I'm not giving you any money.

LADY. Och. That's not fair. If you'd just give me time to think. Or a wee clue . . .

BINKS. Forget it. Just forget it.

LADY. But I get it every week. It's the cat's favourite too.

BINKS *is walking away, twitching.*

LADY. Ach. Ya tight bastard, ye.

BINKS. Mad as a fucking hatter . . . eh, Ronnie?

23

Corran ferry on Loch Linnhe.

ALEX. The Corran Ferry. Nearly a fiver to get across about a hundred yards of water.

BRIAN. What were you expecting? Deckchairs? Duty-free?

ALEX. What's wrong with a bridge?

MIRREN, ALEX *and* BRIAN *are looking over the side.*

MIRREN. Do you know where we are?

BRIAN. Middle of Loch Linnhe.

MIRREN. There's a mountain a few miles down the lochside there, at Glensanda.

BRIAN. Yeah?

MIRREN. They've shovelled most of it away to Europe. High quality aggregate to build the autobahns. To link Brussels and Bonn.

BRIAN. A whole mountain?

ALEX. There's plenty of them left. You surely wouldn't miss the one.

MIRREN. Sorry?

ALEX. Joke.

MIRREN. Oh.

Pause.

ALEX. So, what do you do exactly? For a living?

MIRREN. Lots of things.

ALEX. Nothing in particular.

MIRREN. Bits and pieces. Seasonal stuff in hotels and bars. Sometimes more interesting things.

ALEX. And you just drift from one place to another?

MIRREN. I move on when I get bored.

ALEX. Strange way of life.

MIRREN. Really? Stranger than kidnapping a surf-board?

A mini stand-off between the two. BRIAN is relieved to be able to interrupt it.

BRIAN. Land ahoy! Looks like the cruise is over!

24

On the road. Glen Tarbert. Single track with passing places.

BRIAN. A861 west through Glen Tarbert then along Loch Sunart. Through Strontian. Famous for lead mining. Gave its name to the element strontium which was discovered here in 1764.

MIRREN. They rehearsed the D-day landings on the loch here as well.

ALEX. Stereo now.

MIRREN. If you carried straight on you'd go into Ardnamurchan.

BRIAN. The most westerly point on the British mainland.

MIRREN. Very beautiful.

ALEX. We're going north.

BRIAN. Ardshealach. The end of Loch Shiel.

MIRREN. Blain.

BRIAN. Mingarrypark.

MIRREN. Dalnabreck.

BRIAN. Ardmolich.

MIRREN. Kinlochmoidart.

BRIAN. Kylesbeg.

ALEX. We're overheating again.

MIRREN. You or the car?

25

BINKS *is phoning home.*

BINKS. No . . . No ma . . . Fort William . . . Aye, Glen Coe was
   lovely . . . no, I'm not taking any pictures . . . I'm not on
   holiday, ma, it's a business trip . . . What? . . . Aye, alright
   I'll try and remember . . . but . . . look . . . I haven't got time
   to look for one wi a Highland Cow on it! . . . Sorry . . . No,
   I didn't mean to shout . . . aye, alright . . . Look, I have tae
   go . . . tae Inverness . . . Aye ye go along the loch . . . What? .
   . But they're just stories ma . . . There's no really anything . .
   . Alright, okay, I'll keep an eye out . . . Right. I have tae go.
   Cheerio.

He hangs up.

BINKS. What is she like . . .

26

Outside the car waiting for it to cool.

BRIAN. What a view.

MIRREN. That's Muck. And Eigg. Rum behind that. And that's
   the Cuillins on Skye.

BRIAN. Doesn't look very far.

MIRREN. No not really.

BRIAN. You think your friend will be able to fix this?

MIRREN. Serge? I don't know.

BRIAN. What about Iona? What does she do?

MIRREN. She's a geologist. She's writing a book.

BRIAN. About what?

ALEX. Rocks.

MIRREN. Something to do with continental drift.

BRIAN. That's interesting.

ALEX. It's rocks.

> *Pause.*

ALEX. It's a shame they couldn't use some of that high quality aggregate to improve the roads round here.

MIRREN. What's wrong with them?

ALEX. They're too narrow.

MIRREN. Single-track with passing places.

ALEX. They're crap.

MIRREN. They're fine. If you use them properly.

ALEX. Meaning what?

MIRREN. Meaning it's your driving that's crap.

ALEX. . . . !

MIRREN. You batter along the road as fast as you can and then screech to a halt as soon as you see anything coming towards you.

ALEX. We're in a hurry.

MIRREN. But there's no point in racing and stopping. You want to go at a comfortable speed. When you see a car coming, all you do is judge how fast they're going, work out where you'll meet and adjust your speed slightly so that you meet at a passing place.

ALEX. Really.

MIRREN. They're passing places. Not stopping places. You shouldn't have to stop. Just slow down a bit.

BRIAN. It's Zen.

MIRREN. You need to learn to adjust.

BRIAN. Zen and the art of single-track roads. Optimising the way you meet other traffic. Minimising the disturbance to either side. Oneness.

MIRREN. Common-sense.

BRIAN. It's that yoga stuff, Alex. Breathing, that's the secret. You need to control it. You need to learn how to breathe.

ALEX. I know how to fucking breathe. I've been doing it for years.

BRIAN. It's just a suggestion.

ALEX. Well, I suggest that unless you want to walk the rest of the way you let me worry about the driving.

MIRREN. That's fair enough, Brian. Let Alex worry.

A beat.

D'you think we've cooled down again yet?

27

On the road.

BRIAN. Left on to the A830. Past Arisaig. Yachting centre. And the sands of Morar. Loch Morar is the deepest in Scotland. Supposed to have a monster too.

ALEX. Mallaig. Another fucking ferry.

BRIAN. Brilliant. Over the sea to Skye.

A beat.

ALEX. Where does she live, your pal?

MIRREN. The other side of those mountains.

ALEX. Christ.

MIRREN. The road goes round them, not over them.

ALEX. Just as well.

MIRREN. Forty-five minutes. An hour at most.

BRIAN. Is she expecting you?

MIRREN. She doesn't expect anything. You'll like her.

28

IONA*'s house on Skye.* BRIAN *and* ALEX *poke about.*

BRIAN. Iona's. What a place.

ALEX. Old cottage. Bit run down.

BRIAN. Right on the coast.

ALEX. Wedged between the mountains and the water.

BRIAN. And absolutely full of . . .

ALEX. Mice.

BRIAN. . . . Books.

ALEX. No telly. Lots of rocks.

BRIAN. And the smell. Burning peat.

ALEX. Rising damp.

BRIAN. And Iona . . .

MIRREN *introduces* IONA.

IONA. Hi!

ALEX. You're American!

IONA. Canadian.

ALEX. Oh.

IONA. Is that a problem?

ALEX. No. It's just . . . I wasn't expecting . . . that's all.

BRIAN. We were just saying what a nice place.

IONA. Thanks.

BRIAN. All these books.

MIRREN. Brian likes books.

IONA. Me too.

BRIAN. Good.

ALEX. Great.

Pause.

ALEX. Mirren said you might be able to help us with the car.

IONA. Not me. Serge, my partner. He's the one you want.

ALEX. Right. Serge.

IONA. He's French. In case you weren't . . . expecting . . .

ALEX. No. I . . . well . . .

IONA. He's not here though. He's in Ullapool. They're having a ceilidh tomorrow night. He helps them with the P.A. He's very . . . practical.

ALEX. Ah. That's not much good for us, though.

Pause.

MIRREN. Iona says you can stay here and then go over to Ullapool tomorrow. If you want.

ALEX. We should press on.

MIRREN. You've got no lights. You'll not get very far before dark.

IONA. You can travel in daylight tomorrow. And I'm sure Serge will be able to help.

BRIAN. You're sure it's not a problem?

IONA. Not at all.

BRIAN. It's very kind of you.

MIRREN. We could give Iona a lift tomorrow as well.

ALEX. We?

IONA. I haven't been to a ceilidh for months. What d'you say?

BRIAN. Alex?

IONA. I'll cook you dinner . . .

Pause.

ALEX. Yeah. Why not. We're in no hurry anyway, are we!

BRIAN. He's been doing all the driving. He's a bit stressed.

IONA. I've got just the thing for loosening those shoulders.

ALEX. What would that be?

IONA. A gorgeous fifteen-year old . . .

29

IONA's house. Later. The four are sprawled. Food has been eaten. Whisky is being drunk.

BRIAN. It's one of those whiskies where you can't pronounce its name till you're on your fourth glass.

ALEX. You sound pretty fluent.

BRIAN. Lovely meal.

IONA. Thanks.

MIRREN. It was delicious.

IONA. An old family recipe. From back home.

Pause.

BRIAN. How did you end up here, Iona? From Canada?

IONA. I used to work in the oil industry. Came out to Aberdeen. Spent some time on the rigs then decided I wanted to write.

BRIAN. But why Skye?

IONA. It was the geology first. It's amazing. It's like a crossroads of different rock types and periods. Those mountains are the collision of two different eras. We're right on the edge of the European plate and it's grinding against and buckling under the pressure of the plate moving in under the Atlantic. Like two sides in a war that lasts for millions of years. And this is the front line.

BRIAN. Is that what you're writing about?

IONA. Partly . . .

MIRREN. Makes you a war correspondent.

BRIAN. Geology's answer to Kate Adie!

They laugh.

MIRREN. Alex thinks it's all just rocks.

IONA. It is. But some rocks are very interesting.

ALEX. You're here because of our interesting rocks.

IONA. There's other things too.

ALEX. Like what?

IONA. The people. The quality of life. And because it's so beautiful.

ALEX. Oh.

IONA. Have you been here before?

ALEX. No.

IONA. Wouldn't you say it's beautiful?

ALEX. I suppose it's alright.

IONA. Alright!

ALEX. It's very nice.

IONA. Nice! It's beautiful. Why don't you admit it?

ALEX. I just did.

IONA. You said it was 'nice'.

ALEX. Same thing.

IONA. No way. It's beautiful.

ALEX. Fine. It is.

IONA. So why not say so?

ALEX. Because . . .

IONA. Because?

ALEX. I can't.

IONA. Can't what?

ALEX. Can't say it. O.K? When you say it, it sounds fine. When
  I say it, it sounds . . . wrong.

  A beat.

MIRREN. How can it sound wrong?

ALEX. It just does.

IONA. That's crazy.

ALEX. It's one of those words.

MIRREN. Say it.

ALEX. No.

MIRREN. Go on.

ALEX. I can't. I can think it but I can't say it. It's just . . . It's
  not part of my language, alright?

MIRREN. It's not much of a language if you can't say that.

ALEX. Well, it's the only one I've got.

Pause.

IONA. Brian, what's he talking about?

BRIAN. Eskimos and snow.

IONA. Inuit.

BRIAN. Whatever. The thing is they've got seventeen words for snow, haven't they. But no word for . . . forest. Or something like that. 'Cause they don't need one, do they?

ALEX. You're pissed.

IONA. We're all pissed.

ALEX. Eskimos and snow?

IONA. Inuit.

MIRREN. Are you serious, Brian?

BRIAN. See where we live, right? Seventeen words for dogshit.

ALEX. Rubbish.

BRIAN. It's not.

IONA. Can you say it?

BRIAN. I can say anything when I'm drunk. Especially when I'm drunk on such beautiful whisky after such a beautiful meal with such beautiful company.

BRIAN *and* IONA *fall into giggling.*

ALEX. I think he's had enough.

MIRREN. He's not the only one, is he.

ALEX *and* MIRREN *catch each other's eye. A beat.*

ALEX. Where are we sleeping?

IONA. Oh. You two are in here. There's stuff over there.

ALEX. Thanks.

BRIAN. But it's still early.

ALEX. It's late. Very late.

MIRREN. Yeah. Maybe it is.

MIRREN *gets up to go.* IONA *follows suit.*

MIRREN. I'll say goodnight.

IONA. Oh well. Me too, then.

BRIAN. Night.

They exit.

BRIAN. What's up with you?

ALEX. What d'you mean?

BRIAN. We were having a nice time.

ALEX. You were.

BRIAN. Relax.

ALEX. I can't. I'm scared. I'm scared I'm going to have blunt instruments applied to all my joints. That's not something that's easily pushed to the back of the mind.

BRIAN. Binks isn't going to find us here, is he. Make the most of it. I mean, I didn't ask to be dragged into this but at least I'm going with it.

ALEX. I didn't drag you into this.

BRIAN. You did. You always do.

ALEX. You didn't have to come.

BRIAN. You wouldn't have found your way past Uddingston.

ALEX. Oh, right. 'Cause you're Mister Encyclopedia-fucking-Brittanica and I'm just a stupid bastard?

BRIAN. Shite.

ALEX. How come I got the job then, eh? How come nobody would take on the great brain?

BRIAN. Fuck off.

ALEX. If your brother had a decent capitalist car instead of that heap of communist junk, that's exactly what I would do. I'd phone for a taxi; if there was a taxi. Or a phone.

BRIAN. Well there's not so why don't you just shut up and go to sleep?

ALEX. Don't give me that shit.

BRIAN. Where are you going?

ALEX. I'm not sleeping here. It's like the fucking Waltons.

BRIAN. Too beautiful for you?

ALEX. Hey how about seventeen different words for 'fuck you'.
Fucking eskimos.

BRIAN. Inuit.

ALEX. Fuck off.

ALEX *leaves*.

30

Next morning. ALEX *is hung-over.*

ALEX. I felt bad the next day. My neck was really stiff from
curling up in the back seat and my head was throbbing from
the whisky. I was cold and I felt a bit sick as well. Not a good
start.

Anyway, I struggle out of the car and it's dead early but I
can't sleep anymore 'cause the sun's up. Not that it's warm
mind – fuck no. Just too bright. So I need to have a piss and I
wander down to the rocks by the shore – I'm not wanting to
go back into the house, just yet – and I have one of those
orgasmic early morning slashes that seem to go on for hours
and I start to feel a bit better. I decide a bit of sea breeze
might clear my head and I clamber up a big bastard of a rock
towards the sound of the waves. And I'm up there looking
out.

There's rocks, then a bit of beach, then more rocks and then
cliffs. There's huge seagulls swooping about and the sea
looks chilly but kind of quiet – like it hasn't had to get up
yet. And then there's this seal. I can see its head bobbing in
the water. I thought it might be an otter at first but it's too big
so it has to be a seal. It's not really that close – it's over by
the sandy bit and I'm still up on this big rock – but I've never
seen a real seal before except in the zoo so it's close enough
for me to sit there and watch it bobbing about and ducking
under and coming back up again. And I'm kind of enjoying
it. It feels like a secret. It feels special. It feels warmer. Then
it all fucks up.

It comes in closer to the beach and it starts to look a bit
weird. A bit un-fucking-seal-like. Suspiciously fucking

human, in fact. And it comes even closer to the beach and it
stands up. And the head is connected to a body, with arms
and legs and it's walking out of the water and it's her. Mirren.
Wading out of the fucking sea like Ursula Andress in Dr No.
Except she doesn't have the knife, or the shell, or the fucking
bikini.

And I'm watching her and not feeling a bit like big Sean.
'Cause I'm freezing. My jacket's too thin. My feet are wet.
And my trainers don't have any grip on slippery rock. I'm the
wrong person. In the wrong place. And if this beach had
bouncers I'd never be allowed in. But she's down there, hair
drying in the wind. The Queen of the club. And I hate her.
Because there's a word for it. There's a word. And I'm
thinking it. I'm thinking it. But I can't fucking say it.

31

In the car. On the road to Ullapool.

ALEX. The Skye Bridge.

BRIAN. Opened October 1995. Highest toll in Europe.

ALEX. A87.

BRIAN. Eilean Donan Castle. The view that launched a
thousand shortbread tins. Only built eighty years ago.

ALEX. Left on to the A890.

BRIAN. Loch Carron.

ALEX. Left again onto the A896.

BRIAN. Loch Kishorn. They used to build oil platforms there.
Abandoned now.

ALEX. The Bonnie Concrete Banks.

BRIAN. Shieldaig. Torridon. Kinlochewe.

ALEX. Loch Maree.

BRIAN. Thirteen miles long with twenty-four islands.

ALEX. Gairloch.

BRIAN. Trout fishing and a nine-hole golf course.

ALEX. Inverewe.

BRIAN. Famous house and gardens.

ALEX. Aultbea?

BRIAN. Uhm . . . nothing . . . except . . .

ALEX. Fucking hell!

BRIAN. A very steep descent.

32

Gruinard Bay. A stop for water. MIRREN and ALEX wait for the others to return.

MIRREN. Brian seemed pretty keen to go for the water.

ALEX. Yeah.

MIRREN. Did you two have a fight last night?

ALEX. Sort of.

MIRREN. About what?

ALEX. He thought I should be nicer to you and Iona.

MIRREN. What did you say?

ALEX. I said I'd think about it.

MIRREN. Really?

ALEX. No. I told him to fuck off.

   MIRREN *smiles.*

ALEX. He thinks I worry too much.

MIRREN. What do you think?

ALEX. It's not planned this, y'know. I don't really know what we're doing here. I'm just making it up as I go.

MIRREN. Thrown in at the deep-end. You've done all right so far.

ALEX. Yeah. But what's next?

MIRREN. S'no reason to worry.

ALEX. No?

MIRREN. There's nothing you can do. Just accept it.

ALEX. And relax?

MIRREN. One thing at a time. Try just accepting first.

ALEX. How am I supposed to do that?

MIRREN. You need to learn how to breathe.

ALEX. Are you taking the piss?

MIRREN. Aye.

Pause.

ALEX. Look, last night ... I didn't mean to be ... you know ...

MIRREN. I know.

ALEX. It's just that ...

MIRREN. What?

ALEX. Well. Up here. Like this. I feel a bit ... as if ... I mean, I feel like ...

IONA *and* BRIAN *return with water for the car.*

BRIAN. Hey. You see that island over there. Iona was telling me the government tested chemical weapons on it during the war. They infected it with anthrax and no-one could go on it till a few years ago when they finally cleaned it up. Isn't that wild?

ALEX. Yeah. Wild.

IONA. We got the water. We can get going again.

ALEX. No rush.

BRIAN. You've changed your tune.

MIRREN. He's learning how to breathe.

IONA. Getting in touch with nature, eh Alex?

ALEX. Not exactly.

IONA. Didn't you go bird-watching this morning too?

ALEX. Eh?

IONA. I'm sure I saw you from the kitchen. See anything interesting?

ALEX. No. Not really. I mean, I wasn't looking.

A beat.

Maybe we should get going.

BRIAN. Thought we weren't in a rush.

MIRREN. My Granny always said things would get done faster if everyone just slowed down a wee bit.

BRIAN. My Granny was like that. 'Remember son, the world's your oxter.'

IONA. I don't get it.

33

BINKS *stops on the road to Inverness.*

BINKS. Drumna-fucking-drochit? What kinda name is that?

A SMALL BOY *enters licking an ice lolly.* BINKS *and he eye each other warily.* BINKS *covets the lolly.*

BOY. Are you going to the exhibition? I am.

BINKS. What exhibition?

BOY. The official Loch Ness Monster Exhibition. Over there. Are you going?

BINKS. Naw. Give us a bit of your lolly?

BOY. Naw.

Pause. BINKS *schemes.*

BINKS. I'll tell you a secret if you give us a bit.

BOY *shakes his head.*

BINKS. Two secrets then. For one wee sook.

BOY *swithers.*

BINKS. Three secrets. One lick.

BOY *succumbs and hands over the lolly.*

BOY. Tell me the secrets then.

BINKS. First. Nessie doesnae exist.

The BOY *is crestfallen.* BINKS *sucks on the lolly.*

BINKS. Second. Neither does Santa.

The BOY *is shocked.*

BINKS. Oh aye and third. I'm keeping this.

The BOY *bursts into tears and runs off.* BINKS *enjoys the lolly, pleased with himself.*

BINKS. Eh? . . . Aye, Ronnie son. It's true.

Candy from a baby!

He laughs.

34

Arriving in Ullapool.

ALEX. You come into Ullapool along Loch Broom. It's full of big fishing boats from all over the place. Tied up in rows. Backing out towards the sea. Like a procession.

BRIAN. Established by the British Fisheries Association in 1788.

ALEX. And as pretty as a trawler.

BRIAN. It does look a bit dull.

ALEX. Or it did until we pulled up outside the community hall . . .

BRIAN. . . . and met Serge!

SERGE *emerges like Eric Cantona dressed by Salvador Dali.*

SERGE. Na-na! What are you doing here?

IONA. Thought I'd come to the party.

SERGE. And Mirren! Mon dieu. What a surprise!

MIRREN. How's things?

SERGE. Ça va. You know. Much better now that you are here.

MIRREN. These are some friends of mine. Brian. And Alex.

This is Serge . . .

ALEX. We guessed.

SERGE. So, you are all here for the ceilidh, yes.

MIRREN. Not exactly. We're heading north but we're having some trouble with the car . . .

SERGE. Ah. The Riva. A classic.

He pats the car affectionately.

SERGE. Let me guess. Alternator?

ALEX. And the radiator.

SERGE. Ah. Cooling system and the electrical? Serious. But not fatal, I think. You have come how far?

BRIAN. From Motherwell. Near Glasgow.

SERGE. In this! Then you are officially Heroes of the State. Mad, but heroic.

ALEX. Iona thought you might be able to help.

SERGE. Certainly, but I must first help with the ceilidh. There's so much to do and so little time.

MIRREN. Later maybe?

SERGE. Certainly. Later. But you will stay? You dance, you sing, you sleep. And tomorrow you leave in a healthier car, yes?

ALEX. Tomorrow?

IONA. Go on.

BRIAN. We haven't anywhere to stay.

SERGE. Pas de problème. The hall, I sleep in a back room. It is big enough. Mirren?

MIRREN. It's not up to me. Alex?

Pause.

ALEX. Fine.

SERGE. Bon. Maintenant. Does anyone know something about microphones?

BRIAN. Well, actually . . .

ALEX. Brian knows something about everything.

MIRREN. Yeah. He's your man.

SERGE. Excellent.

He begins steering BRIAN *into the hall.*

BRIAN. It's only been karaoke I've helped out at before . . .

SERGE. Karaoke. Ceilidh. The same. Wan singer wan song, no?

35

The ceilidh.

ALEX. The ceilidh was mad. Really weird. The place was full
of folk from the village. And fishermen and crofters and some
tourists and . . . us. And it was a mix. A huge mix. They
mixed the music and they mixed the people and they mixed
the fucking drink and it was . . . just a bit much. That's all.
Just a bit too much.

ALEX *is in the car park outside the hall.* IONA *comes out to
join him.*

IONA. Hi. You O.K. out here?

ALEX. Fine.

IONA. What are you doing?

ALEX. Practising breathing. It's hot in there.

IONA. Having a good time, though?

ALEX. It's not quite what I expected.

IONA. How so?

ALEX. It seems strange coming to a ceilidh and hearing some
highlander belt out 'Folsom Prison Blues'.

IONA. What would you prefer?

ALEX. I don't know.

IONA. Something in Gaelic, maybe?

ALEX. Yeah. Maybe.

IONA *begins to sing, in perfect Gaelic, a lament.* ALEX
listens in some astonishment. She finishes.

ALEX. I didn't know . . . You never said. That was amazing.

IONA. You didn't understand a word though did you?

ALEX. No.

IONA. But you got every single syllable of Johnny Cash.

ALEX. So?

IONA. So why does it matter what anybody does for their party
piece?

ALEX. It's complicated. I suppose I thought people up here
would be less . . . confused.

IONA. Confused? About what?

ALEX. Who they are.

IONA. Who's confused? Look. See that?

ALEX. What?

IONA. Satellite dish. We're not cut off from the outside world.

ALEX. I know that.

IONA. You think we should be like a big Braveheart theme
park? Pickled in tradition? C'mon Alex. Loosen up. You can
have it all.

ALEX. How?

IONA. Choose your influences . . .

ALEX. I'm not sure you get to choose . . .

Pause.

IONA. What are you looking for?

ALEX. Just . . . somewhere that doesn't make me feel like an
outsider.

IONA. Or someone.

ALEX. . . .

A beat. MIRREN *emerges and comes to join them.*

MIRREN. God, it's hot in there. What are you two up to?

IONA. Just chewing the fat.

Pause.

IONA. Saw you dancing with Brian.

MIRREN. Yeah.

ALEX. Any broken toes?

MIRREN. I think I got off lightly.

IONA. What's he up to now?

MIRREN. He's with the Ukrainians. From the factory ship.

ALEX. I didn't realise they were Ukrainian.

IONA. They've been anchored in the loch for months. No fuel
and no money to buy any. Their government was supposed to
send it but they seem to've forgotten. Their ship's just rusting
away.

ALEX. What are they doing with Brian?

MIRREN. He's reciting Burns. One of them is translating. They're big fans apparently.

ALEX. I didn't know he knew any Burns.

From inside sound of a woman starting to sing a slow ballad.

MIRREN. Oh. I love this song. Come and dance.

IONA. Not me girl. I'm done. Alex'll give you a birl, though. Eh?

ALEX. I'm not exactly Fred Astaire.

IONA. No, but you're not Fred Flintstone either. Go on.

MIRREN. Well?

ALEX. Here?

MIRREN. It's cooler.

ALEX *and* MIRREN *start to dance tentatively.*

IONA. Jeez Alex, it's not basketball. You're allowed contact.

MIRREN. You're trying too hard. Just let it happen.

ALEX *relaxes.*

IONA. That's better. See you later.

IONA *exits.*

ALEX. You're pretty good.

MIRREN. I used to go to classes. When I was wee. You're not too bad . . . once you relax.

ALEX. It'll be all that breathing.

MIRREN. You ought to do it more often.

ALEX. Breathe?

MIRREN. Relax.

ALEX. I'll try.

MIRREN. Don't try, just . . .

ALEX. . . . let it happen.

Pause.

MIRREN. What are you going to do when you get to Thurso?

ALEX. Try and sell the board.

MIRREN. And then?

ALEX. Depends.

MIRREN. On what?

ALEX. Lots of things.

MIRREN. You're not going home.

ALEX. Can't. Not for a while.

MIRREN. Haven't you got family?

ALEX. They won't miss me.

MIRREN. What about Brian?

ALEX. His dad probably hasn't even noticed that he's gone yet.

Pause. Song finishes.

MIRREN. I know some people in Thurso. Surfers. I might be able to help you find a buyer.

ALEX. That'd be good.

MIRREN. There's one guy I could introduce you to. He knows everybody.

ALEX. You're going to come with us to Thurso?

MIRREN. If that's all right?

ALEX. What about Tongue?

MIRREN. I just need to pick a few things up. Flying visit.

ALEX. But this guy . . . Tom? Won't he mind?

MIRREN. That's my problem.

ALEX. Who is he?

MIRREN. He's someone who thinks I've fucked my life up and is determined to save me from myself. I embarrass him. He harasses me. It's a long story.

ALEX. So . . . How d'you know him then?

MIRREN. He's my father.

ALEX. Oh.

Pause.

MIRREN. You surprised?

ALEX. A bit.

MIRREN. Doesn't just happen in Motherwell you know.

ALEX. No. It's not that. I . . .

MIRREN. . . . ?

ALEX. I better go and see how Brian's doing.

MIRREN. Oh.

ALEX. And Serge. He might've forgotten.

MIRREN. Try the bar.

ALEX. O.K. Thanks.

He exits.

36

Inverness. BINKS *has a new pal,* GUNN. *They are pissed.*

GUNN. No. No. No. Definitely not. I'm telling you. Absolutely.
    Under no circumstances. I am quite certain. No.

Pause.

BINKS. Are you sure?

GUNN *belches.*

GUNN. I could be wrong.

BINKS. Christ man!

GUNN. Wait now. Just let me think . . . They had a ladder you
    said.

BINKS. That's right.

GUNN. Tied to the roof?

BINKS. Eh?

GUNN. And what kind of car was it?

BINKS. A Lada.

GUNN. I know about that.

BINKS. Well, why are you asking?

GUNN. I need to know about the car.

BINKS. It had a surf-board tied to the roof.

GUNN. As well as the ladder?

BINKS. On top of the Lada! A surf-board on top of a Lada.

GUNN. Well, I'm sure I would've noticed that. That's not something you see every day, is it. I'm sure I would've noticed.

BINKS. But you didn't.

GUNN. Didn't what?

BINKS. You didn't notice it.

GUNN. Did I not?

BINKS *growls and grabs* GUNN *by the lapels.*

BINKS. You were working. On the roadworks. On the bridge over the Beauly Firth. Right?

GUNN. Right.

BINKS. And you did not see a Lada with a surf-board on top, crossing the bridge. Right?

GUNN. Right.

BINKS. Right!

Pause. BINKS *releases his grip.*

GUNN. Are you sure you don't know what kind of car it was? Must've been awful over-loaded . . .

BINKS' *patience snaps. He produces a knife.*

GUNN. Are we going for a kebab then?

BINKS. Aye. Oh aye.

37

The dregs of the ceilidh.

IONA. Time gentlemen please!

Groans and shuffling as people leave.

MIRREN. Serge, what about the car?

SERGE. Ah. O.K. I remember. I will look at it now. Give me the keys.

ALEX. But it's four in the morning.

SERGE. So?

ALEX. Aren't you tired?

SERGE. I am wide awake.

ALEX. Are you on something?

SERGE. Alex. Too many questions. I am fine. Hunky dory. Trust me. Give me the keys.

ALEX *reluctantly hands them over.*

SERGE. You will go to sleep. You will have wonderful dreams. When you wake up your car will be transformed.

ALEX. Be careful with it.

SERGE. I will be gentle. I am French.

He leaves to attend to the car. ALEX is still concerned.

IONA. It's all right, Alex. He knows what he's doing.

ALEX. Where exactly did he train?

IONA. Nice.

ALEX. Technical college?

IONA. School of Art.

ALEX. Sorry?

IONA. Didn't I say? He's a sculptor.

ALEX. A sculptor?

IONA. But he does do a lot of work with Ladas and Skodas and things.

ALEX. What kind of work?

IONA. Well, normally he cuts them in half and welds wings on to them. Angel-type wings. Or legs. Sometimes it's legs.

A beat.

MIRREN. Alex? Are you all right?

ALEX. Yeah. I'm going to go to sleep and have wonderful dreams and wake up to find the car transformed. Fine.

MIRREN. Are you sure?

ALEX. Just letting it happen . . .

BRIAN spirals over to them very drunk.

BRIAN. Chudovyj! *(tchu-daw-vey)*

He has acquired a Ukrainian word.

ALEX. Yeah. Chudovyj. Very good.

BRIAN. It is. Say it. Chudovyj. Go on.

ALEX. Chudovyj.

BRIAN. Perfect.

They are all now heading off to the back room.

BRIAN. Chudovyj! Doesn't it sound good?

ALEX. Yeah. But what does it mean?

BRIAN. It's Ukrainian for 'beautiful'.

They exit.

Interval.

38

Next morning. SERGE *musters the still sleepy travellers to the unveiling of the car.*

SERGE. Good morning Comrades. You must prepare to witness a transfiguration.

MIRREN. Have you been up all night?

SERGE. I have been creating.

ALEX. But have you fixed the car?

SERGE. So basic! The leaking radiator leaks no more. The alternator is still weak but the battery strong again.

BRIAN. What about the lights?

SERGE. You have no lights. You must be guided by the brightness of your imagination.

BRIAN. Oh.

ALEX. Fuck.

SERGE. Do not worry. The car will carry you where you need it to. I have refreshed its spirit.

ALEX. You've changed the oil?

SERGE. I have changed the car.

ALEX. How, exactly?

BRIAN. Serge . . .

SERGE. The car was unhappy. I asked it why. Then I made it happier.

BRIAN. You asked it why?

ALEX. What was it you took last night?

BRIAN. What did it say?

SERGE. It was unhappy because it was brown. Not even a golden sun-tanned brown but a dark, horrible brown like . . .

ALEX. Shit.

SERGE. Exactly. The car was unhappy because it was the colour of shit. Merde.

ALEX. Oh God.

SERGE. So I cured it . . . Et voilà!

He removes the dustsheet. The Lada is now practically fluorescent with day-glo colours. There is a shocked silence.

SERGE. You have a car with a smile on its face.

MIRREN. Oh no.

ALEX. Fucking hell.

IONA. Serge . . .

SERGE. What is the matter? Don't you like it?

ALEX. It's . . . It's . . .

SERGE. Bright?

ALEX. Mmm.

SERGE. Camouflage for you.

ALEX. Camouflage!

SERGE. You blend in by standing out. You look truly like surfers now. Not robbers skulking around the Highlands.

MIRREN. Certainly going to be difficult to skulk in that.

ALEX. Brian, are you all right?

BRIAN has become catatonic with shock.

MIRREN. Brian? Say something.

There is no response.

IONA. What's wrong with him?

ALEX. I think he's in shock. I've seen it before.

MIRREN. He's been like this before?

ALEX. When his Mum unplugged his computer to hoover his bedroom and crashed a programme he'd been working on for months.

MIRREN. How long was he like this?

ALEX. Well . . .

IONA. Couple of minutes?

MIRREN. An hour?

ALEX. Three days.

MIRREN. What!

ALEX. It's alright. This probably won't be as long.

MIRREN. What do we do?

ALEX. We might as well get going. He'll come out of it when he's ready.

IONA. Are you sure you'll be alright?

ALEX. Any better ideas?

They guide BRIAN *carefully towards the car. He is reluctant to go anywhere near it. They coax him into the back seat and prepare to set off.*

SERGE. The muses shall protect you. You are travelling in a work of art.

ALEX. Well, at least it doesn't have wings.

39

On the road. In the car. BRIAN *in the back.* ALEX *and* MIRREN *in front.* BRIAN *talks directly to the audience.*

BRIAN. I'd been working on it for nearly twelve weeks. It was basically a database with some tricks built in. Horse racing. I had information on over three hundred horses. All kinds of information. It was just getting to the point where the predictions were reliable. The point where I could start to make money.

ALEX. A835. North out of Ullapool.

MIRREN. There's a wee road that turns off at Drumrunie. Goes round the coast to Lochinver. It's a bit of a detour though.

ALEX. What do think Brian? Turn off or carry on? Eh? Brian?

BRIAN. I'd only went to the toilet. Two minutes. I was sitting there working out how much cash I could get together to stake when I heard the hoover. It came to me quite slowly where the sound was coming from. I waited until it stopped before I could bear to go see.

MIRREN. ' . . . a wild and adventurous road with magnificent scenery . . . ' That's what it says. In your book. Look.

BRIAN. She was just plugging it back in when I got there. She switched it on and smiled at me. 'That's the place a wee bit cleaner anyway.' I was looking at the screen. It was more than just a wee bit cleaner. It was blank. I saw all that information, all those facts and figures, all swirling around and down into the big black hole of my mum's hoover bag. I saw her sucking them off the screen and out from between the keys with her handy hose attachment. Nozzling it all into oblivion.

ALEX. Will we turn off then, Brian? You're the navigator. That a no then? Straight on, d'you think?

MIRREN. I suppose it's not so important to avoid the main roads now.

ALEX. Now that we're camouflaged.

BRIAN. She died three months after that. We all stood at the grave chucking dirt down on top of the coffin. Me and George and my Dad. My shoes were leaking and I thought about the money I could've made with the programme. I had an urge to jump into the grave and wipe all that dirt off the polished wood. I wished I had a yellow duster to do the job properly. But I didn't. So my mum disappeared into a black hole too.

ALEX. Look at the mountains, Brian. They're incredible.

MIRREN. Suilven. Canisp. Ben More Assynt.

ALEX. Ever heard of them? Anything interesting ever happen here?

MIRREN. It says here that they 'seem as if they have tumbled down from the clouds, having nothing to do with the country or each other in shape, material, position or character, and look very much as if they were wondering how they got there.'

ALEX. Hey Brian, that's us, eh? Nothing to do with anything and wondering how we got here. That's us.

BRIAN. George joined the army. My dad hit the bottle. He sold the computer to pay an electricity bill. I started spending a lot of time at the library. Nothing got better. Everything just seemed to get worse. I wondered how bad it could get before it would all stop.

ALEX. What?

BRIAN. Stop.

ALEX. Why?

BRIAN. I need some air.

ALEX. O.K. No problem. We'll pull in. Take a wee break.

MIRREN. You're back. Are you all right?

BRIAN. I'm fine. I just need to stretch my legs.

ALEX. All right. Good. Take your time. Take it easy. Remember to breathe and everything.

BRIAN. I'm fine.

40

At the roadside. BRIAN *wanders away from the other two a bit.*

MIRREN. Do you think he's O.K?

ALEX. Yeah. He'll be fine.

MIRREN. Should we go with him?

ALEX. No. Let him get some air.

MIRREN. The car seems better.

ALEX. Serge seems to have done something right.

MIRREN. He's made it happier.

ALEX. Yeah.

   Pause.

ALEX. Where are we?

MIRREN. Assynt. More or less.

ALEX. Nice and quiet. Peaceful.

MIRREN. D'you think?

ALEX. Feels like the middle of nowhere.

MIRREN. D'you know what you're sitting on?

ALEX. A stone.

MIRREN. Gable end of a croft-house.

ALEX. A house?

MIRREN. There's another one over there. And there. Probably another dozen along the glen.

ALEX. Yeah?

MIRREN. Wasn't always so nice and quiet round here.

ALEX. What happened?

MIRREN. Clearances. Whole families packed off to Canada and Australia. Driven out to make room for sheep.

ALEX. Money talks. Nothing changes, eh?

MIRREN. This changed. They changed it into scenery. The Great Wilderness? The Highland Landscape? It's an invention. I don't think it's peaceful. I think it's sad.

ALEX. Where I come from, they took all the jobs away then called it a special development area.

BRIAN, *unnoticed, has found a stream. He sticks his head under the water and keeps it there.*

MIRREN. Doesn't it piss you off?

ALEX. Lots of things piss me off.

MIRREN. I'd noticed. Me included?

ALEX. Well. You did. A bit.

MIRREN. Why? What did I do?

ALEX. You just fitted in, that's all. Looked like you belonged. I feel . . . out of place. A misfit.

MIRREN. It's still Scotland. You're Scottish.

ALEX. I'm a foreigner here. Even the midges know that. Look, my face is like a page of braille. They don't bother you at all.

MIRREN. You think they're picking on you?

ALEX. Insect antibodies. An immune system for repelling invaders.

MIRREN. Maybe, if you stay still they'll leave you alone.

ALEX. We're not very good at that though, are we. Me and Brian. We're running.

MIRREN. What is it?

ALEX. Where's he gone? Hey? Brian? . . . BRIAN!

They run across to BRIAN *and pull him out. He shows no signs of life.* ALEX *shakes him.*

MIRREN. Is he alright?

ALEX. Brian! Talk to me! Say something!

A beat. A cough from BRIAN.

BRIAN. If I'm going to get the kiss of life, I'd rather Mirren did it.

Pause. Then ALEX *starts to hit him.*

ALEX. You stupid bastard. What are you playing at?

MIRREN. Alex. Stop it.

MIRREN *pulls them apart and they calm a little.*

BRIAN. Sorry.

ALEX. Sorry! What were you trying to do?

BRIAN. Drown myself.

A beat.

ALEX. Jesus Christ! It's only a fucking car. It's not even a very good one.

BRIAN. That's not the point.

ALEX. What is the point?

MIRREN. Brian. It's not the end of the world.

ALEX. It fucking will be if you try that again. I'll kill you myself.

MIRREN. Alex.

ALEX. Is this what you've been cooking up in the car all this way? Is that what was going on? What were you thinking about?

BRIAN. It doesn't matter. I didn't realise you were going to get so worked up about it.

ALEX. Thanks.

Pause.

BRIAN. Can we go back to the car now? I'm wet.

ALEX. Yeah, you fucking are . . .

41

Helmsdale. BINKS *at a garage. Chats to the* PUMP-HAND.

PUMP. There now. That's you full. Ten pounds, please.

BINKS. Christ.

PUMP. Aye, it'll be dearer than you're used to. Still, you're lucky you're just passing through. We have to pay these prices all the time.

BINKS. What a shame.

PUMP. It is. It's alright for you. You're going somewhere, aren't you. Where are you going?

BINKS. Thurso.

PUMP. There see. You're going to Thurso and then you'll be going somewhere else no doubt. Then somewhere else. Am I right?

BINKS. More or less.

PUMP. And is it business or pleasure?

BINKS. Business. As in 'mind your own'.

PUMP. Ah. You must be a salesman. I can tell. What you selling then?

BINKS. Private Health Care.

PUMP. Och I've no need for that myself. Fit as a fiddle.

BINKS. That could change. Very suddenly.

PUMP. Not here. Nope. Last sudden change we had round here was decimalisation.

BINKS. Where is this?

PUMP. Helmsdale.

BINKS. How far's that from Thurso?

PUMP. It varies. Thirty miles. Forty maybe if you go via John O'Groats.

BINKS. John O'Groats? Is that near here?

PUMP. Not too far.

BINKS. How do I get there?

PUMP. Ah, you don't want to go there. Nothing to see. A hotel. A woollens shop. A signpost. It's not . . .

BINKS. How do I get there?

PUMP. Well, it's up to you. You'd want to carry on here and go straight through Wick . . . believe me, everyone wants to go straight through Wick . . . and then you can't miss it. Turn left for Thurso once you've seen it.

BINKS. I don't suppose you've seen two guys in a . . .

PUMP. A what?

BINKS. Ach, never mind.

PUMP. Suit yourself.

A beat.

PUMP. Was there something else?

BINKS. I gave you a twenty.

PUMP. Did you?

BINKS. Aye. I did. Give me ma change.

PUMP. Are you sure it was a twenty?

BINKS. Does petrol burn?

BINKS *flips open the lid of a zippo and sparks it into life as he grabs the attendant.*

PUMP. In the name of God! What are you doing? Put it out!

BINKS. Give me ma fucking money before I cremate you.

PUMP. Here take it. Take it all. On the house. Just put that out. PLEASE!

42

On the road. A jet screams past low overhead.

ALEX. What the hell was that?

MIRREN. Jets. Phantoms. They have a base up here. It's a practice area for NATO. Low level flying.

ALEX. God. Any lower and I would've had to pull over to let him pass.

MIRREN. You're getting better, you know.

ALEX. At what?

MIRREN. Passing places. You're using them properly now. It's much better. Eh Brian?

BRIAN. Two steel boxes full of hopes and dreams and fears hurtle towards each other on a narrow road and just as they are about to collide the road widens enough for them to slip past each other with only the lightest of kisses on the cheek. Hello, goodbye, without ever stopping.

Pause.

ALEX. Is that out the Highway Code?

BRIAN. It's life, isn't it.

ALEX. It's only a road, Brian.

BRIAN. The A838. North east from Laxford Bridge. Twenty-five miles to Durness. Then through Sangobeg, all the way round Loch Eriboll, past Portnancon, through Laid then Polla. On to Heilam. The road widens and there it is.

ALEX. What are you on about?

BRIAN. It's on the map, Alex. You can't miss it.

ALEX. Miss what?

BRIAN. The A838. Where it takes you.

ALEX. Thurso?

BRIAN. Before Thurso. Tell him Mirren. Look.

ALEX. Tell me what?

MIRREN. You pass Loch Eriboll and carry on for a bit . . . You come to . . .

BRIAN. Hope.

ALEX. That's stupid.

BRIAN. It's on the map.

MIRREN. It is Alex.

ALEX. I'm surrounded by lunatics. Are we nearly there?

BRIAN. Hope?

ALEX. Tongue!

MIRREN. Not far now.

43

Arriving in Tongue.

ALEX. You come in over a long low bridge that stretches across a kyle of sand and water. The house was on the left before the village itself.

BRIAN. Big grey stone building. Like a manse. A gravel drive and trees.

ALEX. Mirren went to find her dad.

BRIAN. We waited by the car.

ALEX. There was something funny going on with him. I said . . .

BRIAN. 'Are you all right?'

ALEX. And he gave me this look. Like somebody had died.

BRIAN. And he looked worried, so I told him.

ALEX. He told me.

BRIAN. I said . . .

ALEX. 'I'm not going back.'

BRIAN. He says . . .

ALEX. 'What? What d'you mean?'

BRIAN. I said it again.

ALEX. He said it twice.

   A beat.

BRIAN. I'm not going back. I can't.

ALEX. But . . .

BRIAN. I've decided.

ALEX. Is this because of the car? Is that what it is?

BRIAN. No.

ALEX. No? What d'you mean, 'no'? You tried to drown yourself.

BRIAN. It's not the car.

ALEX. Well what . . .

BRIAN. I'm not going back. It's because of me. Not you. Not the car. Me. There's no reason now for me to go back there. It's too far behind.

ALEX. Brian, it's a few hours' drive. In a decent car.

BRIAN. It's too far.

Pause.

ALEX. I knew this would happen. You always do this. You always turn something completely simple and straightforward into a big production number. Some fucking defining moment. Some glimpse into the true nature of the fucking universe. Always. Even at school. A hair in your pie and beans and it's a sign from God. Extra custard and it's an omen of plenty. Well, it's not. A hair is a hair. Custard is just custard. They are not fucking karmic telegrams.

Pause.

BRIAN. I'm not going back.

ALEX. We're only here to flog the surf-board and lie low for a bit. It's not supposed to be a turning point in our lives. Nothing's changed. Nothing.

BRIAN. I'm not going back.

ALEX. That's not an argument. That's shite. You're talking shite.

BRIAN. I'm not going.

Pause.

ALEX. What are you going to do?

BRIAN. Don't know.

ALEX. And what am I supposed to do?

BRIAN. Don't know.

ALEX. Brilliant.

BRIAN. I'm not going back.

Pause.

ALEX. Maybe I should've just let you drown.

44

In TOM*'s house. The atmosphere is a bit strained.*

TOM. I could've made something really special. I don't often get the chance, you know.

MIRREN. We can't stay, dad.

TOM. What about it boys? Can't your business wait till tomorrow? I've got venison in the freezer. Have you ever had venison?

ALEX. We really have to be in Thurso tonight.

MIRREN. Before it gets dark.

ALEX. Maybe some other time.

TOM. Yeah well. I suppose if you're a parent these days you live on the crumbs from your children's table.

MIRREN. Dad.

TOM. Where is it this time?

MIRREN. Don't know. Scandinavia, maybe.

TOM. Got anything lined up?

MIRREN. No.

TOM. What a surprise. I'll give you a name of a guy I used to correspond with at the university in Stockholm.

MIRREN. There's no need.

TOM. He'll help you out.

MIRREN. I'll be fine.

TOM. Doing what? Waiting tables? Washing dishes?

MIRREN. Whatever.

TOM. Right. And after Scandinavia?

MIRREN. I don't know.

TOM. No long term plan.

MIRREN. Not really.

TOM. No. I didn't think so.

MIRREN. Dad. Don't start.

   Pause.

MIRREN. Show Brian your office. He'll be interested in all that stuff.

TOM. Nice that someone is.

MIRREN. We can clear up.

ALEX. Yeah.

TOM. C'mon then, Brian. I'll show you the electric croft.

BRIAN. Great.

45

BRIAN *and* TOM *go to the office.* MIRREN *and* ALEX *wash up in the kitchen. The scene jumps between the two.*

ALEX. He seems alright.

MIRREN. He thinks I'm wasting my life.

ALEX. At least he worries about you.

MIRREN. I don't want him to.

ALEX. It's his job.

TOM. First class honours, you know. Maths and computer science. Could go anywhere with that. Anywhere. Without having to wash dishes.

BRIAN. She never mentioned it.

TOM. No. She usually doesn't. Makes her seem too much like me.

ALEX. You sure you don't want to hang around longer?

MIRREN. It's not worth it. Things tend to get ugly after a while.

ALEX. You're fidgeting.

MIRREN. This place. Him. It makes me restless. What's so funny?

ALEX. Everywhere we've been so far, you seemed so at home. But now you are home . . . !

MIRREN. This isn't home. We moved here when I was thirteen. I left when I was seventeen. I've not really lived here since.

ALEX. So where's home then?

She shrugs.

TOM. We came up here when Mirren's mother died. I needed a change.

BRIAN. Did you bring all this with you?

TOM. No. Got it when I decided to stay.

BRIAN. It's a lot of stuff.

TOM. Nothing special. PC. Printer. Modem.

BRIAN. Haven't you got a satellite dish too?

TOM. Aye, but that's just for the football really.

ALEX. So who's the guy you're taking us to see in Thurso? Your uncle? A second-cousin?

MIRREN. A friend. He's difficult to describe.

ALEX. A lot of your friends are!

MIRREN. He's part of the surfing scene.

ALEX. D'you think we will be able to get rid of the board?

MIRREN. He'll be able to tell you. He's a shaper.

ALEX. What's that?

MIRREN. He builds boards. Shapes them. It's very specialised. A real art.

ALEX. So he's well in with the surfers?

MIRREN. Oh yeah. He's like a guru. Kind of . . . mystic.

ALEX. A mystic surf-guru. Can't wait.

BRIAN. And you work from here now?

TOM. Freelance. Do a lot of stuff for software designers in Silicon Valley.

BRIAN. America? From here?

TOM. It's easy enough. I can phone. Fax. E-mail. I can link the machine straight through. Video conference if we need too. It's no problem.

BRIAN. You don't need to go over there at all?

TOM. I go about twice a year. Just for the sunshine. Who'd be a commuter, eh?

BRIAN. I wouldn't know.

MIRREN. You can't make him go back. It's up to him.

ALEX. He doesn't know what he's doing.

MIRREN. Maybe he does.

ALEX. It wasn't meant to be like this. It was only temporary.

MIRREN. Temporary can be a very long time.

TOM. Portable skills. That's the key. You can take them anywhere. Especially now, with all this stuff.

BRIAN. What if you haven't got any skills?

TOM. Everybody's got them. You just have to bring them out.

BRIAN. How?

TOM. You can learn, can't you?

MIRREN. That's what travelling's all about. Change.

ALEX. Aye. But with Brian it's usually just change for the bus.

MIRREN. Not this time.

ALEX. But it's just a trip.

MIRREN. A long trip.

ALEX. Tell me about it.

MIRREN. You've changed too.

ALEX. But I'm not burning my bridges.

MIRREN. Not yet.

TOM. You're thinking about sticking around up here?

BRIAN. If I can. Somewhere.

TOM. There's a lot going on, you know. I'm sure you'll find something. If you look hard enough.

BRIAN. I hope so.

MIRREN. I think you're scared.

ALEX. Of what?

MIRREN. Being alone. You need him. He looks after you.

ALEX. You think so?

MIRREN. Yeah.

ALEX. What about you, then?

MIRREN. I look after myself.

ALEX. You don't need anyone?

MIRREN. No.

ALEX. And you're never scared?

MIRREN. I've been on my own for a long time.

ALEX. That wasn't the question.

TOM. I just want to know that she's alright, that's all. I know she thinks I interfere but I just want her to be happy. Is she? D'you think she's happy?

BRIAN. I don't know. She seems okay. Maybe you should ask her.

TOM. She won't tell me. I'd be the last to know anything.

BRIAN. I'm sure she's fine.

ALEX. You going to make your goodbyes? We ought to get going before it's too dark.

MIRREN. It won't take long. I've had enough practice.

46

John O'Groats. Bleak. BINKS hovers by a sign-post.

BINKS. Well Ronnie, here we are. John O'Groats. Who'd've thought, eh? The end of the line . . . Aye. I know. Alright. Nearly the end of the line, then . . . Aye. A bit grim is not wrong.

A LADY WALKER clumps up to him in heavy boots.

WALKER. Hello there.

BINKS. . . .

WALKER. I've walked here. All the way.

BINKS. . . .

WALKER. From Land's End, I mean. I've walked all the way.

BINKS. Why?

Pause.

WALKER. Will you take my photograph?

BINKS. I havnae got a camera.

WALKER. With mine. Here. Would you? Go on.

He takes the camera. He takes the picture.

WALKER. Fabulous. No-one would've believed me otherwise.
I've got Land's End to John O'Groats all on one film now.
And there's still one shot left. Shall I take you?

BINKS. I told you I havnae got a camera.

WALKER. I mean with this. I've one left. I could send it to you.

BINKS. I don't think so.

WALKER. Oh go on. You've come all this way. You might not
get another chance. Don't you want something to remember
it by?

BINKS. I'm not bothered.

WALKER. It's no trouble. Go on.

BINKS. I don't want my photo taken.

WALKER. I need to use it up anyway.

BINKS. I told you, I . . .

She takes the picture.

WALKER. There. That didn't hurt did it. Would've been nicer if
you'd smiled though. Your face won't crack you know.

BINKS *moves towards her. Smiling.*

WALKER. There. See. You've got a lovely smile. Now if you
just give me your name and address I can send it to you when
I get it developed.

BINKS. Fuck . . .

WALKER. Is that German?

BINKS. . . . You!

BINKS *grabs her camera. She looks up and is dumb with
terror. He opens the camera and pulls out the film. She
whimpers slightly as he wraps it round and round her head.*

BINKS. I told her, Ronnie. I told her twice.

A gargling noise as the WALKER *is strangled.*

I don't want my fucking photo took.

47

On the road to Thurso. Back in the car.

BRIAN. A strange thing happens on the road between Tongue and Thurso. You move from Sutherland into Caithness and suddenly . . .

ALEX. All the scenery disappears.

BRIAN. You move from mountains into flat peat bogs.

ALEX. The flow country.

BRIAN. So it feels like you're back in the Central Belt again.

ALEX. On the road to . . . Shotts.

BRIAN. Then there's Dounreay.

ALEX. Radioactive dustbin.

BRIAN. Prototype Fast Breeder Reactor. Doubled Thurso's population.

ALEX. More physicists than fishermen.

BRIAN. Till they shut it.

ALEX. And then, finally . . .

BRIAN. Thurso!

ALEX. Viking for 'dull'?

BRIAN. No.

ALEX. Bathgate by the sea.

48

Thurso. The SHAPER*'s workshop. A shrine of surf-boards.*

ALEX *and* BRIAN *hesitate outside.* MIRREN *coaxes them in.*

MIRREN. What're you waiting out there for?

ALEX. Are you sure about this?

MIRREN. I phoned. He's expecting us.

They step into the workshop. Whispering.

BRIAN. What a place. Look at all those boards.

MIRREN. Don't touch anything.

ALEX. Sorry.

A noise in the corner.

MIRREN. Hello? Anybody in?

A beat.

SHAPER. Mistah Kurtz, he dead.

A beat.

MIRREN. Hello?

SHAPER. Hello.

The SHAPER *emerges from the shadows.*

SHAPER. That's better, eh? Mirren. Good to see you. Who're your friends?

MIRREN. These are the two guys I told you about.

SHAPER. Ah. The driver?

ALEX. Eh . . . yeah.

SHAPER. And the guide?

BRIAN. Yes.

SHAPER. You've come a long way.

BRIAN. From Motherwell. It's taken ages.

ALEX. The car's a wreck.

SHAPER. I saw it. Nice paint job, though.

MIRREN. Serge.

SHAPER. Of course.

BRIAN. It's been interesting.

ALEX. And slow.

SHAPER. 'All travelling becomes dull in exact proportion to its rapidity.' John Ruskin.

Pause.

SHAPER. What can I do for you?

ALEX. We need to sell a surf-board. Mirren thought you might be the best person to speak to.

SHAPER. About selling it?

ALEX. I think it's quite a good one. Quite expensive. But I
   don't know how much we might expect to get for it . . .

SHAPER. 'Money is our madness, our vast collective madness.'

BRIAN. D.H. Lawrence!

SHAPER. Absolutely correct, Mister . . .

   The SHAPER *laughs.*

SHAPER. Mirren . . . ?

MIRREN. Sorry. This is Alex and this is Brian.

SHAPER. I'm Frank.

BRIAN. Do you think you'll be able to help us?

SHAPER. Have either of you ever surfed?

BRIAN. No.

ALEX. We're from Motherwell.

SHAPER. See, finding the right board isn't just about buying a
   lump of coloured resin. There's a relationship there. It's about
   compatibility. Personality. Do you know what I mean?

ALEX. Not really.

SHAPER. What you've got to offer is a potential partner. A love
   affair. That's why you shouldn't put a price on it. You can't
   put a price on emotions can you, Alex?

ALEX. We need the money.

SHAPER. Ah. Separate problem entirely.

ALEX. So what do you suggest?

SHAPER. Well, you can't sell love. But there's no reason why
   you shouldn't expect an arrangement fee.

ALEX. A fee?

SHAPER. For bringing the happy couple together. Effecting the
   introduction. Oiling the cogs and wheels of the heart.

BRIAN. Matchmaking!

SHAPER. Precisely. It's not about making boards. Anybody can
   make a board. It's about making a good match. That's what
   people pay me for.

Pause.

ALEX. And you make a living from this?

MIRREN. People come from all over. He's world famous.

SHAPER. Only in Thurso.

MIRREN. Stop being so modest.

BRIAN. It's highly skilled then?

SHAPER. It's an art.

BRIAN. Can you learn it?

SHAPER. If you've got it, you can hone it. If you haven't got it . . .

BRIAN. How do you know if you've got it?

SHAPER. Difficult to say. You can usually tell by the colour of the light round your head.

A beat.

ALEX. So, will we be able to find a match for our board who might be suitably grateful?

SHAPER. We'll talk about it. But not before sunset.

BRIAN. Why not?

SHAPER. 'Cause I have to get to Safeways before it shuts.

49

A hotel in Thurso. BINKS *checks in.*

MO. Good evening, sir. Welcome to Thurso. What can I do for you?

BINKS. I need a room.

MO. Certainly. Single or double?

BINKS. Eh . . .

MO. Sir?

BINKS. Aye. Just a single. Of course.

MO. It's £45.00 a night including full breakfast . . .

BINKS. That's fine.

MO. If you'd just like to sign here. I'll get someone to take your luggage up for you.

BINKS. No luggage.

MO. None at all.

BINKS. No luggage!

MO. Okay then Mr . . . Yamaha. Your key. Breakfast is between seven and nine in the . . .

BINKS. All right Ron! I'll ask! . . . Fuck sake.

MO. Sir?

BINKS. Are there surfers in this place?

MO. Pardon?

BINKS. You know. Surfers.

MO. Yes.

BINKS. Where can I find them?

MO. Uhm . . . The beach.

BINKS. Apart fae the fucking beach. I mean where do they drink?

MO. Oh . . . Well there're a few places . . .

BINKS. Write them out for me and stick them under my door.

MO. Uh . . . Will there be anything else?

BINKS. I'll let you know.

MO. Second on the right at the top of the stairs, then.

BINKS. Ta.

50

The SHAPER *and the others having a drink in a bar.*

ALEX. D'you think she'll go for it?

SHAPER. Alex, it's a matter of alchemy. We'll find out tomorrow. She's nice, Mo. From Cornwall. Been up for about six months.

BRIAN. She came up here to surf. From Cornwall.

ALEX. Don't they have waves down there?

SHAPER. They're better up here.

ALEX. Colder too, I bet!

SHAPER. That's true. Straight down from the Arctic Circle. Huge. Monster waves. But absolutely fucking freezing. That's what always catches the sunshine boys out. Not quite Bondi.

BRIAN. They come from all over then?

SHAPER. Oh yeah. It's a key spot. Best waves in Europe on a good day.

ALEX. So how come no-one's heard of it?

SHAPER. You're here.

ALEX. That's a fluke.

SHAPER. It's 'cause it's not for tourists. You can't mess with the break around here. The waves are big but the water's icy. You can't stay out too long. And they come in over rock. If you get wiped out you can really get wiped out.

ALEX. So why do they do it? If it's cold and dangerous? Why not go to California?

SHAPER. They're on a quest. That's why. They're looking for a wave.

ALEX. But there are waves all over.

SHAPER. They're looking for a particular wave. People come to me and I try and make the board that's right for them, their style of riding, even the particular break they want to surf in. I try and make the perfect match. But each combination'll be best suited for one particular wave. One ideal coming together of elements. One potentially perfect moment where everything in the universe is suddenly aligned. That's the wave they're looking for. That's the wave we're all looking for.

MIRREN. Does anybody find it?

SHAPER. It's not just a matter of finding it. You've got to recognise it when it comes and then you've got to have the courage to get up on it.

MIRREN. Is that what Mo's looking for?

SHAPER. Yep.

MIRREN. Will the board help her?

SHAPER. We'll know after she's tried it. I think they might hit it off.

Pause.

BRIAN. Is that why you came here? Looking for a wave.

SHAPER. Sort of.

BRIAN. Did you find it?

SHAPER. Aye. I found it. Or it found me.

BRIAN. What was it like?

SHAPER. Perfect. And brief. Her name was Elizabeth.

BRIAN. Oh.

SHAPER. It's just the same. It changes everything. What about you two? What're you looking for?

ALEX. Don't know.

SHAPER. A man who doesn't know what he's looking for is usually searching for himself.

BRIAN. Who said that?

SHAPER. Me.

Pause.

MIRREN. What time is Mo meeting us?

SHAPER. Seven.

ALEX. Shit.

SHAPER. You tired? Want to crash?

MIRREN. Yeah.

ALEX. Me too.

SHAPER. Brian?

BRIAN. I'm wide awake.

SHAPER. Well we can take a walk. You two can head back. The door's open. Mirren, you know where everything is.

MIRREN. Yeah. Okay.

ALEX. See you later.

BRIAN. See ya.

SHAPER. Sweet dreams.

    ALEX *and* MIRREN *leave.*

BRIAN. Are you trying to set them up?

SHAPER. Nothing so crude, Brian. It's part of the art. Trust me.

51

BINKS *in a different pub. He is drunk. He approaches the* BARMAN.

BINKS. Oi. Barman. You a surfer?

BARMAN. Pardon?

BINKS. Surf! D'you surf, or what?

BARMAN. Sometimes.

BINKS. Anybody been in trying to sell a board?

BARMAN. No.

BINKS. Are you sure?

BARMAN. I think I would've noticed.

BINKS. They wouldn't have had it with them ya stupid prick!

BARMAN. If someone was selling a board, they'd be at the beach first thing in the morning. Not in here last thing at night.

BINKS. Is it late?

BARMAN. Yeah.

BINKS. Christ it was early when I started. Too many pubs.

BARMAN. Too many drinks.

BINKS. Are they surfers? Over there, with the hair?

BARMAN. Yeah. But I don't want you annoying them.

BINKS. Piss off.

52

ALEX *and* MIRREN *are walking home.*

MIRREN. Big day tomorrow then.

ALEX. Looks like it.

MIRREN. The end of the road.

ALEX. What'll you do?

MIRREN. Haven't decided yet. What about you?

ALEX. Haven't a clue.

Pause. ALEX *smiles.*

MIRREN. What?

ALEX. You're as fucked up as I am.

MIRREN *laughs.*

MIRREN. Never said I wasn't.

ALEX. I thought you were just a nippy bitch.

MIRREN. I thought you were just a sarky bastard.

ALEX *laughs.*

ALEX. I am.

MIRREN. Bastard.

ALEX. Bitch.

They both laugh.

53

BRIAN *and the* SHAPER *are walking by the sea.*

BRIAN. You know that stuff about the colour of the light in your head.

SHAPER. Yeah?

BRIAN. Well, how do you tell?

SHAPER. Good question. Complicated answer though. Let's go down by the water.

BRIAN. Yeah. All right.

SHAPER. ' . . . the sea delaying not, hurrying not whispered me through the night . . . '

BRIAN. Walt Whitman.

SHAPER. Brian, you're a man you don't meet every day.

BRIAN. Thanks.

54

Next day. The beach.

ALEX. The beach was long and wide and windswept.

BRIAN. Dunnet Bay.

ALEX. Five miles out of town.

BRIAN. The Lada slipped into the car park.

ALEX. Sighed a cloud of steam and oil-smoke . . .

BRIAN. . . . and then passed away.

A beat.

BRIAN. It was just after dawn. Cold . . .

ALEX. The waves were coming in like cavalry charges in a cheap western.

BRIAN. Frank and Mirren took the board down to Mo by the water.

ALEX. We stayed in the dunes and tried to keep out of the wind.

A beat.

BRIAN. And?

ALEX. And what?

BRIAN. What happened? Last night. You and Mirren.

ALEX. Nothing.

BRIAN. Nothing at all? Aye right. Go on. You can tell me.

ALEX. Nothing happened.

BRIAN *sniffs. He is unconvinced.*

ALEX. What did you do?

BRIAN. Went down by the castle and got stoned and talked a lot.

ALEX. About what?

BRIAN. Life.

ALEX. Fascinating.

BRIAN. He offered me a job.

ALEX. Eh?

BRIAN. Apprentice shaper. Sort of.

ALEX. Here?

BRIAN. Where else?

ALEX. Are you going to do it?

BRIAN. Yeah.

ALEX. So you really aren't going back?

BRIAN. Sorry. What will you do?

ALEX. I don't know.

MIRREN comes up the sand dune to join them.

MIRREN. She's taking it out. Look. I think she likes it.

ALEX. Good.

MIRREN. It must be freezing out there though.

BRIAN. There's other folk out as well.

ALEX. Mad.

MIRREN. We're just as mad to be up this early watching them.

The SHAPER climbs up beside them too.

SHAPER. She's giving it a go.

ALEX. She's well out.

BRIAN. She looks like a seal.

MIRREN. Why isn't she catching any of the waves?

SHAPER. She's waiting. You have to be patient.

Pause.

ALEX. So there we stood, watching this tiny figure loitering in the swell. Waiting and waiting. The wind was making my eyes water and the sand was stinging my face. I was going to go back to the car and then I heard Frank make this sound like a very quiet moan. And I looked and Mo was moving now, paddling like mad on this lump of green water that was huge and getting bigger and bigger all the time . . .

BRIAN. Jesus.

MIRREN. It's massive!

SHAPER. And she's got it.

ALEX. She was hopping to her feet now on her board . . . our board . . . perched. It looked like she was standing on a plank stuck into the side of a railway embankment. And she was sliding down the face of this glass monster but it was moving so fast it looked as though she was standing still. And then she started to cut across it. Along its length. Swinging up to the lip and then zooming back down into the trough again and it seemed like the sea had stopped to watch her too . . .

SHAPER. Go on girl. That's the way . . .

MIRREN. It's amazing.

ALEX. It's . . . beautiful.

MIRREN. It is. Beautiful.

BRIAN. Chudovyi.

ALEX. And then it began to curl. To roll over on itself into a cylinder of foam. And she pointed herself into the tube and held it there under an overhang of wave.

BRIAN. Bloody hell.

ALEX. And she slipped into the tube so far that we could only see her outline through the wall of water. And everything was blurred. Her. The board. The wave. They merged.

SHAPER. Amazing!

ALEX. We watched all this. Spellbound. Nobody said a word. Until Mo finally came back up the beach.

MO *appears with the board.*

MO. Did you see it?

MIRREN. We saw.

BRIAN. It was spectacular.

SHAPER. Some wave.

MO. It was the one, Frank. That was it. It was just like you said. And the board was brilliant. Just perfect.

SHAPER. That's great.

ALEX. Does that mean you're going to take it?

MO. I can't. Not now.

ALEX. Why not?

MO. That was it, out there. You saw it. That was the one. It won't get any better with this board. Do you understand? I'm sorry.

BRIAN. It's all right.

MO. I am sorry. I'm sure you'll find someone else.

ALEX. Maybe.

MO. I better get dry. See ya later.

SHAPER. See ya.

She leaves. ALEX *is left holding the board.*

SHAPER. I suppose that match was a little too well made.

ALEX. It was perfect. She was right.

SHAPER. So what do you want to do with it now?

BINKS *has appeared behind them.*

BINKS. I'll take it off your hands.

They turn. BRIAN *yelps with shock.*

ALEX. What . . . What're you doing here?

BINKS. I'm on my holidays and thought I'd come for a paddle . . . ! What the fuck do you think I'm doing here dick-head?

MIRREN. You can't just . . .

BINKS. Oh yes I can. I can do whatever the fuck I want.

BINKS *pulls out his gun and cocks it.*

BRIAN. Fucking hell.

BINKS. Eh? . . . Aye . . . Right, bring that over here then back off.

ALEX *obeys.*

BINKS. You little pricks have put me to a lot of trouble.

ALEX. You've got it back now.

SHAPER. I don't mean to interrupt, but did you come on that thing?

BINKS. What's it got to do with you?

SHAPER. Well, it'll be a bit difficult trying to carry a surf-board three hundred miles on a motorbike.

BINKS. Who said I was here to take it back?

He smashes the butt of his pistol against the board several times until the fibre-glass splinters.

SHAPER. You came all this way just to smash it up?

BINKS. Stay where you are.

BINKS *tugs at the splintered plastic and then laughs triumphantly. He jingles a bag of coins at them.*

What? . . . That's right . . . Ronnie says, you never even knew what you had. Did you? You stupid bastards. Think I'd come all this way for a fucking surf-board? I can't even fucking swim.

ALEX. So that's your pension fund.

BINKS. Got it in one shop-boy. Krugerands. South African gold . . .

SHAPER. I thought it felt a bit on the heavy side.

BRIAN. So you can go now?

BINKS. I haven't finished yet sunshine. There's some kneecap business to be done first.

ALEX. Oh shit.

SHAPER. Hold on a minute.

BINKS. Out of the way you, it's got nothing to do with you.

SHAPER. 'Course it has. I'm a witness.

BINKS. You'll be a dead witness if you don't get out of the way.

SHAPER. It's not a good idea.

BINKS. Eh? . . . Get back. Stand still I told you.

The SHAPER is moving slowly towards BINKS.

SHAPER. It's too risky.

BINKS. Stop . . . what you saying?

SHAPER. Listen to him.

BINKS. Shut up you . . . stand still . . . Who you talking about?

SHAPER. Listen to him. He's right.

BINKS. Fucking shut up. Shut up or I'll blow your head off . . .
    What?

SHAPER. Ronnie says it's too risky.

    A pause. BINKS *is taken aback.*

BINKS. You can hear him?

SHAPER. Every word.

BINKS. You can hear Ronnie?

SHAPER. He's telling you it's too dangerous. Too many
    witnesses. No chance of getting away.

BINKS. You can!

SHAPER. You should listen to him.

BINKS. But . . . how can . . .

SHAPER. 'Cause I'm like you. We're special you and me.
    Chosen. And Ronnie's smart. He knows what he's talking
    about.

BINKS. He is. He's fucking smart.

SHAPER. It was his idea to hide the gold.

BINKS. Sharp as a knife.

SHAPER. And now he thinks you should put down the gun.

    Listen to him. Take the money and go.

    But put down the gun.

BINKS. I . . . I . . . What? . . . I don't know . . . I can't . . .

SHAPER. That's it. No rush. It's easy.

BINKS. Stay there . . . I . . . I can't hear you . . . Ron . . . ?

SHAPER. He says don't be stupid.

BINKS. Ron . . . ?

SHAPER. He says it's time to go.

BINKS. Ronnie! Where are you?

BINKS *is immensely distressed and confused. He starts to cry quietly.*

MIRREN. He's mad.

BINKS *hears her whisper and is suddenly raging again.*

BINKS. No! You're the mad ones. You're off your fucking heads up here. All of you. Every last sheep-shagging bastard. D'you hear me? Every. Last. One.

The gun goes off with a huge noise. MIRREN *screams.* BINKS *legs it. A beat.*

ALEX. Frank? Are you all right?

SHAPER. I'm in a better state than that poor guy.

A motorbike revs and roars off.

ALEX. He was going to kill you.

SHAPER. He wouldn't hurt me. I knew his brother.

MIRREN. You mean you really did hear the voices?

ALEX. I don't believe it.

SHAPER. Mr. Binks believed it.

ALEX. But who did he shoot at then?

BRIAN. Look at the car.

The car is burning.

MIRREN. Oh no.

ALEX. Brian. He's killed it.

BRIAN. It was dead already

ALEX. Maybe George can claim on his insurance. Say it was joyriders.

BRIAN. At least he'll never see the paint-job.

The petrol tank explodes with a boom.

SHAPER. Looks like we're walking back to town, then.

BRIAN. Looks like it . . . You coming.

ALEX. In a minute.

BRIAN and ALEX share a look for a moment. BRIAN turns and he and the SHAPER begin to head off. ALEX kicks at the bits of the broken surf-board.

ALEX. It's a shame. All that way for this.

MIRREN. At least it found its one wave.

ALEX. I suppose so.

MIRREN. What now?

ALEX. Don't know. Maybe I'll just keep going north.

MIRREN. Out there?

ALEX. Orkney. Shetland. Scandinavia.

MIRREN. I'm going that way.

ALEX. Yeah? Maybe we could . . .

MIRREN. Maybe.

ALEX. I'd like that. I'd like to be able to say 'beautiful' in Swedish.

Pause.

MIRREN. What you thinking?

ALEX. I'm not. I'm not thinking at all. I'm just letting it happen.

Wind. Waves. Burning car.

Fade to black.

End.

ONE WAY STREET

Ten Short Walks in the Former East

David Greig

David Greig was born in Edinburgh in 1969 and studied at Bristol University. In 1990 he co-founded (with Graham Eatough) Suspect Culture, with which he is now Dramaturg; he has collaborated on and written eight shows for the company, including *One Way Street* (1995), *Airport* (1996), *Timeless* (1997).

His other plays include *Europe* and *The Architect* (Traverse); *Staniland* (Citizens', Glasgow); *Petra* (TAG Theatre Co.); *Caledonia Dreaming* (7:84 Scotland); and adaptations of *The Ubu Plays* (Almeida) and *Oedipus the King* (Theatre Babel). He has written two films: *Nightlife* (BBC Scotland) and *Nothing in the Whole Wide World* (United Broadcasting). For radio: *Copper Sulphate* (BBC Radio 3).

His plays have been seen all over Europe and in the USA. He is currently under commission to the Traverse for a children's play, the Royal Shakespeare Company (for *Victoria*) and the Edinburgh International Festival/Traverse (for *The Speculator*).

For Lucie

'I was sitting inside the café where I was waiting,
I forget for whom. Suddenly, and with compelling force,
I was struck by the idea of drawing a map of my life,
and knew at the same moment exactly how it was to be done.'

Walter Benjamin, *A Berlin Chronicle*

A Note On The Text

I'm not the author of *One Way Street*, I wrote the words. If this piece does have an author then it's a company, Suspect Culture. It may seem perverse for a writer willingly to disclaim some responsibility for work he is proud of. Ordinarily, a writer will 'thank' actors, directors and producers for their guidance and inspiration, even for small changes made during rehearsal, but to assign authorship to a company is clearly uncommon. However, Suspect Culture is an uncommon company.

One Way Street was created collaboratively, albeit with only two collaborators, Graham Eatough and myself. For a month in 1994 Graham and I mucked about in the overwarmed rooms of the Pearce Institute, Govan, exploring the theatrical possibilities of maps and mapping. We had both become seduced by Walter Benjamin's idea of 'drawing a map of your life' and we wanted to make a play which somehow was both map and theatre at the same time. Together, we tried out ideas about tour guides and their gestural vocabulary. We looked at the use of film and video, we confronted the problems of representing different characters in a one man show. We turned over many intriguing possibilities both for performance style and theme. After a month of exploration we noticed we had begun to glimpse a character, Flannery, the strangely lost Englishman in Berlin who leads us through the play. It was only then that I began to write words.

After writing came another month of rehearsal during which the piece took its final shape. It took shape as a piece of theatre first, and a text second. In a reversal of the usual pattern, the writing existed to help realise the performance. The result is, I hope, an unusual and uncategorisable work of theatre. John Flannery's story did not come from me, and it did not come from Graham either. Flannery emerged out of both of us and subsequently returned to inhabit us both, me as writer and Graham as performer.

David Greig

230

One Way Street was first performed by Suspect Culture at the Traverse Theatre, Edinburgh, on 1 February 1995, with the following cast:

JOHN FLANNERY   Graham Eatough

Directed by   Graham Eatough and David Greig
Designed   by Katherine Lindow
Lighting   by Graham Eatough

Setting: Eastern Berlin in 1995.

The Walks

Prenzlauerberg

Dimitroffstrasse and Around

Friedrichstrasse

The Bars of Oranienberg

A Night Walk in the City Centre

A Walk among the Stars

Potsdam

Stalinallee

Rosa Luxemburg Platz

Alexanderplatz

1   Prenzlauerberg

FLANNERY *is sitting in a pavement café. It is an early autumn day. He looks a little shabby, a little distressed, ill at ease with himself. In front of him, on the café table, are piles of maps, papers and notebooks. He has finished a coffee.* FLANNERY *is struggling with a foldaway map, tracing the lines of a route.*

A WAITER *is fussing over his customers.*

The WAITER *approaches* FLANNERY.

In a minute Max, in a minute.

Walk One. The old Cafés of Prenzlauerberg. Take the U-Bahn to Dimitroffstrasse Station.

FLANNERY *writes.*

By tradition, the most radical of all East Berlin's suburbs, Prenzlauerberg has long been home to the city's most exciting cafés and street life.

. . . clatter of horses' hooves on old cobbles, decaying nineteenth-century workers' tenements, clatter of workers' heads on old cobbles, squatters, punks . . .

A sudden moment of discomfort.

Ahhh. Shit.

I don't care what she says, Greta's given me something. A parting gift, souvenir, revenge, 'dear Flannery, goodbye, here's an antique Weimar sex disease to remember me by.' With pus. And hallucinations.

I can't concentrate.

A walk in Prenzlauerberg throws up surprises at every turn of its delightful cobbled streets. Syphilis. You can't catch syphilis nowadays can you? Mind you, she knows where to hunt out antiques.

Begin the walk by approaching Husemanstrasse . . . Max, can you come here a minute?

Can I get you another coffee, Mr. Flannery, or would you prefer the bill?

Syphilis Max. Can you get it?

Not today sir, the chef's not in till five.

Very good Max.

Max. Can you catch syphilis, nowadays, do you think? I'm feeling, you know, unusual. Not concentrating. Seeing things.

MAX *speeds away to clear tables.*

Probably just flu, Mr. Flannery. Everyone's system tends to get iffy as winter's coming on. Cold gets at the bowels. Still, if you have reason to suspect then you must see a doctor. Syphilis. Dear me. It can kill you. Send you mad. Have you got a temperature?

He feels FLANNERY's *forehead.*

I don't think so.

MAX *speeds away again.*

Oh don't breathe on me for god's sake. Bed rest is what I recommend. Although, perhaps in your case, you get quite enough bed rest as it is. Maybe the fresh air would do you good. Syphilis (*Intake of breath.*) nasty. Would you like the bill?

FLANNERY *checks for his wallet.*

Here we go. The sad charade, I don't know why you bother Flannery.

Overcoat left? No.

Overcoat right? No.

Shirt top left? No.

Another one on credit, John?

No, no it's in here somewhere, honestly. Just hang on.

Shirt top right?

Trousers? Right? Left?

Back pocket! It's always the last one you look in, isn't it Max.

I wonder why we don't try looking in the last one first sir?

My Joke.

And they say we have no sense of humour.

Jesus Christ, the wallet's full. Cash in wads. I thought you were broke Flannery. Where did you get the money?

It's . . . it's . . . I suppose you'd call it an advance Max. From Herr Frisch, I told you about Herr Frisch. A job. Work. 'Ten Short Walks In The Former East.' A guidebook, for the tourists. You know. Don't say anything. I know. I know. I can work. I have done jobs before. There's nothing that says anarchists can't write guidebooks. Besides I was desperate Max. You wouldn't believe, I can't live like this anymore. I've got a . . . well I've got responsibilities haven't I?

> MAX *has gone away.*

Note.

Try to avoid talking to the waiters in Prenzlauerberg. They enjoy making you feel guilty.

The waiters of Berlin are your enemy. Two-faced, hate-filled, gliding destroyers of self confidence. It's the first thing you learn when you get here. They never let you leave a café feeling good about yourself. They exact revenge on their customers because their underfed proletarian flesh hangs off the bones of Prussian Aristocracy. They don't know who they are or where they belong. It's why they walk so stiff. There's class battles going on wherever muscle meets bone.

In a city full of revolutionaries, it's a historical fact that the waiters of Berlin have never been on a demonstration. They've never brought their tin trays down on the heads of their customers. Never picked up sir's umbrella only to stab sir through the throat with it. Never placed bombs under apparatchiks' tables or stole the chef's knives. They wanted to, of course. The flesh was willing but the bones wouldn't let them. Prussian bones, holding them back. Watch Max, a body at war with itself. Internal subversion.

I've learned to fight against these waiterly tricks.

Before I leave any café I pull myself together. Use positive thinking. I feel good. I am well. I'm working. Young and free and soon to be sexually active again. I feel good. Now leave.

> MAX *approaches.*

Oh Mr. Flannery! I meant to tell you. A man was in earlier, looking for you. From England. Didn't say what he wanted. Very mysterious. Asked me where he could find you. Gave me this message.

FLANNERY *reads the message.*

Tony. Oh shit.

Bad news?

You could say that Max.

MAX *coughs.* FLANNERY *gives him some money.*

Oh dear. I do hate to be the bringer of bad news.

He glides away. Blackout.

2   Dimitroffstrasse and Around

Walk Two: Dimitroffstrasse and around. Taking in a walk through fire. The Museum of Hairdressing. Corporation Park and ending in the Jewish Cemetery. Take the U-Bahn to Dimitroffstrasse Station.

Something is bothering FLANNERY.

Like the rest of Prenzlauerberg, Dimitroffstrasse is lined with five story tenements built for the workers of the city in the nineteenth century. Left to decay under the Communists the area is now being spruced up and a new generation of Berliners are moving in.

The cobbled streets are . . .

The cobbled streets are . . .

I'm sorry I can't concentrate.

Even today the area attracts Berlin's alternative scene. The so called 'black bloc' of anarchists, squatters and . . .

The cobbled streets are . . .

Art spaces have sprung up in back courts giving the area a lively flavour . . . sorry about this . . . a lively flavour.

I lifted Greta off these cobbles on a wet night. The thump of music and drinking from a nearby club. Her hair so red. Her freckles dots of burnt brown. The street lights reflected in the rain slick. She's dressed in black.

I lift her up.

I hold her.

And she looks straight into my eyes singing 'relight my fire baby, your love is my only desire'.

Anything to make me feel sorry for her.

'Come on. I'll take you home.'

Dimitroffstrasse, named after the Bulgarian communist Gyorgy Dimitrov, the man the Nazis accused of the Reichstag fire. The man who, famously, conducted his own defence and made the prosecutor look a fool in front of the world. Dimitrov, who kept his head, who kept cool. Who walked across the ashes of the Reichstag barefoot and didn't burn.

cool wet grass

cool wet grass

ahh shit.

That was the burn of a black look from behind. I'd know it anywhere. A grab at the ankles with hot hands. She's here.

I knew I should have done a different street.

She's fucking watching me.

Greta?

Greta?

Walk five hundred yards to Husemanstrasse - heads down so you're not recognised. Husemanstrasse, showpiece street of the east. Whitewashed antique shops lining the . . . Keep moving if you don't want to be spotted by an old flame.

On the left the Museum of Hairdressing where the eccentric owner will show you implements . . .

You know she cut off her hair when I left, shaved it, showed it to me so I knew what it meant.

Turn right on to Wertherstrasse, named for Goethe's novel of sorrow and suicide. Right again on to . . . wait . . .

Where are we?

He consults the map again.

How did we get here?

Fuck.

Consults map.

I'm sorry I have to sit down for a minute. My feet are killing me.

He takes notes out. Looks at the map on the ground. Among his notes is the letter from TONY.

Cool wet grass.

Cool wet grass.

Corporation Park. English voices. 'Does anybody want pickle on their sandwich?'

Pickle for me Mum.

Lying in the long grass watching clouds making the shapes of South America and Australia. White continents tectonically drifting on the light blue sea. Only the sound of insects and the breeze in the grass.

'YOURS SON!'

and then . . . what?

The sky's gone black, the sun's gone. An eclipse. A dark sphere crossing the sky. Getting bigger.

'ON THE HEAD SON!'

What?

THE HEAD. FUCK.

FLANNERY is knocked backwards by a heavy football his father has kicked towards him.

Dad!

Did I get you son? Teach you to keep your eyes open for the cross. He was away with the fairies. Weren't you? You all right son? Teach him to keep his eyes open.

It was a proper football. The hard, heavy kind. I swear to god he kicked it knowing I couldn't get out of the way. I swear to god he kicked it hard.

'Keep your eyes open sunshine.'

Maybe he thought I'd forgotten he was there. Thought he'd remind me.

'Come and have a sandwich love. Corned beef. Leave him alone Jim, he's not well.'

Tony takes it.

'Give it here. Yes. Keeper's ball. Shilton, belts it up the park.
Gives it Keegan. He's battling, past one, past the other . . . one
nil, one nil, one nil, one nil.'

'You having a sandwich Gemma? Where's our Gemma?

Cool wet grass. Until the eclipse. I'm sure it was the eclipse that
did it. Sent me spinning. Knocked me out of orbit. Set me
wandering, off course. Like a spaceman when his line's cut and
he floats backwards into nothingness. A look of loss frozen on to
his face until he hits Jupiter sometime next century. That's me.
On the head son.

> *An* ELDERLY MAN *is standing over* FLANNERY *in the
> Jewish Cemetery.*

Young man?

What?

On the head. A cap. There is a sign. Men are requested to keep
their heads covered in the cemetery. For respect. Have you a hat.
We can lend you one if you like?

The Jewish Cemetery. Open Monday to Thursday, 8 a.m. to 4
p.m. Over twenty thousand Jews are buried anonymously in the
old cemetery. Shortly before the war ended the Nazis smashed
all the gravestones into the ground leaving only scattered
fragments amongst the grass and ivy.

You were having a sit down. I do the same myself. It's a
pleasant place to sit. I don't get paid to do this job you know.
I'm a volounteer. The accent? Where are you from?

England.

England, I thought so. Which part of England?

Lancashire.

Lancashire. Would you believe it? Who would have thought?
Lancashire! Would you believe I know Lancashire! Know it
well! Are you . . . Mancunian?

Blackburn.

Oh. I don't. My family spent the war in Manchester, Emigrated.
I was only a boy of course but . . . do you know of a street
called Palatine Road?

Yeah. I know it.

So do I. I don't remember much about it. As I say, only a boy at the time. But I remember the name. Isn't that astonishing. Palatine Road. Small street isn't it?

Big.

Yes. I remember it being small. Of course you're right. But I remember the name. Palatine Road. Palatine Road. Are you feeling all right?

Yes. Thank you.

The maps. Are you lost?

Lost? No. I live here. I know where I am.

An exile. Just like I was. Of course, I was only a boy.

   Silence.

They did a terrible thing here during the War. But we look after it now. It's still a sacred place to us, of course. I don't get paid to work here. I volunteer. I do it to remember. I'm very fond of Manchester. I was only a boy. Six or seven when we came back to Berlin. It was your accent which gave you away. Very fond of the English. Still, you must cover your head in the cemetery. Sit though. If you want to sit, you can sit. The people here don't object to sitting. Well. What a surprise. Palatine Road. Sit. Sit.

I can understand the urge to vandalise gravestones.

You think you've put something safely in the ground and out pops a stone, with a name on it. Like the first burst of earth as a hand reaches up to grab at your ankle. Of course you want to kick out at it.

   Blackout.

3   Friedrichstrasse

Walk Three: Friedrichstrasse. Taking in The Hall of Tears, The Berliner Ensemble. Unwanted Sexual Advice, Elderly Transvestites and my house. Take the S-Bahn to Friedrichstrasse Station.

   A TEACHER.

Flannery! Describe something for me. Describe . . . a railway station. Description lads, John's going to give us an example of description.

A station sir . . . a station . . . trains stop there . . . you get tickets.

Oh dear Flannery. Trains don't 'stop'. They pull in like ancient lumbering beasts. Simile. The jungle scream of their steam whistles merge with the starlings' cries in the vastness of the high glass canopy. Metaphor. People don't 'buy tickets' Flannery, they ebb and flow, tides of humanity surging around the ticket offices. Impression. Do you see?

Now boys. Descriptive essays are the easiest to write. You don't need to make too many things up and you can write about what you know, which is always the best thing. One point. Bear in mind the examiner may be a spinster on the Isle of Lewis so avoid, if at all possible, sex, women, and disturbing thoughts about one's place in the scheme of things. Stick to nature.

He slams the desk hard.

Are you listening to me boy? Hello boy? Knock Knock? Who's there? Are you with us? Are you receiving me? Over.

Sorry.

Friedrichstrasse station. Designed by Johannes Vollmer. It boasts a typical nineteenth–century grand arch of wrought iron and glass over the platforms. The tiled ticket hall . . .

Looks like a lavatory. Looks mucky. It's depressing.

She took me here one day.

We call it 'the hall of tears'.

Difficult to get a ticket?

It's not a joke, John. It used to be the place where trains left for the West. We would come here to see them off, to say goodbye. A lot of crying, obviously, so 'the hall of tears'. When my uncle visited the hall was crowded. People coming off the train. People getting on. We couldn't find him at first. We wandered around till hardly anyone was left. And then, by the kiosk, we saw a skinny old woman in old fashioned clothes, sitting on a little suitcase, looking lost. Uncle Erica.

Who?

My uncle is the oldest working transvestite in Berlin. There used to be many of them. My father was furious. He wouldn't let him walk with us. Uncle kissed me. He smelt of French perfume which I'd never smelt because we couldn't get it here. We all felt embarrassed.

Because he was dressed like a woman?

Because he was better dressed than my mother.

They always think they've got such great stories, Berliners, such interesting families. It gets on my wick.

We had a hall of tears in our house as well. Not so much a hall, in fact, as a vestibule. Mum called it the vestibule. The place where we said hello and goodbye. A vestibule of tears. Well not tears in fact because we don't cry in Lancashire. Not so much tears as silence. The vestibule of silence. The doorbell goes . . .

Get that John.

Oh. It's you.

Who is it John?

It's Gemma.

Silence you see? Telly gets switched off. Silence. She had a little suitcase for coming home.

Obviously the sex disease is eating into my brain even now. Even as we speak. I'll probably collapse before the book's finished. And she'll have killed me. She would if she could. She'd rather have me dead than not have me. It's pathetic.

Cross the Iron Bridge outside the station and a short walk by the river takes you to The Berliner Ensemble. A statue of Bertolt Brecht sits outside the theatre. Quotes from his writings carved around the statue's base. The sayings of the guru. The prophesies of the oracle.

BRECHT *speaks.*

You know. I did a bit of fucking around in my time as well John. It's pretty well known. The theatres of Berlin are crawling with my progeny. Look at me. Short. Fat. I stink. Never changed my clothes. I stink of cigars and sweat. Personally a dog. An offensive, rutting terrier. So why did women swarm around my stink? What is it that they wanted? Satisfaction John. Women may say they like men with a sense of humour but are they doomed to fuck comedians? No. Here's my advice. Sexual satisfaction is an economic system like any other. It circulates like cash between us all. And you know what I say. From each according to his ability to each according to her need. If you want Greta back, you have to satisfy her needs BUT no woman must be allowed a monopoly. If there is a surplus. Redistribute John. Redistribute. It's a Marxist duty.

FLANNERY *steps back and considers.*

Note: don't consult Brecht about your relationships. He likes to cause trouble.

Walk by the river, about a hundred yards or so . . .

By the way, you can see my house from here. A minor landmark in this historic city. I imagine they'll have a plaque there sooner or later. Maybe by the time you read this I'll be nestled in the index next to Isherwood. Das Flannery Haus. See.

The TEACHER *returns.*

So boys, a descriptive essay for next week entitled 'My House.' 400 words. On my desk by Monday.

My House.

My House is a shack in the Allegheny Mountains. By day my daddy hunts coyotes and traps rabbits. My sister Gemma fetches water from a little crick and I . . . I shoot pigeons. My big brother Tony . . . doesn't exist. We all live in constant fear of Injun attack.

No.

I live in the forest, in a camouflaged shelter. My men. My merry men steal from rich merchants who dare to stray into our territory. Our enemy, the wicked Duke Tony, harries us with his soldiers but our forest skills ensure our continued survival. How I long to see again the fair maid Gemma, but alas, she is to be married to wicked Tony.

What are you writing John?

Dad! I didn't see you there.

'My House', a descriptive essay. Why haven't you got anything written down?

I don't know.

You should know.

I don't.

You know where you live Son.

Yeah.

Well describe it then. Isn't that what your teacher wants?

I suppose.

Well . . . why aren't you getting on with it?

I'm going to write about somewhere else anyway Dad. You don't
have to tell the truth. It's supposed to be a sort of trains
screaming like jungle beasts, sort of interesting sort of thing.
Nature he wants anyway. You just have to describe something.
He doesn't care if it's real.

The sooner it's done Son, the sooner it's done.

Oh ancient wisdom.

I don't know John. Sometimes I don't know. You do get some
funny ideas.

No. I don't know either Dad. I'm spinning around in space
somewhere, away with the Germans. I followed the Pied Piper
and danced with the rats across the Channel. I do have some
funny ideas Dad. Like why'd you send Tony? Why'd you send
him?

Anyway. After you've visited the famous house of John
Flannery, plaque and all, take a pause for a beer in one of the
famous Bars around Friedrichstrasse.

   Blackout.

4   The Bars of Oranienburg

Walk Four. The Bars of Oranienburg. Taking in Café Stalin. Fruit
and Vegetables. A slice of Nightlife. Politics. Sex City and a
walk down memory lane. Take the U-Bahn to Oranienburger Tor.

   FLANNERY *is spending a night in the bars.*

A popular first stop is Café Stalin. A lively clientele, locals and
students. Popular with the arty crowd and anarchist musicians.

I'm a writer. Yeah. Well. Travel. I write travel. / Yeah. You're a
musician? English? No. I live here. / Christ I don't look like a
tourist do I? Ich bin ein Berliner? / No I love it. I came because
the dole's better here than it is in England. / It's a better scene
here. Better yeah. Another beer? Sure. Noch zwei bier bitte.

I'm a travel writer. Yeah. Travel books, impressions, descriptions
all that. / Germany. France. China. India. I've done it all yeah. /

I liked China. So strange. Really. There's an incredible pace of change there at the moment. / You're a musician? Pneumatic drills on sheet metal? A sort of drummer then? / Bet it sounds great. I'd love to. Noch zwei bier bitte.

A poet. Sure. / I'm in the writing game myself. Yeah. Fucking bitch of a job isn't it? Sure. From England. England stinks. I couldn't take the mentality anymore. / You've been? Do you know Manchester? Great place. / I fucking love Manchester. / It's got to be my favourite city. / No London's crap. You don't want to go there. / I went to college in Manchester. I studied poetry. Yeah. / Well writing, you know, in all the different varieties that it comes in. / Genres. Genres. Genres. / You having another? Noch zwei bier bitte.

Out into the night. Christ it's cold. Down Oranienburg just like Oxford Road on a Saturday night. Packs of lads loaded up on pils and pills, couples holding on to each other to keep warm. Shady looking men with suede jackets and creased jeans on the streetcorners and the noise of the bars washing across the wide dark streets.

Come home with me.

I can't. I shouldn't.

Come on. Just a coffee.

No.

Look I don't want to pressure you. If you're not ready you're not ready.

It's not that.

One more drink. C'mon. I've got a bottle of wine at the flat.

I don't think I should.

You look so beautiful. I mean it. I know it sounds . . . but I mean it. You're a beautiful woman. I've never met anyone like you before.

John.

Your face is cold. We'd better get the colour back into your cheeks.

I've got to go. Goodbye John. I'll see you.

Fuck.

Why not drop into Fruit and Vegetables. A themed bar. Late night crowd. Quiet relaxed atmosphere. Old fashioned décor.

I met Greta about a month after I arrived in Berlin. She was handing out tomatoes, cabbages and rotten fruit on some demonstration. They were for throwing at the mayor. The mayor and his men had come to evict the squatters from Friedrichshain. Our eyes met over a stinking basket of plum tomatoes. I asked her name and we threw together. Her aim was spectacular.

I had a lot of practice in the DDR.

A spurt of red across the mayor's face, a red stain creeping down his suit. The squatters cheered and the police moved forward. She gave me a little bag of flour. I threw. I was inspired by love. I was devastating. I threw, and Cupid carried the bomb in an arcing flight over the heads of the crowd and it exploded on the face of the mayor. Pale as a ghost and stained with blood red juice, a walking bloody mary, he retreated and the police began the charge.

You hit him.

I hit him.

I love you.

She kissed me.

Run!

They cracked and thumped their way through the bodies of the crowd as though we were a jungle thicket. The noise of the crowd, banners thrown like javelins. She grabbed my hand as we looked for a way out.

This way.

She pulled me, and then . . . a second eclipse. I fell and suddenly there was a space amongst the thicket of legs. I saw the sun briefly. Just for the merest second until once again a black sphere passed across the sky. The blue black helmet of the policeman. Visor down. Arm and stick raised in an elegant curve.

You're one of us now.

I'm sore now.

You were very good back there.

Oww.

C'mon. I'll take you back to mine.

You were on that demonstration? / Yeah. I was the guy that threw the flour bomb. / You threw the flour bomb? Shit man that was on the news. / Yeah fuck. The news man. / You're a hero of the people. A hero of the people fuck man. No shit.

Just a small moment in a history full of little revolutions.

The Autonome Squatters.

The Prenzlauerberg Riots.

Alexanderplatz.

The May Day Anarchists.

The Stalinallee General Strike.

Red Wedding.

Greta says you're not a real Berliner till a policeman's cracked your head at least once.

A great place for a last stop is Sex City. A sleazy crowd. Porn videos and strippers. Popular with men.

Noch ein bier.

Bodies glide into bodies on the small screens, fantastic couplings merge into one another and we all sit and stare at the same cold woman undressing. You can tell she's cold because she's got goosepimples.

This is my place, Greta said when we got back.

A mattress on the floor and walls only decorated with graffiti and stains. On the bare boards a rug and a pile of dirty black clothes waiting to be washed. She hooked an old bedsheet over the window for a curtain and, in the glow of an electric fire, she stripped me. It was fucking freezing and my head still ached from the second eclipse. She didn't say much after.

Are you all right?

She made some coffee.

Greta?

You fucked me like you were angry with me. How do you take your coffee?

Black.

What the fuck did she mean by that? What the fuck did she
mean by 'angry'? I've got to get out of here. Out again into the
wet night. Christ I've got to get myself sorted out. Oh fuck. Oh
fuck.

> FLANNERY *gags. He's going to be sick.*

> *He is sick.*

Everything's got to come up before you feel better.

> *And again.*

Bring it all up in a puddle . . . up it comes. Lovely.

> *He considers the pool of puke.*

My sick has made a little puke map of my life. Ten short walks
through the former contents of my stomach. There's home, all
warm, all pink in the potato hills of Lancashire . . . a little
carrotty college, German language and literature department to
the south . . . a bile dribbling line of the route to Berlin. And
there she is. The black stout splash of Greta's flat.

> *Nausea overcomes him.*

Oh god.

> *Blackout.*

5   A Night Walk through the City Centre

Walk Five: A Night Walk Through the City Centre. Taking in the
Canal and the Rosa Luxemburg Heritage Trail.

> *Night.* FLANNERY *is quite drunk.*

They found the body of Rosa Luxemburg here, in the canal. The
end of the revolution. The Kaiser's militia had beaten her and
mutilated her and blown out her brains. Did they rape her?
You'd think they would. Soldiers don't have qualms. A red
animal like her, you'd think they'd take the time to . . .

. . . anyway, whatever, her body beaten, dragged to the edge of
the canal and dumped. Greta was a big fan. Saw herself in the
same mould. Personally I haven't the courage. People get hurt in
a revolution and I can't stand pain. I wonder if she thought it
was worth it, as they brought the clubs down on her face. If she
thought . . . 'despite the pain, I'm happy because I did the right

thing.' Or if she wished she'd stayed in bed. Still, beaten and her corpse lost in the black water. Very Greta. Very Berlin. Not very me I'm afraid.

Walk along the . . . fuck it. Walk where you like. It's all the same to me. You've seen a canal, haven't you. You know what one's like. Black and still. Inviting. You don't need me to tell you.

FLANNERY *walks precariously along the edge.*

I phoned her. Told her about the brain cancer. She said I was making things up. Drunk. I said I was hallucinating. Itching. She said I ought to see a psychiatrist. I thought she'd be angry with me but she wasn't. She sounded . . .

How are you feeling? I said.

Fine.

Stopped drinking? She had.

Stopped smoking?

I'm trying, I've cut right down.

I can't imagine you not smoking. I've got a job.

Good.

I've got money. Do you want some money?

Silence.

I miss you Greta.

That's your problem John, not mine.

I want you, see me tonight.

If you want me you know where I am. Goodbye John. See a doctor.

She could just get rid of it. Rusty wire, gin, punch in the stomach. It happens all the time. But she won't. I've got money. I could sort her out but she's determined. Obsessed. She wants someone who'll love her back. A little squittery bag of love for her to hold on to. So fucking stupid. So bloody naive.

Attach yourself to me, thing.

Cling to me, thing.

Thing be mine and I'll be yours.

Thing absorb me.

Thing become me.

Forever together the thing and I.

Idiotic. Blind. Greta . . .

He looks at the sky.

6   A Walk among the Stars

Walk Six: A Short Walk among the Stars. Taking in everything.

Lie on your back beside the canal. Feel the damp concrete take your weight and let the beer spin your head. Relax. Watch the stars go round and round. Watch the moon circle pulling tides behind it. Shit. Feel the moon pull tides of nausea up and down your body. Try and get straight. Launch yourself like sputnik into the night. Up over the city. Watch it disappear behind you. A map of streets in orange light laid out beneath you getting smaller, become a single bright point on the curve of the earth. Over Europe, high into the atmosphere, follow the dawn over Warsaw, Moscow and on into Siberia and then out into orbit. Into free space. Floating. Oaaah god.

He feels terribly nauseous.

Try to sleep. Try to float into a sweet blank sleep. Eyes closed. Blank. Think blank. Ooh shit I'm coming down. Coming down fast. Burning up, bloods boiling oahh. You can't escape gravity Flannery. In flames over England. Splashdown in the North Sea. No. I'm heading straight for Burnley. Shit. Oh Shit. The light on the curve of the earth gets bigger and bigger. I can see streets. Houses fuck. Aaaaaaaaah! Splashdown! In the vestibule of silence.

Oh. It's you.

Our Gemma, her black hair sticky yellow now. Earrings she never wore before and a little suitcase for coming home.

Is our mum in?

You'd better come through.

Gemma

Mum

Dad

Me

A study in silence. Silence as a technique. Absorbent silence. A silent sponge heavy with failure and complication.

Why don't you say something?

We're glad you're back love.

Tony barges in. 'What's up?'

A wave of silence breaks over Tony the lump.

'What's up Gemma. Did he throw you out?'

Crash. King Tony Canute orders the sea of silence back.

'Everyone's got a face like fizz. Did somebody scratch the nest of tables?'

I'm pregnant Tony.

'Fuck me! Sorry mum. Heat of the moment couldn't help myself. Well. What a surprise.'

And finally even Tony shut up too. The lump absorbed. The thing accepted.

   Blackout.

7   Potsdam

Walk Seven: Potsdam. Taking in The Offices of Herr Frisch and A Walk in Old Prague. Take the S-Bahn to Potsdamstadt Station.

   HERR FRISCH *is sitting behind his desk studying John's material.*

   He is shy.

Difficulty getting here John? The appointment was at nine thirty, possibly I was wrong. Trains running on time? Trouble. Hmmm? If you don't mind my saying so you don't look well? You look, if you don't mind my commenting, as though you've slept in your clothes. I am paying you, you know.

John . . . it's . . . there's some interesting work but . . . you have to remember this is just a tourist guide, you know. We want to give a good impression. Like I mentioned. We did talk about this. A city united. A city full of history etc. Pleasing walks cafés en route . . . Only you've . . . well you can't . . .

John my writers are artists. I want them to put something of themselves into the writing. I want a personal feel. Idiosyncratic, individual . . . You know I think that. I don't like to interfere. Alexander . . . did you meet him. He's doing Ten Short Walks in and around Dresden. Beautiful prose. Poetry almost. Reflective, elegiac . . . but John you've.

It's too much. You seem to want to drag these people on a journey through Hell. Strip clubs, riots, offensive waiters, murdered revolutionaries . . . do you actually like the city at all? Are you happy John? In yourself?

Have you read Kafka? Now I like Kafka, I think Kafka was a genius but if he walked into my office now do you think I would commission him to write Ten Short Walks in Old Prague. Clearly not. Do you see my problem John? A guide has to show people happy things that make them happy, or poignant things which make them feel a little sad, like a popular ballad. A guide isn't supposed to make people feel angry and depressed. You know that. So John. Back to work eh? Only this time. No nastiness. Can that be possible? Elegiac Descriptions, Quirky Humour, Zany Observation, Human Interest, Architectural History and a 'despite troubled history everything's O.K. in Berlin now' resolution. That's what I want to see from now on. John. Good man. You do look ill. Perhaps you need fresh air. Flush out the system. Good boy. Revitalise! Revitalise! Have a walk in the park.

Blackout.

8   Stalinallee

Walk Eight: Stalinallee. Taking in Stasi Zentrale. The People's Park. Big Rubble Mountain and the Little Rubble Mountain. And a game of chess. Take the U-Bahn to Alexanderplatz.

I'll be with you in a second. I've just got to make a quick phone call.

FLANNERY *in a public phone box.*

Hello? Who is this? Oh. Is Greta there? Can you speak up please. Oh. Are you sure. Yes. Oh I see. Did she leave a

forwarding address? Sorry? I can't . . . Is there a message . . .
Did she say anything? She must have said something for Christ
sake. I'm sorry. What? Thank you. Goodbye. Goodbye.

Shit.

FLANNERY *is with* TONY.

She's . . . not in.

Tone's here. Turned up yesterday. Finally found me. Max no
doubt. He was waiting for me when I got back to the flat. Sat on
my mattress in his car coat and corduroys. I've brought him with
me. Sorry.

Listen John is there any chance of grabbing something to eat
round here? I'm starving.

I gave you tea.

That was hours ago. I'm hungry now. I've got money.

We'll pick up a burger on the way. I'm supposed to be working.

John. At some point. In the not too distant. A bit of a chat's in
order. About things. You know.

Yeah Tone. Not just now.

Sometime though John.

Sure Tone. Top level talks. Full and frank discussions.

Stalinallee. Now called Karl Marx Allee. The showpiece housing
project of the Communist east. A canyon of concrete miles long.
Socialist cubes, dialectically scientific rectangles, towers of
Marxist purity. Buildings to make people feel small.

Jesus these are a fucking disaster. Poor bastards.

D'you think so Tone?

You wouldn't catch me living in one of them. They look as
though they're rotted with damp. They're not sound if you ask
me. They want knocking down.

Tone planning.

They're very popular these days Tone. People queuing up to live
in them.

Poor bastards. There's bits of Burnley better than that.

In 1953 the workers on the Stalinallee project called a general
strike for more political freedom. A crowd of ten thousand

marched down the half completed canyon to the house of
ministries. The Russians sent in tanks.

Poor bastards.

Tony is that all you can say? Poor bastards? Is that the limit of
your analysis?

All right John. I'm just saying.

Three hundred demonstrators were killed. Ninety shot later. It
was an attempt at revolution.

It'd never happen in England. Thank god.

Oh great Tone. Knuckle down. Be a good boy.

Fair enough. John. You know I'm not interested in politics. Do
we have to go all the way down here. It's bloody, a bloody long
way. I'm knackered John. My stomach thinks my throat's been
cut.

Turn right up Lichtenbergstrasse, from here it's a short stroll to
the People's Park.

Very nice. John. Just the spot for a sit down.

The People's Park is the oldest in Berlin. Dominated by two
artificial hills created after the war out of millions of tonnes of
rubble from the bombed city. The park is dotted with worthy
amenities. A boating lake, giant outdoor chess sets and children's
play areas. We sat on top of the rubble mountains and looked
over the city.

It was a hell of a job finding you John.

You can see the old Stasi headquarters from here.

I had to track you down. I didn't even know you'd left the
country.

Greta read her files. I went with her. Source F155b described her
as: 'A woman who craves reassurance.' 'Constantly at war with
authority' F120h. 'Immature' F70. Surprisingly accurate I
thought.

Your mate from college said you'd gone to Berlin.

She laughed when she read about her past boyfriends. The Erics,
the Mikhails, the Helmuts and the Gerds. One of the Erics
turned out to be an informer. F70. She said she wasn't surprised.
I imagined all the Erics and the Mikhails writhing in slippery
repulsive ecstasy in front of the fire in her flat.

I always knew you were a lazy bastard so I looked in the cheap
areas. Asked for an English guy. Eventually I got a lead. I met a
waiter. It was quite exciting in a way. I've been here weeks
John.

Her files were piled up in front of us. A mountain of the past. On
paper. I felt sick reading. Unauthorised biography. Eric, Gerd,
Helmut and Mikhail. Fucking her brains out in foolscap. Having
opinions on her in ink. Spewing out details over coffee.

I had to take time off work and everything John. I haven't got
long.

On a mountain built out of Berlin's past piled up and grassed
over. Tone and me. Sit. Silent again. Conversational entropy.
Words decay in our family.

Let's go on a pedalo. I fancy a go on a pedalo. I haven't been on
a pedalo since we were kids. Do you remember when dad took
us to . . .

Sea salt in the swimming trunks. Sunburn scratched by sand.
Fighting Tony on the beach. 'Stop it lads. Stop it.' Tony laughed.
Each laugh fills me with more violence. I hit him but I'm too
small. 'That tickles.'

His DAD *drags him off* TONY.

'CALM DOWN JOHN.'

I was shaking.

'CALM DOWN. GO AND SIT BY YOUR MUM. JUST
COOL IT.'

Yeah I remember the pedaloes Tone.

JOHN *and* TONY *are on a pedalo.*

John. They want you to come back.

Who?

Who do you think? Mum and Dad. All of us.

Why?

John.

I mean it. Why?

You can't escape gravity Flannery. Newton's Law of Attractions.
Fat Tone's mass is pulling me back in. Lumbering through the
streets of Berlin pulling me back into orbit.

John. You haven't even met our Gemma's kid. You're her uncle.
Don't say that.

You're her uncle John and she's not even met you. That can't be right.

Uncle. Jesus. I am not an uncle. I am a free man.

They just want to see you. Say hello. It's natural enough John.

You know what Mum's like.

Stop it. Stop it. I can feel the black hole sucking at me. Fire booster rockets. Warp factor six Chekhov. I don't care what Mum's like. I've left.

John! Stop pedalling so fucking fast. We're going round in circles.

   JOHN *stops. Exhausted.*

Look at the state of you John. You're a fucking mess. Who's your bird?

Bird?

The one you tried to get on the phone.

She's not my bird.

Problems?

What would you know.

I know about birds mate. I can tell when you've been caught and hooked. You've got the look of it. Birds do that. Don't fight it. You need looking after. I'd like to meet her. You could both visit.

Battle has been entered for my soul. They've sent in the heavy battalions. Fat Tone the tank. The stakes are immense. Have you ever played outdoor chess with the devil?

Go on then. It'll be a laugh.

He moves his pawns forward. Cagey.

Mum's not been the same since you stopped writing. She's worried. She blames herself you know.

Sneaky.

I stopped writing because I couldn't stand writing all that rubbish just to please them. Nothing stuff. No truth in it. 'How are you? I am fine.' Meaningless crap. I was drowning in it. Choking.

Write what you want John. Pawn again. Say what you want, just ring her . . . say something.

There's things you can't say. Tony. Right in the middle of us. On the rug. On the kitchen table. Next to the telly. Wherever our family gathers Tony, there's a hole that sucks everything out of us. Thoughts. Hate. Pain. Differences. Sucked out of your brain before you even get a chance to think them. Even Gemma. Even Gemma. The Flannery who dared to be different. Who went to London. Even our Gemma got sucked back in. Got herself pregnant. Went all milky and mothery on us. It's not going to happen to me. I'm not going to be like you, Tony. Never.

Tony moves the bishop. I don't know what you're talking about John. Families are just like that. It's hard going. I'm not stupid. I know I say stupid things. I put my foot in it and all that. I know I'm not as bright as you. You're a clever lad. But I'm just saying. They need to see you. Need to know where you are. You can't just disappear. You can't just fuck off. It's not right.

Pawn. I can. I did.

John. Just come back for a visit. No one's asking you to live at home. It'll do you good. You're in a mess. Saying all this stuff. It's mad. You're losing it.

He's got his knight paired with the bishop. How the fuck could I miss that. I'm not concentrating. I CAN DO ALL RIGHT ON MY OWN. I'M DOING FINE.

Why don't you bring your bird with you. They'd love to see her.

Queen attack.

She's not my bird.

John they love you. Check.

Tell them to stop.

They're nice people. Just like everyone else. That's what home's like. It's difficult. You put up with stuff. I know that. But you put up with it. They're just nice people.

I don't like nice people.

No. Well that doesn't surprise me. You're not a nice person yourself, John. It's taken me a long time to get here. A long time to find that out. But I've come all this way and I've found it out. You're . . . you're not a nice person. But that's what you want isn't it. That's what you want people to think. Go and fuck yourself John. You deserve yourself.

TONY *is leaving.*

What about the game?

What game?

Tony! Tony! Come back! Tony . . .

His car coat disappears over the horizon.

Mate.

Blackout.

9   Rosa Luxemburg Platz

Walk Nine: Rosa Luxemburg Platz. Taking in a chat with Max. A Sensation at the Theatre.

FLANNERY *is in the café again.* MAX *is serving him.*

Everything all right Mr. Flannery?

Oh . . . yes Max. Yes . . . fine.

It isn't fine is it?

No.

Do you want to talk about it? Max pulls up a seat.

I'm, not a nice person Max.

I can't find her.

She's gone.

Left.

No address.

No message.

Nothing.

I want to . . . I have to speak to her.

Say something.

Sorry.

Do you know where she is Max? You found me for Tony. Could you find her?

It might be too late but then again. It might not.

What do you mean?

Oh I don't know . . .

You know something don't you.

I notice things.

Tell me Max.

He puts some money down on the table.

It's just I noticed a red haired woman was in here earlier on.
That's all.

He puts more money down.

A red haired woman with freckles. She was sitting just over there.

He puts more money down.

She was with friends. Funny looking crew if you ask me. All dressed in black.

He puts more money down.

They seemed to be planning a trip to the theatre. Tonight. Top the Volksbuhne. Some show or other. Ghastly I imagine. The sort of thing people who dress in black enjoy. With lots of blood, I imagine. That's all. I didn't think you'd be interested.

He puts down the last of his money.

I've just got time. Max you're a thief.

He leaves.

Run down Shonhauserallee. Breath coming hard. Painfully.
A few weeks of poor living take their toll. Shit I'm bleeding from the lungs.

Stops. Coughs. Spits.

Rust red. Fuck. I'm dying. Maybe I'm dying. She's got to be there. Keep running. Keep fucking running. On to Rosa Luxemburg Platz. In the shadow of the television tower, Christ I can barely breath, the Volksbuhne sits, a concrete box. The big sign . . . 'East' on a banner on the front. Worst seats in the house. There's one left. I can't see her . . . I'm right at the back . . . only heads. Sit down and watch the show.

Lights dim for the start of the play.

FLANNERY watches for a bit. Then he stands up to look around. He is shushed back into his seat. He fidgets. He tries to look. He turns to the person next to him.

They do go on don't they?

Fuck me. Look at that. He's gone and poured blood all over his head. Is he supposed to be dead now or what?

Sits a while.

Laughs.

The audience also laugh.

Fair enough that was pretty good.

He looks again.

I heard her. That was her laugh. I swear. Shit where is she . . . I can't see a fucking thing from here.

Excuse me . . . do you know if there's an interval in this play? Really. Bollocks. An hour and a half without an interval, they've got a bloody cheek. What is it. Theatre of cruelty?

He has another look for GRETA.

Excuse me. Excuse me. Sorry. Sorry.

He gets up and edges past the people in the row.

Down the aisle. It's embarrassing but it's got to be done. People are looking. Coughs into programmes. Up on to the stage.

Excuse me . . .

Audience hisses.

GRETA! ARE YOU OUT THERE? IT'S ME . . . GRETA
I HAVE TO TALK TO YOU!

Audience boos.

I'M SORRY GRETA . . .

FLANNERY is manhandled off the stage.

Just a minute . . . will you . . . I'm looking for someone. In a minute. Shit you can't see a thing from up here can you? The lights are blinding me. GRETA? ARE YOU THERE . . . fuck! Get off. Get off me you fucker. Get off . . . and so the third eclipse.

10   Alexanderplatz

Walk Ten: Alexanderplatz and the City Centre. Ending with
Dinner in the Revolving Restaurant.

FLANNERY *and* GRETA *revolving in the revolving
restaurant.*

You came. I wasn't sure if . . . you look . . . it's good to see you.
I missed you. What do you want to eat? I'll pay . . . the food's
not brilliant but the view's lovely . . . I thought we could talk.

I moved out of the flat John . . . I got a new place in the west.
It's all right. It's home. The old flat didn't feel like a home any
more. I wanted to lose you. You kept ringing. Stupid letters.
Abuse. You frightened me. Only you looked so desperate on the
stage. You looked so . . . helpless. Did they hurt you badly?

Greta. I made a mistake. I shouldn't have left. I was just . . .
you know. You know what I'm like . . . I can't say . . . I don't
have the words for . . . I don't like to admit I like people. Or
things . . . But I do. I like you . . . I . . . well you know. You
know what I mean.

I don't think I can take you back John. Not just now. You can
visit. She'll be your daughter as well so you can visit of course.
But . . . you have to be there. Even if it means you're stuck.
I have to trust that you'll be there . . . and you like to run away.

I know I'm not a nice person Greta . . . but . . . I'm changed . . .
changing. I write happy things to make people happy, or
poignant things . . . I'm trying.

Maybe. O.K. You can visit. But . . . well let's see. We'll see
what happens. I gave everything to you John. I handed myself
over. And you ran away. You can't just leave people. A person
isn't like a place you can just leave behind.

The restaurant spins a mile up above the city. Round and
round at a steady one revolution an hour. Only slightly more
revolutions an hour than the city's had. The carpet of lights
stretches to the horizon and we look out over the east, slowly
turning into the west . . . and back again. Somewhere in the
puddle of light below us the black hole Tony is moving, trying
to pull me down to Earth. Up here Greta touches my face.
We don't speak. Silently she draws me into her orbit.

End.

QUELQUES FLEURS

Liz Lochhead

Liz Lochhead is a poet, playwright, performer and broadcaster. She studied at Glasgow School of Art and lives in Glasgow.

Her theatre plays include: *Perfect Dogs* and *Blood and Ice* (Traverse); *Shanghaied* (Borderline, and revived at Royal Lyceum, Edinburgh); adaptations of *Dracula* and *Tartuffe* in Scots (Royal Lyceum, Edinburgh); *Mary Queen of Scots Got Her Head Chopped Off* (Communicado); *Quelques Fleurs* (Nippy Sweeties); a version of *The York Mysteries* (York Festival, 1992); *Cuba* (BT National Connections at the Royal National Theatre, London). Her film work includes *Latin for a Dark Room* (BBC Tartan Shorts).

Publications include *Dreaming Frankenstein and Collected Poems* and *True Confessions and New Clichés* (Polygon); *Bagpipe Muzak* and *Penguin Modern Poets 4* (Penguin).

Quelques Fleurs – in a slightly different form from the text here printed – was first produced by Nippy Sweeties Theatre Company at the Assembly Rooms, Edinburgh Festival Fringe, on 10 August 1991. The cast was as follows:

VERENA	Liz Lochhead
DEREK	Stuart Hepburn
GUARD (*voice recording*)	Billy Riddoch

Note The set for this play is two isolated spots, one containing an armchair, rug and coffee table bearing, initially, a small imitation silver Christmas tree (Verena's home); the other a double Intercity seat and table (Derek's 'Rattler' train). Verena's costume changes indicate her passing year. Verena's scenes span from 23 December 1990 till 23 December 1991, the date of Derek's single journey – shown backwards from drunk till sober and measured by a dwindling mountain of beer-cans – from Aberdeen home to Glasgow.

Scene One   23rd December 1990

At home, VERENA *quells those nagging doubts, speaks.*

VERENA. His mother's a problem. Always has been. I don't
know what she wants. (*Pause.*)

Take last year, racked my brains, no help from Him as per
usual, left to him we'd end up getting a bottle of Baileys, a
gift voucher and a petted lip all through Christmas dinner!
Anyway I done my best, lovely wee lambswool cardi, sortofa
mauvish, a *blue*ish mauvey no' pinkish, nothing too roary,
not my taste but then I'm not seventy-four in February.
Self covered buttons, none of your made-in Hong-Kongs.
So. I goes into the top drawer of her tallboy looking for clean
guest towels for her toilet and there it is. Still done up in the
blinking glitterwrap the following November! Says she's
keeping it for a special occasion. I felt like saying where
do you think you're going, your age, crippled with arthritis?
But I bit my tongue.

Thing is too, only the week before – well, He was home at
the time, you know, one of His weeks off – and we'd went
to the bother of driving over there, and we'd picked her up
in the car and we'd took her along with us to our Stephen's
engagement party – aye, my mother's losing her baby at
last – well, anyway we thought His Mother would be company
for My Mother while the young ones discoed. Plus it would
be a wee night out for her. And naturally it was an occasion
for the gladrags, Big Night for The Wee Brother exetra – even
Our Joy had made somewhat of an effort. Good appearance,
my sister, I'll admit that. If she bothered. I says to her: Listen
Joy, I hope you have not bankrupted yourself paying through
the nose to get that wee costume on tick, I says (because it's
a false economy yon Provident cheques and whatnot, you
know!). I says: Joy, I'm sure I could've gave you a loan of
something perfectly acceptable to put on. Because I've got
the odd silky trouser and matching top, several dressy wee
frocks jist hinging there since the last time I wis down at ten-
below-target . . .

Anyway I was telling you about His Mother: we get there, she takes her coat off and, honest-to-God, I could of *wept*.

I says to her, I says: What's up wi your wee lambswool cardigan, wee brooch on the collar and you'd have been gorgeous? She says: Och I thought I'd let my hair down, you're only young once, and she winks at Him. I says to Him afterwards I says: Your Mother. What was she like? Telling you, talk about mutton dressed as lamb? Crimplene Trousers. Thon stretchy efforts with the underfoot stirrups. And this sortofa overblouse affair that quite frankly lukked like it came from Whateverrys. Big blooming Dallassy shoulder pads, hectic pattren, *lurex* thread through it, sent away for it out Myna-Wylie-Next-Door's catalogue, cheaplukkin wisnae the word for it. I was quite affronted, you'd think we never bought her anything decent. I caught our Steven's fiancée's mother looking at her, eyebrows raised. Although what right *she's* got to be so blinking snobbish, all *she* was was a manageress in Robertson's Rainwear . . . Aye, I think my young brother'll no' have his troubles to seek dealing with that one! Looked to be the type that likes to *control* everything, get everybody dancing to *her* tune. *(Pause.)* Fiancée seemed to be a nice enough lassie. Pageboy. Good bonestructure, but. Suited it.

I mean, you want to give, but – basically – you want to give something *acceptable* . . . So. Our Steven's no problem for once, something-for-the-house, naturally. Well they're both *modren* so the electric wok seemed the obvious thing. *My* Mother's easy pleased, she's had nothing all her life, give her a good thing she's delighted. With His Mother I give up. Designer thermals. At least I'll no' know if she's wearing them or not! For Him *this* plus the exact same golfing sweater Moira-McVitie-round-the-Crescent-in-the-cul-de-sac got for her man Malcolm last Christmas. Well, *he's* been threatening to take up golf for yonks and if not . . . well it would always do for lounging around the house. When *he's* home. Plus, I've got some stocking fillers for Him, nice wee items in the novelty-line hid away for months up the back of my night-dresses. Well, the July sales can be a very good time for Christmas Shopping. Particularly in the discontinued toiletries.

Actually I got Moira's wee minding then as well. We just tend to exchange a wee token thing, just to be neighbourly, nothing pricey – well what with her Malcolm only being on a teacher's salary I think Moira was frankly quite relieved when I suggested putting a ceiling on it. Because the whole thing can get out of hand. Overcommercialised. Which is a pity.

I hope I done right. I asked Him when he was last home, I said: Country Diary of An Edwardian Lady Drawer Liners, does that say Moira McVitie to you? He goes: *Drawer liners?* I said: *Don't* start, you know fine well it's for fragrant clothes-storage. He says that sounds like Moira to me. Defin*ate*ly.

Big sigh. Several beats.

So, basically, that just leaves me with the recurring nightmare of Our Joy and family. Because recently I've frequently had the feeling I just cannot say or do anything right as far as my sister is concerned.

I blame my Mother. I mean to her my man's God Almighty. Fair enough. He is a Good Provider, unlike some.

I said to my Mother though, I said: Fair enough you worshipping Him, *fine* you being over the moon we've a new shagpile but, mum, I said, there's no need to rub our Joy's nose in it! Causes resentment. (*Shakes head.*) I said: Mum, think about it. Use your imagination.

Families, eh? This is the pretty one. This is the clever one . . . (*Shrug.*) Basically Our Joy's always been jealous. Don't like to think that about my own sister but I'm afraid it's true.

Naturally, we're good to the kids. Me and Him. Having the none of a family ourselves. Although Simeon's geting to be a wee shite! Semi-adolescence I suppose . . . Kellymarie, and Kimberley, and that wee monkey Charlene are gorgeous all the same. Easy! Money, record tokens, clothes, merr money . . . (*Big sigh.*) . . . My Little Pony . . .

But that wee new one! Now he *is* a sweetheart. I could *eat him up*, so I could! Went to yon designer-baby shop in Princes Square, yon, you know, that imports everything from Milan and France exetra. Well, I'd got him this, you know, downfilled mini-ski-suit, arm-and-a-leg-time, still it's not every day you become a godmother, all the thanks I got from Our Joy was her sneering at the make: and turning her nose up at the pattren, which was of Babar the Elephant skiing down a hill saying French things in a bubble. Goes: Oh, a ski-suit, *very* handy in Easterhouse! My, that must've cost your

Auntie Verena a not-so-small fortune! (*Pause.*) Which I don't think was a very pleasant remark.

Consequently I've restrained myself Christmas-wise with regard to the baby. *Well* that was the master-plan, just the matching hat-and-pawkies to complete his ski rigout . . . *Until* the girl says to me: Have you seen our wee Italian dungarees? Just in. I says: That's his *name,* she goes: What? I says: *Justin,* my new wee nephew. (*Beat.*) Fatal. (*Beat.*) Born to shop, that's me! Honest to God if Magnus Magnusson done a Mastermind on Brand Names and Merchandise of the House of Fraser I'd be champion, no question. I can resist everything but temptation I'm afraid, so basically I'll just have to reconcile myself in advance to another slap-in-the-face from my sister . . .

Her man's no bother. Bottle of Bells and he's happy, wee Tommy. Pleasant enough, mind. Basically a nonentity. Hate to say it about my own sister's husband, but she could've done one helluva lot better for herself than yon. Chances she had. *Her* looks! And smart! All brains, nae bloody common sense . . .

So. Five weans. Man that's no worked since nineteen-canteen. Steys in a three-up in Easterhoose that's that bogging damp the paper's curling aff the walls, has to humph that pram doon three flights past pish, broken glass, auld hypodermics and Alsatian-shite. Excuse my French.

Beat.

Anyway I thought I'd get her something nice. Something-nice-for-herself . . . Upshot, I splashed out over-the-odds at Arnotts, got her a jumbo gift basket. Matching cologne, talc, perfume-creme and body lotion. Gorgeous. 'Quelques Fleurs.'

Scene Two   23rd December 1991

Between Springburn and arrival at Glasgow Queen Street.

On the Rattler, the Aberdeen–Glasgow train, DEREK *by the end of his journey, is very, very drunk and giving it laldy. Although it will only be apparent by the end of the play, it is one year later.*

DEREK. In the meadow we can build a snowman
    And pretend that he is Parson Brown

He'll say are you married you'll say No, Man!
But you can do the job while you're in town.

Later on
We'll conspiy-er
As we sit
By the fiy-er
To face unafraid
The plans that you've made
Walking in a winter wonderland

He breaks off his singing, speaks out.

My wife is a dog. Merry Christmas.

*He is interrupted by the two blows into the intercom and the
pre-recorded voice of the GUARD announcing –*

GUARD'S VOICE. This train is about to arrive in Queen Street
Station where this train will terminate. This is the sixteen
thirty train from Aberdeen to Glasgow Queen Street. Would
all customers please check that they have all luggage and
personal belongings with them before they de-train. We hope
you will travel with British Rail again soon.

*Halfway through he lurches to his feet, gets himself drunkenly
together and exits belting out his version of –*

DEREK. C'mon over to my place
Hey girl! We're having a party.
We'll be swining
Dancing and singing
C'mon over tonight.

*He remembers he has forgotten a small white teddy with
Christmas hat, goes back for it, picks it up.*

Oh, fuck! (*Shakes teddy, its bell jingles.*)

Scene Three   6th January 1991

Twelfth Night. VERENA *takes down the tree, talks.*

VERENA. Of course, one year we dispensed with the tree
entirely. Tried something I seen in a magazine. Just this
barren branch flat-whited with emulsion, *very* sparingly glit-
tered up, you know, just where the twigs forked and just . . .

very, very sparsely hung with just – mibbe five or six, maximum seven – giant silver mirror-balls. Sort of monochro*matic*. Quite effective, but. *(Pause.)* Depressed me. It wisnae the same.

Moira McVitie came round this morning for a cappuccino. Phoned up and said: Is that your man away back? I says: Uh-huh footloose and fancy free that's me! She says: Yes I *thought* so. Saw you both getting into the car together and I thought that's unusual. I suppose that'll be her driving into Queen Street for the Aberdeen train? I says: Do you fancy coming round? Sample my new Beverage-Master? Because it even foams the milk. Of course, in the event I spoke too soon and we were reduced to Marvel because I could tell Him till I was blue in the face, but he will be over-lavish with milk in his cereal. Moira can talk though. I've had more black instant than I've had hot dinners round at her house.

So round she came. Wee Scott in tow. I think she's lonely. Says she gets bored, nothing but a two year old's conversation *all* day. I mean he's *lovely*, but he can be quite wearing. Will of his own as well! I said: Do you miss the staffroom? She says: Well . . . I do and I don't. The *banter*, uh-huh . . .

Usual from her: *I've* got a beautiful house . . . *I've* got marvellous taste . . . *hers* is like a *bomb*site but what's the point with young Genghis Khan scattering his Duplo all over the shop? Plus apparently he's felt-tipped all over her anaglypta . . . says the seven year old is *worse*, if anything! Face like a wee angel as well. Goes to ballet . . .

Course, my tree was much admired. I do try and stick to a different theme every Christmas. Obviously this year I'd stuck to the cherub motif only. Nothing gaudy, no baubles, no fairy lights. Nothing.

Less is more. We had an English teacher at the school was always saying that. *(Pause.)* I think it's true.

Course, wee Scotty was into everything what with me being in the middle of dismantling the decorations. Ever noticed how fond mothers tend to just content themselves with the odd don't-son and basically just let the wee buggers run riot?

Moira says to me: I'm full of admiration, she says. See if it was me I doubt I'd bother to go the effort of a tree. Not if it wasnae for the weans. *(Pause.)*

I don't think that's the attitude. Course I couldny be doing wi pine needles. Clogs your tube.

Moira says: Different story from last year! Mind how your sister was quite the celebrity. The big TV star! I says: Don't start me. She says: I think she was excellent. Very articulate.

Oh she's that all right. Always was. Never short of some bloody thing to say, Our Joy . . .

This was yon 1990 TV special. Channel Four, Contrasts . . . *A Tale of Two Cities.* Joy had to swap wi some other wummin they'd found born the exact same time as her in a private ward in Guy's Hospital, Honourable Felicity something and they put them through a full twenty-four hours of each other's lives – well, with *limits,* they didnae go the lengths of making them shack up wi each other's *husbands* nor nothing!

Anyway, at the time thon TV programme took quite a trick with the world and his wife. Evening Times called Our Joy 'a passionate spokesman for the unemployed, the poor, the polltax rebels'. Said she'd of brought a lump to the throat of the most hardened Tory. They called her a 'bonny fechter'. Practically know it off by heart because everybody wis stuffing that blinking cutting down my throat till I was sick – fed up looking at it – Him, Moira McVitie, Our Steven, Isobel Hislop at the check out round the delicatessen . . .

Thing is, Our Joy's obsessed with poverty. Makes a meal of it. I mean, I was embarrassed for my Mother. Dragging us up she had nothing, because my feyther – God forgive me speaking ill of the dead – but he'd have took drink through a shitty cloot. She kept the three of us beautiful, nobody knew the heartache when wan of us grew out our shoes just when she had the Co dividend earmarked for something else . . . Nae money in her purse to give us our dinner money she'd say: Tell your teacher you've got sangwidges because your mum doesn't have change of a five pound note! That's my mother.

And when I seen Our Joy sat there on that television on the Honourable Felicity's horse in Dorset done up in the breeches, the riding hat, describing day to day in Easterhouse, how you're at the mercy of the medical profession, the social workers, the social security . . . Rhyming it all off. No shame. I mean, how did she think my Mother would of felt, watching that?

Funny programme. Not what you'd call festive. Actually it was on the night before Hugmanay among all yon kinna gloomy programmes, you know, resumé of the eighties, lukkin back on all the disasters exetra. Lockerbie. Piper Alpha. (*Sigh.*) You tried to switch channels but they were all at it . . .

Funny thing is, Joy says she was sorry for that Honourable Felicity, would not cheynge places wi her for all the tea in China. Man's a bad yin, never there, leaving her languishing in the sticks, up at his London flat all week, getting up to all sorts, palling about wi MPs exetra. (*Beat.*) Stepson a heroin addick.

Course, that'll be how they tracked Joy down for their programme. Be that Mothers Against Drug Abuse thing that Joy is so involved with in Easterhouse. Aye, she's a volunteer at the Community Flat place, aye campaigning against dampness, sticking up for tenants' rights exetra, single-handed she actually fought through the Rid Tape and won some grant off the EEC only the shortfall had to be made up by the Housing Department and they said their hands were tied. Blamed Central Government. Anyway, Our Joy was up to ninety about the whole thing at the time. Like I said, she's obsessed.

Pause of several beats shaking head over perverseness of her sister.

Moira McVitie was asking would I like to join her Book Group seeing I was all on my ownio? Just a few folk she's knew since the Uni, couple of lassies she taught with and three likeminded types she met at the playgroup. They all read the same paperback every fortnight, meet in each other's houses to discuss it and not be cabbages. Turns out it's at Moira's this Thursday that's why she thought of asking me. Left me a loan of the book they've been reading. I took a wee peek at it over my lunch, but I couldny really be bothered. 'Woman at the Edge of Time' or some damp thing . . .

Anyway, that's Him away back this morning. So that's me. Auld claes and parritch! Never really slept right last night, well, you don't, do you? (*Pause.*)

Och, I hope that's not me heading for another dose of yon honeymoon cystitis . . .

Scene Four   23rd December 1991

Somewhere between Perth and Stirling.

Continuation, moving backwards in time of DEREK*'s single journey.* DEREK *is much less pissed. That many less cans cover the table. He speaks to an (invisible) person opposite, trying hard.*

DEREK. Good book, eh? Good book? Like reading? Engrossed, eh? I used to be a big reader. Aye wance upon a time but I've gave it up. 'M I annoying you? Interrupting your concentration? Because I wouldnae like to think I was disturbing you. I've seen it often, guys on the Rattler, pestering women, making right tits of theirselves forcing theirselves on innocent fellow-travellers with their sob-stories. A liberty. You from Perth yourself? Going to Glasgow? Stirling? You stay in Stirling? Going home for Christmas?

Danielle Steele, eh? Is that a love or a murder?

Nothing but cowboys. Nothing but cowboys and science fiction in the liberry up therr on the rig, and nine times out of ten you get to the lass page and some bastard's torn it out. I mean, imagine a whodunnit. Whodunnit? Don't ask me pal, the lass page is missing. I don't understand the mentality. See, what some folk love more than anything else is to destroy other folk's pleasure. Do you like happy endings? I like happy endings, I'm a simple sort of guy. You look like a happy ending kinda person. Lovely smile. Whit's your name? That's lovely. Lorraine, eh? When I marry sweet Lorraine. Nice song. Derek. But I'll answer to anything.

Naw, you look like a happy ending person. I think women generally are, eh? Unless it's a weepie yiz want. Yiz like that. Aye ye dae, don't come it. I canny greet. Wish I could. Sometimes I wish I could kinna . . . get it out my system.

Yeah, yeah, that's right, Lorraine. Offshore. For my sins. Oh aye two weeks on two weeks aff – well, for the roughnecks and the roustabouts and that, my line of work it's four and four, Lorraine. Want a can? Want a wee gin and tonic well? Lorraine?

Sure? You're sure you're sure? Just to be seasonable. It's nice to be nice. You don't mind if I do? That's right. That's right, up therr's totally T-total. Funny thing is you don't miss it.

You really don't. That's the amazing thing. Or the fags. No, because I'm not allowed to smoke, no in my line of work. Diver. Yeah, yeah up to a point it is dangerous, but they certainly pay us for it. Have to! Yeah the other guys up there they hate us, but they've got it dead cushy compared wi us.

O.K. it's nae teddy berr's picnic the twelve hours on twelve hours aff, but they've the rec room and the videos, even a wee blaw of the wackybacky noo and again on the fly, try to make up for the lack of bevvy. But in sat. it's a different story. Even your meals come in through a err-lock . . . 'S like outer space. Walkin' aboot in your woollyberr . . . Makes you talk like Donal Duck . . . the *helium*, you know . . .

Naw, it's borin' doon therr and bloody dangerous but I wouldnae say you get used to it. The dive is the dive. Thank fuck for your umbilical, eh? You just get yoursel out the bottom, five hunner feet of black watter above you, you climb to the tap of the bell and you dive . . .

Well, thing is obviously up therr you've got all this stuff deep deep down below the surface on the seabed. Needing maintenance, Well, say your concrete casing gets damaged, say by dragging anchors of mibbe fishing boats or something and the installations need to be inspected constantly so you're continually cleanin' up the welds to bright metal. Particle inspection exetra. I don't want to get too technical . . .

Back to the book? Eh, eh? Ut a good bit? Seen in a book wance . . . wis reading this book, know, quite interessin . . . on the History o' Oil. Here there wis this guy used to hink the earth wis this shuge creature, the waters wis its blood, the rocks its bones, the grass and trees its hair, the hills were pimples on its face and Vesuvius and Mount Saint Helens 'n 'at wur boils and big pus-y abscess-hings erupting all over its skin and all you had to do to get oil was to bore through the skin intae the stinkin blubber of this huge animal. Whit do you think of that? Eh? Plus 'zis bam minister or sumphn . . . Texas . . . says that oil was the oil that kepp the fires of Hell burning, and the fires of Hell wid go oot if . . . eh . . . petroleum kepp getting sooked oot tae the surface for, lik, Profane Purposes. And then wherr would we be, Lorraine? Withoot the Fires of Hell!

Aye, we've to live doon therr.

In saturation . . .

He abruptly switches from the glittering eye approach and the horror story back to the bragging.

But it's all down to us. The Divers. Headbangers the lot of us, darlin, you don't have to be crazy to work here but it helps!

Aye the high cost of oil, right enough. In shuman terms. Well I think that's wan thing – you interested in politics? – that Gulf cerryoan showed up didn't it? Wir priorities. A lot of folk up therr that time were scared nae doot aboot it. Theory wis Saddam Hussein would take out a rig or two in the North Sea nae bother. A possibility. Could of. Safety up therr the best of times 's a joke . . . Joke: J.R. has this big blowout at one of his oilwells. Flames everywhere, it's costing him billions every day, a disaster. He says to his right hand man: Get me Red Adair, his man gets on the phone and gets back to him, says: if you want Red Adair it'll cost five billion and you'll huv to wait eight months, he says: Red Adair's very busy puttin' oot the fires of Kuwait. But the good news is I can get you Green Adair, he's willing to come the morra and it'll cost you twenty five thousand. J.R. goes: get me Green Adair then. Well, so the next day this big Hercules Transport comes fleeing in, big shamrock painted on the side of it and it comes screamin intae land in this airfield right next to the fire, back door of the plane flees open and this jeep comes fleein oot hits the tarmac and goes fleein intae the heart of the fire, four guys in welly boots and donkey jackets come leapin oot start stampin and jiggin and jumpin all over fuck on the flames stampin them out. Here it's oot in nae time, they walk back oot aw black, kinna coughin' a bit. J.R. goes up to them goes: Guys that is fantastic you've earned every cent, now what are you gonna do with your twenty-five K? Green Adair goes: Well the first thing Ah'm gonny do is get the brakes mended on that fuckin jeep!

Disappointed with the response to his joke, he tries yet another tack.

Tell you a *true* story, well. Guy I came over wi on the Chinook therr. Wee Eddie, A berr.

First wife wis a cracker! When Eddie went offshore she used to wave him tata, take the train tae Edinburgh, book into a B&B and go on the streets down near Leith Docks. Never knew a thing about it. Not for years. Eventually, well he's no Epstein, but even Wee Eddie got suspicious, he'd rang up jist

wance or twice too often and naebody therr so he gets the
idea she's having an affair. Asks her. She denies it, naturally,
he gets a private detective and the whole story emerges.
Waved her bankbook in his face. She's only amassed a small
fortune! . . . Eddie's shattered.

Ma Big Mate, Big Malk jist goes: Listen, Eddie son, how
should it worry you? What you don't see disnae hurt you. She
disnae see you covered in muck, grease and snotters
clamping pipe on the drilling flair and spitting intae the hole
for good luck. So how no jist let her screw on regardless? On
the wan condition she makes it a joint account, like. And he
winked at us. Christ, I thought Wee Eddie was gonnae
murder him, midget or no.

Big Malk, but . . . Jist recently therr got hisself hitched to
Mrs Malk Mark Three. 'Nuther sunbed kid. No three month
merrit an' he's flashing photaes of her topless all over the
module . . . Wee Eddie but, Eddie . . . Kinna guy Eddie is:
this is years later, right – he's married again, lovely girl,
primary school teacher, she's expecting their second, Eddie's
on his way home, meets this burd on the Rattler, lassie fae
Dundee, jist gets aff wi her. Gets aff the train and gets aff wi
her. Twenty-four hours from Tulsa style. Shacks up with her
for six or seven month afore she chucks him out on his ear
and nae wonder. I mean, nae herm to the guy but some of his
personal habits . . .

Quite unconsciously DEREK *scratches himself.*

Men kin be horrible, hen. Watch yirsel.

DEREK *is by now getting desperate. He's tried the chat-up,
the smarm. The offer of a drink, the brag, the impress-you-
with-technology, the gothic-horror approach, the political
discussion, the stand-up comedy act, the true stories with a
sleazy hint of sex, the avuncular watch-yirsel . . . Now his
self-dramatisation just goes for broke, he's inventing wildly,
on the hoof, he'll try anything.*

Spain. Yup. Yup. That's wherr I live. Aye, aye right enough
naw I huvnae much of a tan . . . Naw. I havenae been back
there recently. No since the tragedy.

Aye, few years ago we decided what's the point the four
weeks off, the money I was making, as well travelling hame
to Spain as somewhere in Scotland or England, eh? How No?
Sold up, Costa del Sol. Costa del Crime as it's widely known,

several of the neighbours well known wide boys from
gangland and that. Used to drink wi that Barbara Windsor's
ex husband . . . To drink with, many of them the nicest guys
you could ever meet . . .

Aye we couldnae of been happier . . . the wife, the kids,
everybody brown as berries and happy as the day was long.
Beautiful lassie my wife. Ex model. Former Miss Scotland in
fact. Gorgeous nature as well, Claudette. A angel. Everybody
loved her. Accident on her motor bike. Head on. Her and a
juggernaut. No chance. Mangled.

Got the news and I was in sat. Well that's you. You're
scuppered. No way of getting back to the surface. Beam me
up, Scottie, but they canny . . . They lifted that hatch four
days later and I was a crazy man. Insane. Three years later
think I was still in shock. I still didny know what hit me.
All I could think of was Claudine, ma Claudine.

My wee daughter and the wee filla they were my whole life
after their mother died. No that I can have been that much
use to them state I was in, thanks to the drink.

That's what kills you . . . it's the regrets, it's the regrets that
get you, isn't it?

I can just see that wee lassie, the herr in bunches, doing
wheelies on her BMX and the wee filla wi his waterwings
on jumping into the pool. The image of his Maw, the blond
curls, a wee cherub. Burnt to death the baith o them in a fire
in the basement while that bitch of a nanny was oot by the
pool chatting up the Spanish gardener . . .

Pause.

Roy Orbison? Roy *fuckin' Orbison*?????

GUARD'S VOICE. We are now approaching Stirling station.
Stirling . . .

DEREK. Aye. Aye well screw you sweetheart sorry I spoke.

Aye, well this is where I get aff as well, darlin.

Only spoke to you because I was sorry for you, you're that
pigging ugly, Merry Christmas. (*Pause. Total switch.*)

If sixteen year of this life have taught me wan thing it's this:
you're better aff cutting your life into two weeks on, two
weeks off and never the twain shall meet. I mean: hauf your

life is hauf the time in a force ten gale and hauf the time in a four bunk boax in ablow a guy that never cheynges his soaks or wyes in a hale fortnight.

Opposite you is the yap whose wan topic of conversation is how his daughter used to winch the Yorkshire Ripper.

As-nice-a filla-as-you'd-ever-want-to-meet, big-Peter, his-lorry-was-never-out-the-layby-along-the-road-he-was-that-daft-aboot-oor-thingwy, used-to-sleep-in-the-house-but-never-shacked-up-wi-her-or-nothing, coorse-me-and-her-mammy-wouldnae-huv-allowed-it-but-he-always-treated-the-lassie-like-a-lady. Say-whit-you-like-but-I-ayeways-thought-Sutcliffe wis-a-great-block.

And you're thinkin to yirsel: out of five hunner blocks on the flotel how come yet again you've ended up wi Ma-Daughter-Almost-Married-A-Monster and how come he canny mind how often he's telt you the same fuckin story?

Gets so you think you're gonnae lam the other poor bastard that never says boo, the big silent cheuchter type, jist a laddie, the wan that's no botherin emdy, jist lyin' on his back on the bunk whistlin through his teeth while he works his way through a big pile of fishin magazines and old Fiestas.

You know you've been up therr too long when even the dogs in the Fiesta begin to lukk attractive . . .

I *am* morbid wi the offshore carryon. Up to here wi it.

Big Derek Jimmison forty-two, failed fitter. Correction, it wis the fittin' that failed me . . . So offshsore.

Supposed to be short term mizzure. Jist till the economy takes a wee upswing. Jist till we get a few bob thegither, get a wee start. Jist till we get the hoose up to Ags's standards and I'd start my ain business. Ha. Ha. Then it would be no longer the roughneck. Tata the Rattler. I wish.

Sixteen fuckin year. Young man's gemme as well, definately.

So's fatherhood son. As you are just about to find out . . .

Scene Five   March 1991

VERENA. Coourse, I'm used to it now, after all these years,
never give it a thought. Since ever He first went up there on
the rigs it's been much better. Definately. Well, financially
speaking anyway, I mean see before, with his other job,
before, on shore . . . honest to God the mortgage was a
millstone.

Him away, the diet is a piece of cake. I mean, you've no
distractions. Well, until he bought me this blinking Easter
egg! Plus a big bunch of flowers! Wonder what he's feeling
guilty about!

And I am out a lot.

Och just round to my mother's basically, just to get out of the
house. An Ann Summers the night, round my mum's next
door neighbours. Although I hope their lingerie's better
quality than yon Pippa Dee party. Set of French knickers you
could spit peas through.

Telling you though, He is that jealous, always was, vernear
divorce proceedings he phones up and I'm no' in!

Although as I try to tell my mother and Our Joy, I'm convinced it's with us having the none of a family ourselves I've
adjusted so well. (*Pause.*) Means I'm a free agent. (*Pause.*)
Moira was just asking me when I was round there the other
day, she says: Did you never think to *investigate* it, if that's
no' too cheeky a question . . .

I says, no, I don't mind telling you I says, it was a *night*mare
Moira, I says you know nothing about indignity if you've
never had your tubes blown.

Doctors! Och it was into the ins-and-outs of everything.

Could find nothing wrong. Nothing wrong with either of the
two of us. Not that they could put their finger on. Suggested
we might simply be missing the moment, what with the two
weeks on, two weeks off, mibbe he should think of changing
his job, or something?

But och, it's security isn't it . . .

And is a kid compatible with an off-white fitted carpet, that's
the question . . . ?

Because I gave Moira a wee tinkle this morning, asked her round, she said she would love to if it was just her, but wee Scotty was having one helluva hiccup with his toilet training. (*Pause.*) Hope she wasn't offended I bodyswerved her Book Group . . .

Scene Six   Between Montrose and Dundee

DEREK. The first I mind of noticing Joy – well, apart from her being Ags's young sister – was funnily enough the night Dixie and me were arranging my stag. There was this pub, the Dagwood Bar, near wherr I grew up, bit of a dump it was in many ways but they had this upsterrs room they let out for like meetings, clubs, twentyfursts, and me and Dixie, he was my best man, huvny seen him in years, imigrated to South Africa, anyway, we'd went to the Dagwood to book it for the Wensday before the wedding. Because no way was I gonny be daft enough no to leave the two or three days recovery time before the Saturday. I've seen too many grooms green about the gills. Foolish . . .

Anyway, fair enough, we'd fixed it up, we're just ordering up a pint and Dixie spies through the alcove in the lounge this burd. Dixie was always spotting burds. He goes: You know who that was, Big Man? I go naw. He goes: Big Gwynneth. Big Gwynneth Thingwy. I says: Gwynneth Inglis, Big Gwynneth that was at the school with us? I says: I very much doubt it, last I heard of her she was living down in Maccles-field. He goes: I tell you, that was Big Gwynneth in therr. Big Gwynneth that used to wear the *nylons*.

Oh aye! The diamond mesh nylons. With the wee rips stopped with the wee dabs of nail varnish. Big Gwynneth had a stoatin' perra pins, no skinny, dead shapely wi good firm muscles an that, she used to be great at the P.T., a runner as well . . . Wore high heels even at the school, all the old bag wummin teachers used to go crazy, big spike stilletos, thirteen year aul' . . . Likely all the men teachers used to go crazy an all. That wee hollow in behind Big Gwynneth's knees . . . She was a right big ride goes Dixie. Although that used to be what we said about everybody. A mixture of wishful thinkin and pure resentment of the fact when we were fifteen she wouldny even have looked at us. I mean ever looked recently at a school photo of back when you were fifteen? I mean there's just all these big women, some of them look about forty, the bouffongs, the perms, the big pointy tits, and guys? – ther's always this wan neanderthal type with eyebrows that meet in the middle and black hair curling out the neck of his shurt – and then aw these Wee Boays . . . A joke! Dixie goes: Mibbe we should go in and buy the lassie a drink for old times sake. But mind, Big Man, you're a married man as near as dammit he says. I'm like that . . . I says next month, Dixie, next month anyway I'm not interested. I'll believe you, thousands wouldny says Dixie and anyway mibbe she's got a pal with her, mibbe I'll be well in therr or mibbe she's in wi a block or her mother in which case I don't like the wan you're getting.

So through we goes. Ben the lounge. Usual shite from the barman about how it's couples only through therr, you need to be in with a partner and anyway it's waitress service so you're no allowed to take your pint in from the public or everybody would be doing it because it's three pence cheaper. So ends up Dixie slapping ten pee on the bar and telling him we're meeting somebody and in we go.

And who should Gwynneth be sitting with but Joy. I was amazed. Because Joy is out the house at this time, her father and her have had one of their famous fa-outs. Every hoose is different I suppose but, Jeezus, in Ags's family the Third World War was never mair than a nasty remark away. Well, Joy and her da had had a big falling out, he'd threatened to put her out the door and here she'd upped and went just to spite him. Nobody knew where she was, she'd left the college, mibbe that was what the fight had been about in the first place, nobody had seen hide nor hair of her for about three weeks or somethin. And there she is, sitting wi Big Gwynneth. Aw naw, goes Joy. I goes: Well hello stranger, your Ags is up to ninety about you, you've missed about three fittings for your bridesmaid's thingwy. She says: Gwynneth, you don't know thame do you? Of old, says Gwynneth, worse luck. Joy says: Well you can tell our Agnes Verena – from me – that apple green is a bogging colour. I go: Joy, Joy, it's Ags's big day, c'mon noo, I'm gonny be all done up like a dish o' fish in the Moss Bros masel, the brown tuxedo, the cumberbund I don't know all what. Well, says Joy, I wish you health to werr it.

Turns out she's working beside Big Gwynneth. In a bookies.
And she's sharing a flat with her over the South side somewhere. Talk about the odd couple! I mean Gwynneth's got to
be my age at least! Twenty-four or five. This is – whit? – the
middle seventies, and she's in a time warp. Froze in the kinna
style she hud at fifteen. Dusty Springfield. That kinna sketch.
The pale pale pink lipstick, the two black eyes like burnt
holes in a blanket . . .

And Joy, she's seventeen or eighteen but looks about fifteen
or somethin. Dead young for her age. That wis Ags's theory
anyway. Easy led. But there she is, a pint of Guinness in front
of her, a pint, in a pint mug, the freckles, the fork and knife
herrcut. The bibfront dungarees.

Dixie's like that. I hate to see that, he says, a wummin wi a
pint tumbler. I thought you'd chucked the yoonie. Joy just
makes a face and says nothing. Him and Gwynneth seem to
be getting on just dandy, although I notice he's elevated
himself to a draughtsman . . .

I mean why do guys do that? Pub in the Torry docks. Union
Street disco, the guy's a K.P. in the caterin, he tells the burd
he's a roughneck, roughneck's a mud-engineer, mud-
engineer's a diver, diver's a chopper pilot. I mean burds aw
know that. He knows they know that. Mibbe he's feart he
says he's a roughneck she'll think he's only a bender kitchen
porter.

Anyway that night . . .

Course in the finish up we go round there to their flat wi a
carry out. Well I know for fact Joy wasnae very pleased but
she never says nothing. Well it was Big Gwynneth's flat
originally. Few cans, some Carlsberg Specials, a quarter
bottle of Bacardi for them, a quarter bottle of whisky for us
and a boattle o'ginger. Flat was basically just the wan big
room. Gwynneth goes dancing over to the settee picks up a
perr y tights wi the knickers still in them rolls them up into a
ball and chucks them over this partition along a bit from the
fireplace. There was a partition hing normal wall height that
didnae go right up to the high ceiling – that cut a corner out
the room, took a big bite out of it. Dixie goes: That your
bedroom in therr? Wouldn't you like to know goes
Gwynneth. I sat on the settee and picked up a woman's
magazine. As if I was interested. What to do if he wants oral
sex and you don't. The usual.

Dixie makes a beeline for the record player and starts slagging the record collection. Amazing sound system, Gwynneth. The hifi dansette, haveny seen wan y these for dunkeys and geez oh, some ell pees! Dave Dee Dozy Beaky Mick and Titch, Wayne Fontana! Bob Dylan? Whit's he dane here? That's my album, says Joy. Oh *album*, sorry I spoke says Dixie, have yous nothing good? How about some of the late great Jimi Hendrix or somethin?

This is what I'm thinkin when I'm sittin on the settee with the magazine. I'm thinkin' *burds' flats* . . .

The wee frilly bags of rollers lying about the place, the inside out jerseys drying over towels on the backs of chairs, the durty coffee mugs on the ironing board, wan of they big paper lantern hings, slightly tore, the light blue Tampax box among all the make-up and stuff on the dressing table. Burds' flats . . .

Of course I've been up in plenty burds' flats over the years. Several. But no enough. No really. And I'm thinking about the room and kitchen Ags and me have been dane up for about three month, the silk finish woodwork, the breakfast bar I'd aw the bother wi the rawlplugs for . . .

Later on I come back in from having a slash. And there's no sign of Gwynneth or Dixie. Just Joy . . . I go: Where urr they? But Joy just shrugs. She just sits there on the settee hunched up round her cup of coffee singing along to the Bob Dylan record, and when she turns it over she ups the volume a wee bit, but nothing too obvious. Otherwise – it's ridiculous – but we just sit there completely ignoring the noises from the other side of the partition while Dixie and Big Gwynneth get down to it and do the business. I mean I'm thinkin this is my burd's wee sister here. She's starin down into that coffee cup as if it's got the answer to somethin in it and mouthing along to Positively Fourth Street.

Eventually – everything's quietened down a bit through there by this time – she looks up at me. Light clear eyes she hus. She says to me: One thing I just don't understand about guys she says. What's that? says I. She says: Why is it some guy's called Deans everybody's got to call him Dixie?

The next mornin, Joy's got this mark on her face from where she's been lyin all night on my corduroy jacket. It's imprintit. I touch her face and I can feel it. The wee ridges, the grooves.

I kiss her and say it's gonny stay like that, wee pal. And she just smiles at us. She says: Gonny no tell Verena or my ma or my da or anybody where I am? I say: Don't worry . . .

Course in the event at the wedding three weeks later it's all blew over. Like most of the big dramas in their family. Joy's there, in the identical-same bridesmaid dress as wee fat Alma, Ags's pal fae work. Just the way Ags wanted it. End of story.

GUARD'S VOICE. Will all passengers who boarded the train at Stonehaven or Montrose please have their tickets ready for inspection . . .

DEREK. Nothing actually happened, but . . .

Scene Seven   July 1991

VERENA. Hired a sunbed. Well, you don't want to give yourself a ridneck turning up totally paleface at the beach day one, do you? Although possibly we'll generally use the pool at the hotel, because – if you can trust the brochure – it looks immaculate. Kinna Kidneyshape. Although if it's anything like Portugal there'll be a shortage of sunloungers.

So I was saying to Moira if she wanted to come round, because I've the six weeks hire of the blinking thing, and there might as well be somebody using it. It's not as if I can just lie there all day toasting myself. Over thirty and your skin can get yon leathery way. Not attractive.

But she's no turned up. So far. Shame because it'd help her acne.

I suppose we'd better enjoy this holiday, Him and me, because it'll be our last fling before the joys of parenthood. (Pause.)

Aye it'll be changed days. Funny how it's all worked out. It was in the March or April there, just around Easter anyway, Moira and I went along to see yon Destinastra.

Moira had said to me Scotty's wee pal Chloe at the playgroup's mother was having a night in the house where she was getting in a clairvoyant and she was looking for one or two to bring up her numbers. Because with Destinastra it's minimum a dozen before you can get her to come out to you.

Moira says apparently she's excellent, prophesied Pauline
Patullo would be crossing water for profit in connection with
a Leo with the initial R. And here, her husband's boss –
Roy – turned down the promotion he'd been offered (and
had at that point in time accepted!) at head office in Florida
because his wife's mother took Parkinson's – so her Harry
got it and him and Pauline were sold up and off in jigtime.
I mean how could she have *knew?*

So we went. Top whack, she reads your palm, does the
crystal ball and gives you a choice of either the cards or the
Tarot.

She takes my hand and she says: I see here a secret sadness. I
says: I don't think so. I says: I tend to be quite content with
my lot, anyway I don't go around with a long face moaning
about things. Unlike some.

She says: No, I can see that you are self-effacing, tendency
to sacrifice yourself for others – and was I Taurus? I says:
No – Gemini – but funnily enough I am frequently taken for
one and mibbe it's because I am on the cusp. Anyway, she
says, I see a Big Joy in your life and it's in connection with
the patter of tiny feet. Could it be a sister, or someone close
because it's not actually in your own personal house of
happiness, but it's a very very close run thing, and it will
deeply affect you? You *and* a partner, but I'm not getting him
very clearly, is he fairish, anyway that's all very shadowy, am
I right to get water, and a brownish car? She said complete
change of lifestyle coming within a nine.

Amazing. And to think that it was only a coupla month
before I so much as got wind of Joy's Big News.

Although – and here's where I think you have to believe in
something, call it fate, call it what you like, but – Well this
day Moira had been going down the shops and she said can
I bring you back anything? I says och, mibbe the Woman.
If you're passing. Upshot she brings a Woman's *Own* because
turns out they'd ran out – and is there not this big article
about surrogate mothers? It's very big in Australia apparently,
and they'd two or three case histories, one woman it was her
own egg and you know yon in-vitrio fertilisation with her
own husband's sperm and her sister – I think it was mibbe
her twin – carried it for her, because there was some blockage
or something in her fallopiums and a badly tilted uterus.

Another case, the woman didn't ovulate herself, so her sister (who actually had a grown-up family of her own) had a baby for her by artificial insemination off the woman's husband. Own husband didny mind, thought it was just a case of womb-leasing, a favour one woman could do for another, sister or not and nobody's business but their own.

So I had been reading that on the Tuesday. Yet when – this was the Wensday – Joy let the cat out of the bag by no means did the penny instantly drop.

Well, she was looking hellish, but I didn't think anything of it. Well, I knew she was worried about the poll-tax. I mean it was all very well, but when push comes to shove and the chickens come home to roost they'll seize your television as soon as look at you. Politicians. I mean it's folk like Our Joy are going to suffer.

Plus Joy runs herself ragged all that volunteering and social activating and whatnot she does locally. Newsletters. So it's not unusual to see her looking kinda peely-wally and washed-out.

Of course, you've guessed it, it was quite the reverse and she was pregnant! Up to high-doh she was, I mean the baby's only what? Nine or ten month old, wee Justin, and when she fell she must've been actually still breast feeding. I says: Could you not persuade that man of yours to get a job so the time doesny hang so heavy on his hands so to speak? She says: Very funny. Turns out according to my mother he'd actually hud the vasectomy, but they were still waiting for it actually to be finalised, because it takes a month or two before you can be certain that they're firing blanks, as her G.P. put it . . . So it was rotten luck.

I mean obviously they'd the five kids already, and Justin, gorgeous as he is, was a mistake.

But, although the G.P. said he'd put her in for a termination no question, say the word – thing is, she said, I'm torn.

Mibbe it was the fact that – vasectomy exetra – it felt like slamming the door on her last chance, mibbe it was just that whatever her head thought about it – because definitely they couldn't *have* it – her heart thought different.

My Mother was surprising. She said: Jesus Christ, Joy, get rid of it or you'll never get out the bit.

Joy just sighs and says: I know mammy, I know, you're right, O.K.

Pause.

It was driving the car home later that it came to me. Thing is He was due home the next day and I knew I could put it to Him. Discuss it.

Course in the event the money that we're actually giving her isn't a payment. How could it be, between sisters?

And it's as old as the hills this kind of arrangement, sister for sister, servant for mistress, all through history. Since Bible Days. A lot longer than test tubes or U.S.A. palimony lawyers that's for sure!

No, a friendly arrangement, enough to keep her comfortable while she's carrying – because obviously it's hard work, blossoming or not blossoming! Plus a wee nest-egg for the rest . . .

Scene Eight   Aberdeen to Montrose

GUARD'S VOICE. This is the 16.33 Inter City train from Aberdeen to Glasgow Queen Street stopping at Stonehaven, Montrose, Arbroath, Dundee, Perth, Dunblane, Stirling and Glasgow Queen Street. This train is about to depart so would anyone not wishing to travel please leave the train immediately.

DEREK. I do admit I am somewhat of a settee spud. At home, the tendency to turn into quite the couch potato and I freely admit it.

Has caused problems in the past. The way Ags is as well, she's very unlikely to come straight out with something, could be something schunnered her the last time I wis hame and – since then – it's been sorta simmering. A possibility!

Ach, who am I trying to kid? The way she lit into us on the phone last night, I doubt it was about me forgetting to flush the toilet . . .

Queued up, queued up the regulation three quarters of an oor waiting on the phone, nae answer. I gies up, tries again later, nothing. Thurd time, thurd time lucky she picks up the phone.

I goes: Fuck you been? She says . . . (*He shakes his head.*)

I mean: What was all that aboot?

I hope to fuck nothing has happened.

I hope naebody has said nothing.

No with this wean due in a coupla weeks.

I don't think so.

Surely no . . . Nah.

Christmas fuckin' Eve, eh?

Alang Union Street therr lukkin for a jewellers. Get Ags a eternity ring. For her Christmas . . . Ended up wi eighteen carat set wi zircons and synthetic sapphire . . . Bar that I've a coupla bottla scent out the Bond. Obsession. Better be the right thing. Big Malk says wan thing each and every wan of his wives wanted that wis a eternity ring.

Sometimes I think I'm the only person offshore that has been married jist the wance. To the wan lassie.

I don't think I'd ever split up wi Ags. No at this stage in the gemme.

I've been off the drink as well. Off the drink for vernear nine month. So what has induced you to start the night, son? Ach, I dunno . . . Perhaps it is the Christmas spirit. Cheers! Gaun yirsel!

See when oor Ags comes oot wi the suggestion we should adopt Joy's wean. Out of the blue. Joy's wean . . . I'm like, eh? Joy's pregnant? You have got to be fuckin jokin? I thought I was gonny burst a blood vessel. I'm like that . . . Ags goes: You are as white as a sheet. I go naw, it's jist the shock of this adoption caper. I thought we'd thought about that and thought that it wasnae for us.

This wis what? – three-four years after we got married, round about the time of all those tests and everything, when she was desperate to start a family and we were never away from yon Southern General. I couldnae love a stranger's wean, Ags said, could you? I goes: I don't know. The consultant suggested for starters mibbe Ags should give up her work, relax, let nature take its course so she did. Nothin.

Now this about us adopting Joy and Tam's wean!

Well, I'm out of there and down the pub and I phone up Joy.
I goes: Get out of there, get a taxi, meet us in the city centre,
I'll meet you upstairs at Sloan's. She goes: Whit am I gonnae
yase for money? I goes: I'll pey it, just get there. Whit the
fuck is going on?

It was only the wan night. Well, no the night, the efternin.
Out of the blue an all. It was April. April Fools Day. I'm no
kidding, I wish I wis. Wan y my weeks aff. Hitting the heavy
bevvy at that time an all. You don't notice, creeps up on ye.
Anyway, I'd put away two-three Superlagers, I'm lying aboot
on the settee in my stoakin soles watching a video I've seen
umpteen times already. When the doorbell goes. It's Joy.
I goes: Well hello stranger. Because I hadnae seen hide nor
hair of any of them for donkeys. Anyway, there she is, on the
doorstep. In a right state an all. She goes: Oh you're home
urr ye, where's my sister? I says: Come in, come in, you've
no long missed her, away intae the shoaps wi yon Moira
McVitie. She says: When will she be back? I says: Well, as a
matter of fact I'm no expecting her, no' till later on the night
because she was talking about going on to some fortune teller
or something. Girls' Night Out. And you know what they're
like. Nuh, goes Joy. And I suppose she doesnae.

Anyway she's up to ninety, anybody can see that. Shaking.
Eventually – oot it comes – she's just – oot the blue – had
a wee visit from the mammy of the wee fourteen-year-aul
lassie that lukks aftir the weans for her while she's oot at the
Tenants' Association and the Community Council and
whatnot. Babysitter's mammy has found condoms in the
lassie's bag and read the riot act and here has it no emerged
that she's been kerryin oan wi Tam. Who is auld enough to
be her faither and merr than auld enough tae huv a loat merr
bloody sense. Shiting on his ain doorstep like that. I canny
believe it. I tell her that. I says: Whit did he say? But
she's no confrontit him yet. Lassie's mammy's jist away
and Joy's come running ower here in case she stabs the
bastard wi the breid knife when he comes in the door fae the
Job Centre.

Gies her a drink. To calm her doon. There's a bottle of
Bezique in the sideboard been lying there since Christmas.
Normally she is fanatically anti. Guzzles the loat y it this
time, but, state she's in.

Don't really know how it happened. Wan minute I'm
cuddling her, patting her on the back, trying tae get her to
stop greeting . . .

First thing I mind is coming to on the carpet. Nae Joy. In she
staggers wi' the basin and the disinfectant, white as a sheet,
says: Get up, get up, we'll huv tae clean up this mess. Huv
you ever tried to clean a carpet when somebody's boaked up
a boattle y Bezique?

Course ever since then I'm waiting for seventeen shades of
shite tae hit the fan. Two weeks on. Nothing. Two weeks aff.
Nothing. Ags never mentions her sister, nor her sister's
marital problems, nothing. Until – this is June – Joy's-
pregnant-and-I-want-us-tae-adopt-the-wean. Hullo?

Well when Joy turns up at Sloan's that night she is very quick
to disabuse me of any notion that it is my child. No way. A
wummin knows these things. The dates don't tally, forget it.
She is adamant. So that's that.

Thank fuck. I suppose.

Never really done it right we were that drunk.

Anyway, turns oot there was no truth whatsoever in the
business about Tam and the babysitter either. Naw, it was
Simeon – thirteen year aul! – Simeon and the babysitter had
been mucking aboot, and when the lassie's mother fun the
packet of three, lassie just panicked and blamed Tam, because
she knew she would get nothing but sympathy fur getting
abused by an adult whereas if they fun oot it was wee Simeon
she would get a tanking for leading *him* on. Which she did.
Joy says: I don't know what gets into the young wans . . .

Listen, says Joy, I feel terrible about thon day, I don't know
how I could have done that to my man and my sister. She
says: If you ever tell anybody what happened I will kill you,
because a lot of people would get hurt, including my kids,
and nobody hurts my kids. She says she's thought about this
surrogate business and she's thought about her sister and she's
going to go through with it. I go: Let her have our wean?

She goes: It's Tam's. Can't you get that into your thick skull?

Do you know the funny thing? I tellt her. I tellt her how I'd
felt ever since yon night up at thon flat. Her and Big
Gwynneth. And she couldnae remember it. At first I thought
she was acting it. But she wasnae. She couldnae remember.

Ags is ecstatic aboot this wean. Place is like Mothercare.

I don't think she cares whether it's a boy or a lassie. Well, nane of the two of us do, really.

Beryl, Beatrice, Claire, Mabel, Maureen, Renee. Brent if it's a boy? Mibbe Ninian . . .

Scene Nine   December 1991

VERENA – *dull-eyed, dirty, barefooted and rat's nest hair – slumped.*

VERENA. Bought a big bunch of flowers, got myself over there, says where's the labour ward, where do you find the women that have just had their babies, they said Thirteen B upstairs. Think I knew alreadys, my heart was hammering, tried to tell myself it was just I was just dying to see her. Seven pounds nine ounces. Perfect.

But I knew.

Knew ever since the phone went that morning. Out of the blue. No warning. Everything great. I'm driving over there every day feeding the rest of them. Getting mucked in. Three and a half weeks to go. Her totally serene. Blossoming. First thing I knew, he phones me. Her man. Eleven o'clock in the morning and I'm just about to go over for the three girls coming home from the primary when he phones me. Says don't bother because he's gave them their dinner money. Thing is Joy went into labour last night at six o'clock and had a wee girl at quarter past midnight. My heart stopped. Says: Why didn't you phone me? Supposed to let me know. I wanted to be there. He says: I know. I know that. Obviously. Just Joy wanted to be on her own. Didny even want *him* there . . . Scratched his face and fought like an animal, doctor hud to ask him to leave because it was upsetting her. I says: I'm going in there, he says no, no the now, she's sleeping. Joy is exhausted.

Christmas. No bloody Christmas. Never be Christmas again.

He can go to his mother's. Go wherever the hell he likes. No use to me. Never had been.

I told him: You can drill a big big hole for yourself deep at the bottom of the big black North Sea.

Lights come up on DEREK*'s spot. Stay up on both places till end.*

DEREK. Beryl, Beatrice, Claire, Mabel, Maureen, Renee. Brent. Brent. Brent.

I am totally and utterly morbid wi the whole offshore carryon, I'll tell you . . .

VERENA. And my Mother, coming round here greetin' saying she's sure Our Joy will see sense. Don't want her. Don't want Our Steven or that passremarkable smart-arsed tart he's shacking up with. Fostering. Adoption. Knows fuck all about anything. Any of them.

Told Moira McVitie where to go and take her fat brat with her.

DEREK. Tartan, Glamis, Claymore, Crawford, Forties, Heather, Brae, Glen.

VERENA. Go in there and out it all comes. She's hysterical. Private room. Sister says you can't go in there, no the now, but they can't stop me.

Pause.

Out it all comes.

Pause.

He's shattered, Tommy. Can't believe it. Knows it's true. Keeps on telling the two of us to calm down. Calm down – when it's my Derek's wean they won't let me have?

Tommy goes: Every single penny will be paid back to you . . .

She asked me please would I be godmother. Please. Felicity. Felicity Verena.

DEREK. Brent, Alpha, Brent Bravo, Brent Charlie, Brent Delta. Piper. Piper Alpha.

VERENA. Felicity Verena. Our Joy thinks of nothing but herself. Selfish to the core. God forgive her because I never will . . .

Black.

End.

ONE GOOD BEATING

Linda McLean

Linda McLean's work for theatre includes: *One Good Beating* (Traverse); *The Price of a Good Dinner* (Derby Playhouse); co-author of *The Corridor* (Benchtours). Radio work includes *Take One Egg* (BBC Radio 4). She is currently under commission to Derby Playhouse and Paines Plough.

One Good Beating was first performed in a workshop production at the Traverse Theatre, Edinburgh on 13 December 1996, with the following cast:

ROBERT, *father*   Tom Watson
ELAINE, *daughter*   Jennifer Black
STEPHEN, *son*   Frank Gallagher

Directed by Philip Howard

ELAINE *and* STEPHEN *are standing outside the coal shed.*
The coal shed is sideways on with the front door facing the left.
The wall facing us is cut away so we can see into it. Inside the
shed sits ROBERT, *their father, listening to them.*

ELAINE (*whispering*). I want to hit him.

STEPHEN. Me too.

ELAINE. No. Really. I want to hit him. Hard.

STEPHEN. What? You mean . . . go in there . . . and give him
   one.

ELAINE. More than one.

STEPHEN. How many?

ELAINE. I don't know.

STEPHEN. Three? Five.

ELAINE. I don't know. Till it's over. Till I'm done. Can I?

STEPHEN. It's not for me to say.

ELAINE. You would have to hold him. I couldn't do it myself.

STEPHEN. It's a bit . . .

ELAINE. What?

STEPHEN. A bit . . . sick. Elaine.

ELAINE. I feel sick. Don't you? Didn't today make you feel
   sick?

STEPHEN. Not sick exactly.

ELAINE. What then?

STEPHEN. Sad, I suppose.

ELAINE. Well I'll hold him while you cry if you hold him while
   I give him a good thumping.

STEPHEN. But he never hit you.

ELAINE. Don't do that.

STEPHEN. What?

ELAINE. The past is the past. Refuse to discuss it.

STEPHEN. I don't understand. I thought the past was why we put him in there.

ELAINE. No.

STEPHEN. It's why I put him in there. See how he likes it.

ELAINE. Well you'd better bugger off then. You'll be useless.

STEPHEN. I'm a lot stronger than you.

ELAINE. If he thinks for a minute that you're stuck in the past he'll beat you. He'll talk rings round you. Explanations. Justifications. No. Ignore any remarks about the past.

STEPHEN. Why did you do it then?

ELAINE. We did it.

STEPHEN. Yes, but . . . I told you. I thought it was for/

ELAINE. /I'm angry. That's why I wanted him in there. Because I'm angry. Today. Now. This minute. Not then. Not way back then. Now. I'm bloody raging at him. I want to hit him. Hard.

STEPHEN. Yes.

ELAINE. When I just think of his face I want to smash it.

STEPHEN. Yes.

ELAINE. When I think of that . . . that . . . bloody box.

STEPHEN. Bloody awful box.

ELAINE. Yes. So. Can I?

STEPHEN. . . . Yes.

ELAINE. You'll hold him?

STEPHEN. I want to hit him too.

ELAINE. O.K. but me first.

STEPHEN. He's a . . .

ELAINE. He's a bastard.

STEPHEN. A bad tempered old bastard.

ELAINE. He deserves a good kicking.

STEPHEN. A bloody nose.

ELAINE. She was too good for him.

STEPHEN. Far too good. Bloody bastard.

ELAINE. Bloody nose.

STEPHEN. Good bloody kicking.

ELAINE. Get him then.

STEPHEN. Aye. Get him.

ELAINE. Come on then.

STEPHEN. Come on.

They run at the coal shed and pull back the bolts to open the door.

ROBERT is sitting on the ground huddled in a ball with his hands wrapped over his head.

ROBERT. Don't hit me. Please don't hit me.

STEPHEN. Shit.

ELAINE. Come on then.

STEPHEN. Shit.

ROBERT. I beg you. Please. Don't hurt me.

ELAINE. Hold him.

STEPHEN. Fuck.

ELAINE grabs hold of him and shakes him.

ELAINE. Come on. Pull yourself together.

STEPHEN. Look at him.

ELAINE. It's an act.

STEPHEN. He's pathetic.

ELAINE. It's an act.

STEPHEN. I can't.

ELAINE. Bugger off then.

She pushes him out of the shed. ROBERT unfolds his arms and looks up at her. He winks.

ELAINE. You old bastard.

She kicks him and leaves. STEPHEN is sitting outside, head in hands. She slaps him.

STEPHEN. Hey.

ELAINE. You bastard.

STEPHEN. I couldn't.

ELAINE. You know what he did? Soon as you were out of there? He winked at me. Bloody well winked at me. That was you. You let him do that to me. You bastard.

STEPHEN. He was crying.

ELAINE. Crying my arse. He's laughing at you. Go on. Take a look. Laughing.

She shoves him.

ELAINE. Go on.

STEPHEN *pulls open the door to the coal bunker and* ROBERT *is smiling at him.*

STEPHEN. I'll hit him now. Come on.

ELAINE. Aw shut the door. Before the smell gets to me. Have you shit yourself, father?

STEPHEN. I can. I can hit him now.

ELAINE *shuts the door and bolts it.*

ELAINE. All you had to do was hold him. Hold him till I hit him. It was that simple. And quick. I would've hit him. Then you would've hit him. And that would've been it. One good beating and we would've been finished.

STEPHEN. I can do it now.

ELAINE. Do you know what you've done?

STEPHEN. We can still do it.

ELAINE. No we can't. The moment's gone. The moment when we could have beaten him. A good beating. Is gone.

STEPHEN. We can still beat him.

ELAINE. He beat us.

STEPHEN. But . . . you kicked him. You've done your bit.

ELAINE. That was different. I kicked him because he beat me. And I'm a bad loser.

STEPHEN. He winked?

ELAINE. Yes.

STEPHEN. Bastard.

ELAINE. Yes.

STEPHEN. I should never have fallen for all that begging and crying.

ELAINE. No.

STEPHEN. So what do we do now?

ELAINE. Exactly.

STEPHEN. I'm going to phone Holly.

ELAINE. No.

STEPHEN. Why not? I need to tell her. She doesn't even know.

ELAINE. Don't phone her yet. Till we know. What we're going to do.

STEPHEN. Well I'll need to phone her sometime.

ELAINE. We'll all need to phone some time. But not now. Not yet.

STEPHEN. What are you going to do?

ELAINE. We.

STEPHEN. Yeah yeah. We.

ELAINE. I don't know. I don't suppose you can make tea?

STEPHEN. Of course I can make tea. What kind of remark is that?

ELAINE. Well I don't know whether you make tea or not. Maybe somebody else in your house makes the tea. Maybe what you make is piss water.

STEPHEN. Just because I couldn't hit him doesn't mean I can't make tea.

ELAINE. Good.

STEPHEN. Right. I make good tea.

ELAINE. Well make it then.

STEPHEN. Don't.

ELAINE. What?

STEPHEN. Don't do that.

ELAINE. Do what?

STEPHEN. Order me about. I'm in this too, you know. It's not just you. She was my mother as well.

ELAINE. I'm pleased to hear it.

STEPHEN. I loved her too.

ELAINE. Don't get upset. Not yet. Look, I'm sorry. I was just . . . I'm a bit . . . thrown.

STEPHEN. O.K. Well. Do you want tea?

ELAINE. Yes. Please.

STEPHEN. Right. I'll get it then.

STEPHEN *leaves*.

ROBERT. 'Lainey. 'Lainey. What are you doing hen? What are you thinking? Hey. You used to be ma wee girl. Remember, 'Lainey.

Lay Lainey
Ower the glen
Daddy's pet
An Mammy's hen.

Remember 'Lainey? On the swing? Come on. You remember.

ELAINE. I don't remember anything.

ROBERT. Of course you do. Up the Cathkin Braes on a Sunday. 'Swing high, Daddy. Higher.' And up we went. Just you and me.

ELAINE. I don't remember.

ROBERT. Let me out, Elaine.

ELAINE. No.

ROBERT. There's a terrible smell in here.

ELAINE. Good.

ROBERT. Rot. Some kind of rot. Like . . . dead mouse.

ELAINE. Maybe there is a dead mouse. Place has never been cleaned.

ROBERT. And you're a clean girl aren't you? You like things clean.

ELAINE. Yes I do.

ROBERT. My nice clean girl. Honest and straight, that's my girl. No sides. No behind the back dirty dealing. Eh, Elaine?

ELAINE. So?

ROBERT. So. How you going to square this one up? Eh? I'd like to hear that? Locked your Da in the coal shed. The stinking coal shed. For why? For a joke? Ha ha. Kicked him an all? Not so funny joke. You know how it'll look, don't you?

ELAINE. I don't care.

ROBERT. It'll look like revenge.

ELAINE. It's not revenge.

ROBERT. Revenge for the times YOU sat here.

ELAINE. It's not revenge.

ROBERT. In the dark. And you were afraid of the dark, weren't you, 'Lainey?

ELAINE. I'm not afraid of the dark.

ROBERT. No? You were.

ELAINE. I like the dark.

ROBERT. First thing you did when you got out was jump straight into a bath. Scrub yourself clean.

ELAINE. There's comfort in the dark.

ROBERT. Comfort in it? You might be right.

ELAINE. And I like the smell of coal.

ROBERT. There's none of that here. No honest black coal. Dead something. That's what there is now. Dead something. Puppy maybe.

ELAINE *thumps the door of the coal shed.*

ROBERT. Maybe not. Maybe it's mouse.

ELAINE. You didn't even give her a proper funeral.

ROBERT. The puppy?

ELAINE. Don't act smart. My mother. I'm talking about my mother.

ROBERT. She was my wife.

ELAINE. A rotten cardboard box.

ROBERT. She was a rotten wife.

ELAINE. You're a mean old bastard.

ROBERT. Not at all.

ELAINE. You are so.

ROBERT. Your mother was an environmentalist, Elaine. Never out of bloody bottle banks and recycling dumps. She would've been happy with the cardboard box.

ELAINE. You never even told anybody she was dead.

ROBERT. I told you.

ELAINE. This morning. When I got here.

ROBERT. I told Stephen.

ELAINE. Was it the money? Were you scared people would be looking for a meal. Or a drink.

ROBERT. Tut tut. Now now. They don't cost nothing these cardboard coffins, you know.

ELAINE. Bloody cheapest thing you could get.

ROBERT. Not by a long chalk. There were at least two cheaper – not to mention the recyclable bag.

ELAINE. Even you wouldn't have buried her in a bin bag.

ROBERT. It's not a bin bag. It's a highly sophisticated piece of modern technology. Biodegrades in rhythm with Mother Nature. And I would've but they were out of stock. They're very popular you know. All the rage. But it was going to take two weeks to order another one. Couldn't have her hanging about the place for two weeks.

ELAINE. You're disgusting.

ROBERT. Not that you'd have noticed any difference. Your mother has been silent for so long now that sometimes I forgot she was there. But two weeks. She would've went off. And you know me, Elaine, I canny abide bad meat.

ELAINE. You'd think. This once. You might have not let her down.

ROBERT. Aye.

ELAINE. You might have done this one thing properly.

ROBERT. She did like things done properly. Didn't she?

ELAINE. What's wrong with that?

ROBERT. So do it then.

ELAINE. What?

ROBERT. Whatever you're going to do. Do it properly and get it by.

ELAINE. Aye you'd like that, wouldn't you? Short sharp shock. Well, I don't think I will. I've no made up my mind, mark you, but I think I'll let you sweat it out a bit.

ROBERT. Smacks of petty revenge. I always thought you were capable of greater things. I hate to see you petty. Your mother was petty.

ELAINE. She was not.

ROBERT. Oh Christ, Elaine. She counted the bloody toast. There I'd be. Dipping my toast in my egg. And I'd reach for another bit. Just to mop it up. 'Two,' she'd say. 'That's your second slice.' And even when I told her to belt up she'd still mouth it. Couldny even get peace to eat my breakfast.

ELAINE. Your fault. Your fault. You always took more than your fair share. We'd have had nothing if she hadn't counted it.

ROBERT. So you remember something then?

ELAINE. . . .

ROBERT. She wouldn't have been happy about this.

ELAINE. Happy? She's delirious. Can you not hear her?

STEPHEN *comes back with tea.*

ELAINE (*loud*). Oh a cup of tea. Lovely.

STEPHEN. What?

She nudges him.

ELAINE. And toasted cheese and tomato.

There's no toast.

I bet he'd like some.

STEPHEN. D'you think so?

ELAINE. Would you like some toasted cheese Father?

ROBERT. Piss off.

ELAINE. He doesn't want any.

ROBERT. You haven't got any.

ELAINE. 'Course we have and we're going to eat it while you
sit in there and think about your actions.

ROBERT. Liar.

ELAINE. And then, when you're ready, you can come in and
apologise and we'll say no more about it. Are you ready to
apologise?

ROBERT. . . .

ELAINE. I don't hear you.

ROBERT. I AM sorry.

> ELAINE *and* STEPHEN *don't expect this.* STEPHEN *makes
> a move towards the shed.* ELAINE *holds him back.*

ELAINE. Say that again.

ROBERT. I never made you say it twice.

ELAINE. But you made me explain what . . . For what?

ROBERT. What?

ELAINE. What are you sorry for?

ROBERT. That all my efforts to turn you two into decent human
beings were obviously wasted. You're useless. And I had
such hopes. Especially you, Elaine.

ELAINE. You're sick.

ROBERT. I'm telling you. There is nothing more disappointing
in this life than watching your children fail. Naw. That's no
quite true. Sex with your mother. Now there was/

STEPHEN. Shutup.

> *He bangs on the shed.*

STEPHEN. You better shutup. How come, even when he's in
there. Even when he's . . . how can we shut his mouth? I
want to shut him up.

ELAINE. Shut him up then.

STEPHEN. Shut his mouth.

ELAINE. Stick it shut.

STEPHEN. Well and truly.

ELAINE. Shut.

STEPHEN. For good.

ELAINE. Stuck.

STEPHEN. Shut.

ELAINE. Right.

STEPHEN. Right.

She goes out.

ROBERT. This was her idea, wasn't it, son?

STEPHEN. . . .

ROBERT. You would never have done this yourself.

STEPHEN. . . .

ROBERT. She talked you into it, didn't she?

STEPHEN. . . .

ROBERT. She can be very persuasive.

STEPHEN. . . .

ROBERT. But she'll leave you to carry the can. Always did.

STEPHEN. How come you never saw that before? How come I
    was always the one that got belted while she got a hug?

ROBERT. She had me twisted round her wee finger. You saw
    that. Besides. I don't hold wi hitting women.

STEPHEN. . . .

ROBERT. If you open the door I won't do anything.

STEPHEN. No.

ROBERT. I'll just slip off.

STEPHEN. No.

ROBERT. You can tell her I overpowered you.

STEPHEN. No.

ROBERT. Whatever you like. Make something up.

STEPHEN. I can't.

ROBERT. Naw. Right enough. You never had an original idea in that thick skull of yours. Did you son?

STEPHEN. So you say.

ROBERT. Take after your mother. Always have. Weak genes.

STEPHEN. Shut it.

ROBERT. Do you not want to talk about your mother?

STEPHEN. I mean it.

ROBERT. She was a beautiful woman. Was she not?

STEPHEN. . . .

ROBERT. Ah. How would you know? You never saw the best of her. When I first met her she was . . . a wee cracker. God she was brilliant. Her eyes shone and her cheeks glowed. She was perfect to hold. Soft and round in all the right places.

STEPHEN. . . .

ROBERT. Not like women these days. Aw thin and pointy. Melt right into her, you could.

STEPHEN. . . .

ROBERT. You loved it, when you were a wean. Couldny get you off her. Suck her to death, you would've.

STEPHEN. . . .

ROBERT. Even after the milk dried up.

STEPHEN. . . .

ROBERT. Are the tears tripping you yet?

STEPHEN. You're a bastard.

ROBERT. So your sister tells me.

STEPHEN. She's grieving.

ROBERT. We're all grieving, son.

STEPHEN. We've just lost our mother.

ROBERT. And I've just lost my new found freedom. I had plans you know.

STEPHEN. I'm sure you did.

ROBERT. How long are you going to keep me in here?

STEPHEN. Till you rot.

ROBERT. Elaine'll never go through with it.

STEPHEN. Elaine hates you.

ROBERT. Nah. She's just annoyed. She'll come round.

STEPHEN. Even more than I hate you.

ROBERT. It's temporary. Elaine knows I loved her.

STEPHEN. There was nothing to love.

ROBERT. That's why she's stronger than you.

STEPHEN. Nothing.

ROBERT. And weaker. In my hands.

STEPHEN. Don't be so sure. She'll never forgive you for today.

ROBERT. There have been worse days.

STEPHEN. We're finished with you. Both of us.

ROBERT. Liar. If you were finished with me you wouldn't have shut me up in here. But here I am. If you were finished with me you would be gone. But here you are. You are stuck.

STEPHEN. We can go any time.

ROBERT. I can go at any time.

STEPHEN. No. You are stuck.

ROBERT. I can get out of here any time I like. The game is no when. The game is how.

ELAINE *comes back with a roll of tape.* ROBERT *hears her.*

ROBERT. And don't let Elaine find you weeping. She canny abide it either. Tears. Sentimentality.

ELAINE *signals shh.*

ROBERT. She's never shown me one moment of sympathy. Ma whole life. She's hard.

STEPHEN. She's not hard. She's hurt.

ROBERT. Is that what she says? Hurt? Naw. Naw. I was in the army son. I met a lot of hurt men. Met a lot of hard men. None of them as hard as her.

STEPHEN. If you hurt people often enough they toughen up.

ROBERT. What happened to you then? How is it you're still soft?

STEPHEN. I'm not soft.

ROBERT. You must be joking. You're plasticine, son.

STEPHEN. If you say so.

ROBERT. I've a tin full of tenners says so.

STEPHEN. ?

ROBERT. Can you guess where I got them? Stevie boy?

STEPHEN. . . .

ROBERT. Och aye, the penny drops. I can hear it. Clunk. You guessed it. I got them from your mother. Courtesy of your good self.

STEPHEN. I don't believe you.

ROBERT. Aye, you'll like this, Elaine.

ELAINE. . . .

STEPHEN. My mother wouldn't have done that to me.

ROBERT. She did what she was told.

STEPHEN. She wouldn't.

ROBERT. She said, 'Stephen, I hate to ask you. I know you're no well off.'

STEPHEN. You . . .

ROBERT. Have I got it right so far? Word perfect?

ELAINE. You gave him money?

STEPHEN. I gave HER money.

ROBERT. And she gave it to me. I've still got it. In a tin. A wee fortune.

ELAINE. Aw Stephen.

STEPHEN. You're lying. She wouldn't have kept taking it.

ROBERT. She had no choice.

ELAINE. You should have known.

ROBERT. Don't be too hard on him, Elaine. I do need the money. No work way out here. No big pension. And him nothing but a big sooky wean. A big sooky wean that loved his mammy. Had to be dragged to school every day. Waa waaa. Eh son?

STEPHEN. It's my turn.

ROBERT. How come you've no weans, Stephen? You and that Holly? Yous are getting on a bit. Leaving it late. Bit thin and pointy for ma taste, that Holly. Bet she's the boss, eh? If she wanted weans you'd have them. Am I right? Maybe no. Ho. Stephen. Trouble in the willy department? Is that it? No hard enough? Plasticine willy an all?

STEPHEN *strides to the shed and pulls open the door.* ROBERT *is standing right there, looking at him.*

ROBERT. Please don't hurt me. I beg you.

STEPHEN. Shutup.

ROBERT. Make me. Make me.

STEPHEN. I'm your son.

ROBERT. I know. (*To* ELAINE.) He's waiting here for the chance to forgive me. Did you know that? If I put my arms around him and tell him I'm sorry, truly sorry, he'll forgive me. After aw the beatings and bad mouthing, aw the nights he spent in this crap hole of a shed. He's prepared to forgive me. He might even forget. Can you believe that? Five minutes from now he could be saying 'My father belted me but it never did me any harm.' Don't you find that amazing? Bloody amazing. Would you forgive me Elaine?

ELAINE. Fuck off.

ROBERT. See. Do you see that son? And do you know what? It's her forgiveness I want. I don't give a toss about yours. I'm sorry. But I don't. I couldn't give a tuppenny damn whether you forgave me or not. In fact, I'd rather you didny.

STEPHEN *punches him in the stomach. Not that hard. And shuts the door. He's shaking.*

STEPHEN. What? What are you looking at me like that for?

ELAINE. I don't understand why you care.

STEPHEN. I can't help it.

ELAINE. But he treats you . . . worse than a dog.

STEPHEN. All I wanted from him . . . I wanted him to love me. Why can he not love me? Am I not good enough?

ELAINE. It's just him. He's an animal. If he thinks you're weak he has to prey on you. You can't be weak.

STEPHEN. But I'm not. Out there. I'm as tough as the rest of them. Really.

ELAINE. You were never tough, Stephen.

STEPHEN. I am.

ELAINE. You work in a library for Christsake.

STEPHEN. Oh what? That's not tough enough?

ELAINE. I didn't say that.

STEPHEN. You think because you work in a fancy office with consultants that you've cornered the market on toughness?

ELAINE. I run that office.

STEPHEN. You see. That matters to you. You run it. You're as bad as him sometimes.

ELAINE. Don't. This is what he wants. You and I to fight. Don't give it to him.

STEPHEN. I don't know what he wants. What do you want Dad? What do you really want?

ELAINE. Stephen, don't. Don't let him do this to you. Here. I'm going to tape his mouth. That'll shut him up. Give me a hand.

STEPHEN. Not before he tells me.

STEPHEN *opens the door of the shed once again.*

STEPHEN. What is it you want?

ROBERT. Shut the door.

STEPHEN. What is it you want from me?

ROBERT. Shut the fucking door.

STEPHEN. No. In fact. You can walk out it if you like.

ELAINE. Stephen.

ROBERT. Is that right Elaine. Can I go?

STEPHEN. I said you can go.

ROBERT. Elaine?

ELAINE. Answer him.

ROBERT. What?

ELAINE. Tell him what you want from him so he can stop turning himself inside out trying to be it.

ROBERT. It's pathetic.

ELAINE. Tell him.

STEPHEN. Tell me.

ROBERT. I canny.

STEPHEN. Tell me.

ROBERT. There's nothing to tell. I want nothing from you.

STEPHEN. That's a lie. Nothing I ever did was good enough. That's why you loved her.

ROBERT. Naw. Nothing you did was good enough because you were you. I don't like you.

STEPHEN. That's it?

ROBERT. I never did.

STEPHEN. You mean it didn't matter what I did?

ROBERT. Naw. I tried to tell you. But you kept coming back, like a wee puppy dug. It just annoyed me.

STEPHEN. But why d'you not like me?

ROBERT. Who knows?

STEPHEN. And I'm supposed to just live with that? Could you not try?

ROBERT. Elaine. For Jesus sake, this is pathetic, hen.

ELAINE. Let him finish.

ROBERT. He'll just get worse. I'll end up hurting him.

STEPHEN. Let me finish. What about Mum?

ROBERT. She loved you.

STEPHEN. No. I mean, did you love Mum?

ROBERT. I don't need to answer that, do I?

ELAINE. I think you should.

ROBERT. I don't know. I don't know what it means. I lived wi her. I slept wi her. Wasny always brilliant but it was enough. Did I love her? I don't know. She was a bit thick. Like you, son.

STEPHEN. I'm not thick. I've got a brain.

ROBERT. Naw, naw. Thick - as in slow moving lava. Painful to watch, sometimes. Predictable.

STEPHEN. And that's it? That's what I've got to take away from here? That. And I can't change that.

ROBERT. Here's progress.

STEPHEN. Well, it's your loss.

ROBERT. I won't feel it.

STEPHEN *walks away from the shed leaving the door open.*

ROBERT. Shut the door.

ELAINE. Happy now? Is that what you wanted? You made him say it, didn't you?

STEPHEN. Why don't YOU have any children, Elaine?

ELAINE. What?

STEPHEN. I know why I haven't got any. Because I'm too scared. Too scared that I'll turn out like him. But why haven't you?

ELAINE. I've no partner. You know that.

STEPHEN. You don't need one.

ELAINE. I have no lover.

STEPHEN. Why?

ELAINE. I don't know. Haven't found the right one I don't suppose.

STEPHEN. Really?

ELAINE. Stephen? It's not my fault. It's him. Don't blame it on me.

STEPHEN. Doesn't it worry you that he does love you?

ELAINE. He doesn't love anybody except himself.

STEPHEN. I'm going home.

ELAINE. But we're not finished.

STEPHEN. I'm finished. Well and truly. I'm going home.

ELAINE. What about him?

STEPHEN. What about him?

ELAINE. We can't just leave him there.

STEPHEN. You do what you like. I'm off.

ELAINE. That's not fair. We put him in there together. We should see it through together.

STEPHEN. Didn't you hear him? There is no us. There is only you.

ELAINE. That's him. Not me.

STEPHEN. I can't do anything. You saw that. I have no power. You do what you have to.

ELAINE. Don't let him win now, Stephen. We've always seen it through because we were a team. Us against him. Don't let him win.

STEPHEN. You're kidding yourself on, Elaine.

ELAINE. I'm not.

STEPHEN. You fight him if you want. But understand that it's because you want to.

ELAINE. What do you mean?

STEPHEN. Has it ever occurred to you that maybe he's the only thing we've got in common? That if it wasn't for him there wouldn't be an us?

ELAINE. That's a lie. Come on. We have fun.

STEPHEN. When? What fun?

ELAINE. We have a laugh.

STEPHEN. WE don't have a laugh. You say very witty things about how stupid the man in the street is, how easy he is to con and I laugh because I'm glad it's not me you're talking about.

ELAINE. Stephen?

STEPHEN. You know what I think?

ELAINE. Those are funny stories. Everybody's got a funny story. You do it too.

STEPHEN. But you sound like him.

ELAINE. What?

STEPHEN. When you're telling your stories I see him – him belittling us – not you, never you – me and Mum. Making a fool of us.

ELAINE. They are just funny stories.

STEPHEN. It's what I see.

ELAINE. Why did you never tell me?

STEPHEN. I didn't know. It's only now I see you here. Still wanting to beat him. You can't walk away from it. Can you?

ELAINE. He deserves it.

STEPHEN. You enjoy it. Nobody else can beat you. Can they? You've tried and nobody comes up to quite his standard.

ELAINE. I have to beat him because he's wrong.

STEPHEN. Still?

ELAINE. If I don't fight him it means that what he did . . . to you . . . to Mum . . . it's all O.K. He can't get away with thinking it's O.K.

STEPHEN. It's over. He only does it for you now.

ELAINE. That's a lie. What about this morning? What about that? That was to get at you as well.

STEPHEN. I'm going home.

ELAINE. What does that mean, Stephen?

STEPHEN. It just means I'm going home.

ELAINE. For us? What does it mean for us?

　　STEPHEN *walks away.*

ROBERT. Good riddance to bad rubbish.

ELAINE. Shutup. You miserable old pig.

ROBERT. So. What you gonny do now, 'Lainey?

ELAINE. I'm going home too.

ROBERT. But you're not finished.

ELAINE. I'm finished with you.

ROBERT. You have to let me out.

ELAINE. I don't need to let you out. The door's open.

ROBERT. I need your permission.

ELAINE. Piss off.

ROBERT. I'll stay here till you tell me.

ELAINE. You will not. You're too fond of your dinner.

ROBERT. I will. Your permission is the only thing I want.

ELAINE. I can't.

ROBERT. You can't just walk away from me.

ELAINE. Watch me.

She walks.

ROBERT. You say you don't remember.

ELAINE. I don't.

ROBERT. But you will.

ELAINE. It's too depressing.

ROBERT. Not all of it.

She stops.

ELAINE. You killed my dog.

ROBERT. I hit her too hard. That was all.

She walks.

ROBERT. I love you Elaine.

ELAINE. Fuck off.

ROBERT. You loved me once.

ELAINE. I'm sorry for that.

ROBERT. You don't stop loving somebody.

She stops.

ELAINE. Yes you do.

ROBERT. Naw, hen. You just put it away somewhere till it's safe to bring it out and look at it.

She walks.

ROBERT. It's no for me. The permission. It's for you. It's a gift from me to you.

She stops.

ELAINE. Keep your gift. They always come with a price.

ROBERT. A free gift.

ELAINE. There's no such thing.

She walks.

ROBERT. Your mother then.

ELAINE. What about her?

ROBERT. You loved her. Right?

ELAINE. Of course.

ROBERT. Of course. Some day, when you're really grown up, you'll be able to take an honest look at her. Nobody's perfect.

She stops.

ELAINE. In comparison to you she was a bloody saint.

ROBERT. In comparison to me. But I know you. And come that day when you're pulling her apart and wondering why she didn't do more or how come she let this happen and that happen. That day. You'll start to think.

ELAINE. About what?

ROBERT. About who you are. Are you as good as her? As bad as me?

ELAINE. . . .

ROBERT. I just need your permission.

ELAINE *turns.*

ELAINE. I can't forgive you.

ROBERT. Who's asking?

ELAINE. And I don't want to see you.

ROBERT. Don't look then.

ELAINE. I mean . . . I'm not coming to visit. Don't come and visit me.

ROBERT. I don't go where I'm no wanted.

ELAINE. You're not wanted.

ROBERT. So.

ELAINE. What?

ROBERT. Can I come out?

ELAINE. . . .

ROBERT. Elaine.

ELAINE. Just . . .

ROBERT. Elai/

ELAINE. /Give me a minute. I need a minute.

ROBERT. . . .

ELAINE. Right.

ROBERT. Say the words.

ELAINE. . . .

ROBERT. Say it.

ELAINE. Come out then.

   Black.

   End.

LAZYBED

Iain Crichton Smith

Iain Crichton Smith was born in Glasgow in 1928 and brought up on the Isle of Lewis. He is one of Scotland's leading writers, in both English and Gaelic. He taught English in schools from 1955 to 1977, after which he devoted himself full time to writing. His plays include *Lazybed* (Traverse) and *Columcille* (Stray Theatre Company).

Publications include several collections of poetry and short stories; his novels include *Consider the Lilies* and *An Honourable Death*.

His honours include an OBE, FRLS, and Honorary Doctorates from the Universities of Dundee, Glasgow and Aberdeen. He lives in Argyll and is currently under commission to the Traverse and Tosg, Scotland's Gaelic Theatre Company.

Lazybed was first performed at the Traverse Theatre, Edinburgh, on 10 October 1997, with the following cast:

MOTHER	Ann Scott-Jones
NEIGHBOUR	Anna Mhoireach
MURDO	Iain Macrae
INSURANCE MAN	Callum Cuthbertson
MINISTER	Tony Kearney
BROTHER	Tony Kearney
DEATH	Alexander West
SPECIALIST	Callum Cuthbertson
JUDITH	Iona Carbarns
IMMANUEL KANT	Ann Scott-Jones

Directed by   Philip Howard
Designed by   Evelyn Barbour
Lighting designed by   Renny Robertson
Music composed and performed by   Anna Mhoireach

A room. A man lying in bed.

MOTHER. There he is, in his bed.

NEIGHBOUR. Should we not be speaking quietly?

MURDO. Not at all, gossip away.

NEIGHBOUR. How strange. And you say there's nothing . . .

MOTHER. There's nothing wrong with him. He took to his bed a week ago.

MURDO. There's nothing wrong with me except metaphysically. Otherwise I am as sound as a bell or a tinkling cymbal.

NEIGHBOUR. Did he say physically?

MOTHER. No, there's nothing wrong with him physically.

NEIGHBOUR. Why is he in bed then?

MOTHER. He says, I don't understand it, that there's no point in getting up.

NEIGHBOUR. What?

MURDO. That's it. The day of the spade is finished. That is my discovery. Others have discovered the Internet. My discovery is the vanity of the spade.

NEIGHBOUR (*ignoring him*). Is he just lazy then?

MURDO. I've just told you I'm not lazy. I've explained to you. Why don't you listen, you contingent creature. The spade and the graip are finished. And the hoe and the harrow.

NEIGHBOUR. He goes to the bathroom, doesn't he?

MURDO. Of course I go to the bathroom. The body still hangs about.

NEIGHBOUR. And he takes his food?

MOTHER. Oh, yes.

MURDO. Why don't you address your questions to me instead of through an intermediary. I know the earth has been displaced from its privileged position. Nevertheless I am here in the flesh, as you can see.

NEIGHBOUR (*ignoring him*). And he eats?

MOTHER. I bring him his food though he never ate much. Even before this happened.

NEIGHBOUR. I think this is scandalous.

MURDO. And of course it will be your mission in life to tell everybody. Naturally.

NEIGHBOUR. That your mother has to bring you your food!

MURDO. She doesn't have to do it.

NEIGHBOUR. What do you mean?

MURDO. She could take to her bed as well but then she doesn't suffer metaphysically. And so could you instead of nosing about. We could all take to our beds. Certainly that will come as time passes.

NEIGHBOUR. Are you insulting me?

MURDO. Not as exquisitely as I would like. No, I think the day will come when everybody will take to their beds.

NEIGHBOUR. Then nothing would be done at all.

MURDO. Quite right. There would be no wars, no Scottish dance music, no ceilidhs and no-one taking anything on board. There's no end to what wouldn't be done.

NEIGHBOUR (*to* MOTHER). How old is he?

MURDO. Why don't you ask me directly? I'm thirty-nine years old and a great reader of Beckett and Kafka and other such reclining people. And of course I liked the Russians before they disintegrated. I have worked hard as a crofter. And then I had a vision. I could see no point in my work. My foot moved away from the spade. It froze in mid air.

MOTHER. He did work hard.

MURDO. Then just like a clock I stopped.

NEIGHBOUR. I don't understand it. If he's not ill why is he in bed?

MURDO *takes out a bell and rings it.*

NEIGHBOUR. What's that?

MOTHER. He rings that when an interview is at an end.

MURDO. I call it Timor Mortis Conturbat Me.

NEIGHBOUR (*gets up angrily and goes out*). I don't call that polite.

MURDO. Neither do I. (*Gazes after her.*) A simple and angular woman.

MOTHER *goes to see the* NEIGHBOUR *out. Comes back in.*

MURDO. What are you doing today mother? Nothing strenuous, I hope.

MOTHER. I have to tidy up the garden.

She goes.

MURDO. So what does she do? She weeds the garden. Then after a while the weeds grow and she weeds it again. And this goes on all the time. Maybe instead of weeding she should be reading, adding to her knowledge. But then perhaps the weeds would grow so high that we wouldn't be able to look out the window or see the road, and the postman wouldn't be able to find the letterbox. Not that we get many letters.

(*Thoughtfully.*) It's as if I'm chained to my bed. One minute I was digging happily and the next I came to a stop.

Knock on the door.

VOICE OF INSURANCE MAN. Anyone in?

MURDO. No there isn't. Go away.

INSURANCE MAN. I'm selling insurance. Can I come in?

MURDO. Certainly not.

INSURANCE MAN. I can give you excellent rates on life insurance.

MURDO. I told you, go away. You are the last person I want to see.

INSURANCE MAN. O.K. then but you're missing a great opportunity. Our spring bargains. I'll come back when you are in a better mood.

MURDO. Not on your life. Or your life insurance. Clear off. There he is, so enthusiastic, selling insurance. He gets up in the morning and he looks at his pimply face in the glass, and he thinks, 'I am going to sell insurance today'. And he loves it. How does he do it? How does he convince himself? How does he have the energy? Of course he might be able to insure me against working. But that can't happen, ever since our expulsion from the Garden of Eden, or so they say. When Adam and Eve left Paradise the accountant and insurance agent and lawyer were created, and they sold services to those who were once happy in a garden. For work came then, and shortly afterwards Death.

Pause.

My mother doesn't know this but Florence Nightingale spent a lot of her time in bed after she gave up nursing. The Lady with the Lamp. The Lady with the Limp. The Lady with the Lump. She would fire off missives to the War Office from her bed. That's true, absolutely true, not a word of a lie.

Phone rings.

That will be my revered auntie wondering how I am. On the other hand it might not be her at all. It might be a Malayan or a small South Korean. Phoning from a rice paddy somewhere in Asia, his back bent with toil. A miniature digger of the soil as I was, erstwhile, myself.

Phone rings.

Whoever it is expects an answer. But why should I answer it? Ring on, you intrusive bugger.

The phone stops ringing. MURDO *sits up in bed.*

Not a lot of life around here. Not much stirring. But the clock ticks on.

He picks up the clock and listens to it.

The mystery of time. Who can solve it? Only the Readers' Digest.

He switches on the radio.

VOICE OF ANNOUNCER. Roderick MacDougall in second place with one hundred and eighty points. The adjudicator commented favourably on his expression. In third place was Hector MacDonald of Kilmarnock. Hector learnt his Gaelic from his Harris grandmother who is, alas, now dead.

MURDO. The bloody Mod. Held this year in Kilmarnock. In riveting Kilmarnock, home of Gaelic.

He switches off the radio. He lies in his bed, hands behind his head. He twitches his toes for a while. These can be seen beyond blankets.

Physically I'm in good shape. It's metaphysically that I don't know my shape. My toes are in good health. No, it was the central engine that went, that ceased to function. Impotence of the will, that's what I've got.

MOTHER *comes in; her hands are dirty.*

MOTHER. Do you want tea?

MURDO. If you do. Are you tired?

MOTHER. There are a lot of weeds.

She goes.

MURDO. Each with its own life. Determined. Resolute. I am me. I may not be a beautiful flower, but I am me. I will not be put upon.

Pause.

No I am not lazy. I literally can't operate a spade, I am paralysed in front of graips as well. Actually, my mother doesn't have to weed if she doesn't want to.

MOTHER *comes in with a tray with tea and biscuits on it.*

MURDO. Are you tired of my being in bed and munching Kit-Kats?

MOTHER. Well, people are talking about you.

MURDO. What are they saying? As if I didn't know.

MOTHER. They're saying that you're lazy. Either that or you're mental. We never had anything like this in the family before.

MURDO. Maybe we had worse, who knows. Still, our family has never been a metaphysical one. It has been straight-forwardly peasant. It never sat down in a furrow and asked itself about the meaning of things.

MOTHER. You could sit up and watch TV. People would understand if you watched TV.

MURDO. I hate TV. You know that.

MOTHER. Well . . . you could go for a walk.

MURDO. No, you don't understand. I can't do anything. I have, however, given in to you on one thing. I do shave. Imagine if I had a long beard like Robinson Crusoe.

MOTHER. You certainly will not grow a beard. Are you trying to shame me completely.

She takes the tray.

I have to go. I can't sit here all day.

She goes.

MURDO (*thinks aloud*). It would be a long beard. Down to the foot of the bed. Like Freud. A Highland Freud. How is your id today Mrs MacLeod? And your superego, is it as inflexible as ever? How about Deep Heat for it? Eh?

VOICE. Murdo.

MURDO (*sits up*). Who's that? Who's that?

VOICE. You may call me what you like. The devil maybe.

MURDO. You can't be the devil. I'm an atheist. What do you want?

VOICE. The devil finds work for idle hands. You say you don't believe in God.

MURDO. No I don't.

VOICE. Even I believe in God. Why don't you?

MURDO. There is too much sorrow in the world. Too much pain. Anyway you rebelled against God yourself.

VOICE. I did. Actually it was more from boredom.

MURDO. Exactly. That's what I often feel.

VOICE. Everything was too perfect. There was never any rain. Sunshine every day – who can stand it.

MURDO. No that's not the boredom I felt. The land so stony for a start. And there was no-one I could discuss my boredom with. Who here reads Kant?

VOICE. I haven't read him myself. I find him too difficult. I've read *Faust*.

MURDO. Anyway if there's a God why is there so much pain? So much carnage?

VOICE. God blames it on me.

MURDO. Are you responsible then for the deaths of the children?

VOICE. I was acting on orders.

MURDO. It's always the same. Everyone says that. Anyway, I don't believe in you either. Why are you here?

VOICE. I don't suppose you'd noticed that my voice is quite like your own.

MURDO. Clear off.

There's a flash of light and the MINISTER *appears.*

MINISTER. I came straight in to see you. Your mother's in the garden. I don't think she saw me.

He comes in, takes off his hat, sits down.

MURDO. Did you see anything just now?

MINISTER. No.

MURDO. Or hear anything?

MINISTER. No.

MURDO. Or smell anything?

MINISTER. No.

MURDO. That's interesting. How could one not smell sulphur?

MINISTER. I don't understand what you're talking about. Now what's all this?

MURDO. What's all what?

MINISTER. This lying in bed. I'm told there's nothing wrong with you.

MURDO. There is something wrong with me.

MINISTER. Well what is it?

MURDO. Metaphysically there's something wrong with me. I can't get up from my bed.

MINISTER. What on earth are you talking about?

MURDO. I've just told you. Actually it has to do with earth. I can't turn it.

MINISTER. Do you read the Bible?

MURDO. Not a lot.

MINISTER. Well if you read the Bible you would find in Genesis that Adam and Eve were put out of the garden for the sin of disobedience. And thereafter they and we have had to earn our living by the sweat of our brow. After the Fall everyone has to work.

MURDO. Do you have to work after the Fall?

MINISTER. I do work. My task is to save souls and preach the Word.

MURDO. To women with nice hats and suitable hair styles. My work was hard and physical. When did you work with a spade? It's easy enough to write a sermon which avoids all the real questions. And the people here treat you like a God. I've seen your photograph on the walls of their bedrooms and their living rooms.

MINISTER. My work is spiritual and mental.

MURDO. Anyway this is a pointless argument. The fact is that I see no reason for work. Indeed for anything we do. There is no purpose.

MINISTER. The purpose is the Kingdom of God. And anyway what of your mother? She's working in the garden. I didn't think she looked well.

MURDO. That may be the case. All ministers however look well. In the old days they looked gaunt and lined. Thin and Calvinist. Now they look innocent and babyish. And they don't hear the gunfire or the screams. Anyway if you saw my mother working in the garden why didn't you help her?

MINISTER. I haven't the time. I have to visit the sick, of whom you are not one. How old is your mother?

MURDO. She is sixty.

MINISTER. Are you not ashamed to have her work while you lie in your bed?

MURDO. She can go to bed as well if she wishes to. Christ himself let his mother work.

MINISTER. Are you comparing yourself to Christ?

MURDO. Of course not. I was giving you an analogy, a theological analogy, an analogical theology. I was speaking in parables, not to say parabolas.

MINISTER. I think you have delusions of grandeur and that you are a blasphemer. Do you wish me to read a portion of the Bible?

MURDO. Not aloud. Do you wish me to read you a portion of Dostoevsky?

MINISTER. I'm beginning to think you are a limb of Satan. What if everybody in the village took to their beds?

MURDO. That is their choice. Do you know what Pascal wrote? That it is because people will not stay in their own rooms that the disasters of the world have happened. Alexander the Great should have stayed in his own room. And so should Napoleon. And Calvin in his Swiss but and ben.

MINISTER. This is monstrous. You are a real limb of Satan.

MURDO. But which limb? That is debatable. Anyway I never asked you to call. You people seem to think you are welcome everywhere and that you can invade people's privacy with your superficial agenda.

MINISTER. I pity your poor mother.

MURDO. And I pity your mother. Who would have thought that her son would have turned out a dogmatist, and a fundamentalist. Dull, inflexible, unimaginative and intrusive.

MINISTER. I can't listen to any more of this.

MINISTER puts on his hat and stamps out.

MURDO. And good day to you too, sir.

Pause.

I wonder if I should stop shaving and let my beard grow. My mother wouldn't like it. On the other hand she doesn't like me lying in bed either. I must go to the bathroom.

Gets up unsteadily.

Oops, I wonder if my legs will stop functioning eventually. That's a thought. I suppose it's a bit late in the day for shaving. I should have shaved in the morning, not when the shades of night are drawing in.

Goes into the bathroom. Comes out after a while.

When I was young I used to sing in the bathroom. I was so happy. Not any more.

He gets back into bed.

The sunset is upon us. See, there's a cloud in the shape of a trust hospital.

The stage darkens. The moon hangs ahead of him.

The moon of my precious youth. I remember the autumns and the dances on the wooden bridge. Where have they gone, the strip the willows of yesteryear?

The moon suddenly turns into a skull. We hear the noises of the night, the cry of an owl, the sudden screams of cats, rustling.

VOICE. This is Nature red in tooth and claw. And Murdo sleeps on in the protection of his mother. Poor Murdo.

A light picks out MURDO's *face momentarily.*

Oh how calmly Murdo sleeps. Like a child. Like a corpse. Except that now and again he twitches like a mouse below the owl.

Some time passes. Daylight comes up. MURDO *rubs his eyes, sits up in bed. He looks and listens for a while. Then he takes out a pair of field glasses. He looks through a window ahead of him.*

MURDO. Seagulls. I thought I'd have seen a squire seducing a simple maiden. Or a maiden seducing a simple squire. But no. I see rabbits chasing each other while a cat looks on. And a buzzard sitting on a fence. In the olden days there were contented peasants scratching their backsides.

Door opens suddenly and a man comes in like a whirlwind. This is Murdo's BROTHER.

BROTHER. What's this? What's this I hear, eh?

MURDO (*puts down the binoculars*). I don't know what you hear my dear brother.

His BROTHER *is in perpetual motion.*

BROTHER. Get up out of that bed.

He tries to haul him out of bed but MURDO *clings to the headboard.*

MURDO. It's no good. I've got the strength of the effete.

BROTHER. What's all this about? (*Looks at his watch.*) I can't wait here long. I should be on the building site already.

MURDO. Still building houses eh?

BROTHER. That's not the point. The point is, why are you in bed? It's a beautiful May morning. There's nothing wrong with you.

MURDO. There is something wrong with me. Why are you in such a hurry?

BROTHER. I have work to do. These houses have to be finished in a week's time.

MURDO. Why?

BROTHER. Why? What do you mean why? People have to have houses.

MURDO. And then what?

BROTHER. What are you talking about? They have to have houses. That's what.

MURDO. And then they'll sit in them and watch TV and pass the time.

BROTHER. I don't know what you're talking about. But then you were always odd. Reading books at the peatbank. I was the one who had to cut the peats. You were useless. What does mother think of this?

MURDO. Not a lot.

BROTHER. It's disgraceful. A fully grown man with nothing wrong with him lying in bed. Father would have killed you.

MURDO. Well, where is he now after all his busy-ness. And where will you be after all your busy-ness. You're dashing through life at a tremendous pace. You'll fall down and look up at the sky as father did. And there will be a look of surprise on your face but not on the face of the sky.

BROTHER. I think you're a nutcase. It comes from reading all those books. And in any case you're depending on mother.

MURDO. You don't understand, I'm really ill. I can't move from my bed.

BROTHER. I think you're a selfish bugger. (*Looks at his watch*.) Anyway I can't stay. I have work to do. You always were an idiot.

He goes.

MURDO. Why he's like a whirlwind. What energy! How astonishing. Am I really a selfish bugger? All I know is I can't face the spade. It has broken in my hands. Sceptre and spade must tumble down. Spectre and shade must tumble down. Would it be a great danger to the village if everyone took to their beds? But why shouldn't they? What is their reason for getting up in the morning? It is harder and harder to get up. And yet people used to get up at five a.m. and think nothing of walking twenty miles. Sometimes with a boll of meal on their shoulders. And they would have thirteen or fourteen children, sometimes more. What energy. I have written my will. Here is an excerpt from it.

To whomsoever it may concern. If anyone can tell me why we're alive I'll give him two pounds. All my own money.

When we were young we were created of flesh and lightning. And in the fullness of time the flesh and the lightning grew old. And also we are working in a world without meaning.

Yesterday I looked at an egg and I couldn't understand why it was in the place that it was.

And the same could be said about Bovril. And salt. And Sanatogen. We cannot do without some belief. And that is our tragedy.

DEATH *dances in with his scythe. He parks it carefully against the foot of the bed.* MURDO *gets his toes out of the way.*

MURDO. Hey, watch what you're doing.

DEATH. You were thinking of me and here I am.

MURDO. And here you are, as you say.

DEATH. On a fine May morning. I think you were thinking how successful I am.

MURDO. Yes, you're the most successful of the lot of us these days.

DEATH *does a little dance.*

DEATH. Without being particularly proud, Murdo, I know you are right. This is an especially good time for me. I am happy as the flowers in May which is, indeed, the month we are in. Even Death feels happy in the spring. The air is warmer. The world has a holiday atmosphere. I feel as if I'm back in the Middle Ages again.

He does another dance, clutching his scythe like a guitar.

DEATH. In May in glorious May
Death feels fresh and free
O what a fine day
He says to bush and tree.

In May in glorious May
Death feels fresh and gay
And dances in the clay
And sings a roundelay.

O Death is like yourself
He'll even shed a tear.
Sociable is Death
In a cheerful atmosphere.

MURDO. What a brisk sunny fellow you are.

DEATH. And here you are lying in bed. Did you think you'd
escape me?

MURDO. I'd like to kick you, that's what I think I'd like to do.

DEATH. That wouldn't be any good. I'm a happy fellow really.
The successful are always happy. You, on the other hand, are
very unhappy. I can always tell.

Pause.

Your father, I think, is one of mine.

MURDO. Yes, he died of a stroke.

DEATH. Not a stylish way to go. Some die stylishly, e.g. Charles
the Second. He had a little soundbite for the newspapers of
the day. Anyway your father's time had come. He worked
from morning to night or to put it more poetically from morn
to dewy eve.

MURDO. He was trying to lift a huge stone. A ridiculous death.

DEATH. He didn't have much time for you. You were the
clumsy aesthetic one. You hated the spade. And yet the spade
has its uses as I should know. And so you buried yourself in
books. You drew them over your head. Was my daylight too
bright for you? Anyway why should I be here insulting you
when I have so much to do?

DEATH *does another little dance, puffs his chest.*

The scythe is my guitar
My sun my guiding star
Below my scythe and spade
All things grow and fade.

MURDO. You are a smug bastard.

DEATH. Murdo, au revoir
I'm off to peace and war
My scythe like the curving moon
Plays its necessary tune.

There is maybe medieval music. Pause. Lights go down, come up again. The curtains are right round MURDO's *bed. His* MOTHER *in a flowery dress comes in. She sweeps the floor. She gives the impression of not being well. Stops as if she feels dizzy. Clutches at her heart. The* NEIGHBOUR *enters. She looks at the bed with the closed curtains.* MOTHER *stops sweeping the floor.*

NEIGHBOUR. You're busy.

MOTHER. Yes, I'm expecting someone.

NEIGHBOUR. Oh. Do I know who it is?

MOTHER. I don't think so.

Silence.

NEIGHBOUR. And is there an improvement? (*Nodding towards the bed.*)

MOTHER. No.

NEIGHBOUR. If I may say so you look a bit puffed out.

MOTHER. I'm all right.

NEIGHBOUR. We bring them into the world and we suffer for them. I always thought that he was a sensible person.

MOTHER. He always read. All the books piled up in the attic. You should see the place. I think they turned his mind. His father used to get very impatient with him.

NEIGHBOUR. His father was a real hard worker. Always on the move, just like your other son. I suppose there is really nothing wrong with him.

MOTHER. No there isn't. I should know if there was. He was always very close to me. Far closer than he was to his father whom I used to protect him from.

NEIGHBOUR. I remember the day he had his stroke. Such a great nose bleed. Blood everywhere. All over that big stone . . . He's never thought of marrying?

MOTHER. Who?

NEIGHBOUR. Murdo.

MOTHER. No.

NEIGHBOUR. He's too fond of you. I mean he should be married now. At thirty-nine. A good wife would have got rid of all those books.

Silence.

MOTHER. Yes he was always very close to me. He was a very imaginative child. If only we had had money maybe he could have gone to university. He was always very sensitive. When I was ill it was always him who looked after me. He once told me when he was very young that he had seen a funeral passing and the coffin was red and there were dancers instead of mourners.

NEIGHBOUR. A red coffin?

MOTHER. Of course it was his imagination. He always had a strong imagination.

NEIGHBOUR. Maybe he's got the second sight.

MOTHER. No, nor the first. For a long time he worked peacefully on the croft. And he worked very hard, though sometimes I would find him staring into space. Then one day he said he couldn't work any more. When he tried to raise his foot to work the spade he couldn't. It was as if his leg was paralysed, he said. It wasn't laziness he told me. He used to go on about his father, how he had worked till he dropped.

NEIGHBOUR. All that blood would have upset him. I mean, there was such a lot of it, pints and pints.

MOTHER. Maybe.

NEIGHBOUR. It's strange right enough. Talking about strange things, my mother, when she was very old and sitting in her chair beside the fire, said to me, 'Where will I put my face?' And another time she said, 'The earth is tired of me.' She lived till she was ninety. We used to let her smoke. Silk Cut. One time she put the carpet on fire and she said, 'Isn't that lovely.' Maybe Murdo should see a specialist. An ordinary doctor wouldn't do. He would need a specialist.

MOTHER. The doctor told me that a specialist would come today.

NEIGHBOUR. Is that why you're tidying up? (*Pause.*) I always liked that blue vase. (*Pointing.*)

MOTHER. Yes, it is nice isn't it?

NEIGHBOUR. When are you expecting him? The specialist.

MOTHER. Shortly.

NEIGHBOUR *makes no move to go.*

NEIGHBOUR. Aye, a specialist will cure him right enough.

MOTHER *doesn't answer.*

He'll be coming from the city, I shouldn't wonder.

Silence.

A specialist is not like a G.P. He's got more certificates.

Silence.

It stands to reason that if they do the one thing all the time they should know a lot about it.

Silence.

And here is a green car. What a big car.

SPECIALIST *enters.*

SPECIALIST. What a lovely, lovely day.

NEIGHBOUR. I'd better go and leave you with him.

She goes.

SPECIALIST. You live in a beautiful part of the country, Mrs. Mackay.

MOTHER. Macrae. Mrs. Macrae.

SPECIALIST. So sorry.

MOTHER. Would the gentleman like some tea?

SPECIALIST. No, no, I won't put you to any trouble. We are talking about your son, aren't we?

MOTHER. Yes, sir.

SPECIALIST. He won't leave his bed, I gather.

MOTHER. That's right sir.

SPECIALIST (*looking at his watch*). May is such a beautiful
month. Imagine staying in one's bed on a day like this.
Usually we find these cases in the winter, not in summer,
such a fine money-making time.

MOTHER. Excuse me, sir?

SPECIALIST. Did I say money-making time? How odd. I meant
of course, sunny waking time. The yellow month. Many in
the trust hospitals would be glad of such a day, of such a
landscape. How is the patient? Has he always been like this?

MOTHER. No, he used to work quite hard.

SPECIALIST. A rural yuppie, eh? A conscientious, simple rustic.
A fanatic with the spade. And one day he said, the world has
no meaning in it. And thought he was being original. In the
nineteenth century a discovery like that was new but not
nowadays. Some people are idealists, they don't want to
make money so they stay in bed. But then again can you lie
forever in your bed if you're poor? Madam, why has your
son turned his back on this beautiful meaningless, I mean
meaningful, landscape? Is he a remarkable person! He's not
by any chance a genius?

MOTHER. I don't think so, sir. He's not very practical.

SPECIALIST. On the other hand if he was a genius he wouldn't
be here in this non-profit-making part of the country. He will
in my opinion be a lazy sod and not a genius at all. The fact
is he won't have any money and therefore he is of no medical
interest. I shouldn't be talking and meditating so much. Every
second is a golden coin. I shall have to look at him. My fees,
though not paid by him, are high. Still, you won't have to sell
your house to pay me. (*Laughs.*) Now where is your son?

MOTHER. Over there sir. Behind the curtains.

She leaves.

SPECIALIST *pulls the curtains aside.* MURDO *is lying with
his hands under his head.*

SPECIALIST. And how are you, my middle-aged friend?

MURDO. I'm not your friend particularly.

SPECIALIST. Don't take that tone with me. I'm here to study
your case. Do you have a disease of the mind? It saves time
if you tell me.

MURDO. I don't know that I'd tell you if I had.

SPECIALIST. Well then let me ask you a question. Which is the odd one out in the following: Beethoven, Brahms, Haydn and Shakespeare?

MURDO. Shakespeare, of course.

SPECIALIST. Not at all, Beethoven it is. He was the only one who was deaf.

MURDO. You're insane. You shouldn't be a specialist. You should have a higher position.

SPECIALIST. A palpable hit. Not bad for a rural cud-chewing intelligence. Now, man to man, admit that you're a conman. You're suffering purely from laziness.

MURDO. Man to man, I'm not. It is a metaphysical, not a medical, question. I cannot lift a spade.

SPECIALIST. What nonsense. There is no such thing as metaphysics. There's blood, bones and organs, that's all.

MURDO. Not at all. There is more than that as you well know. But I suppose that people like you feel that your patients would be better off dead. And many feel the same about you, though I don't know you well. Why should you save them you ask, there is no money in them. Where is your Hippocratic Oath then?

SPECIALIST. We don't use it in the private hospitals. There is a certain truth in what you say. Patients are no longer cost-effective. However what I have to find out is whether you're sane or not. And there's no point in asking you directly. What colour is that wall?

MURDO. Green.

SPECIALIST. I reserve my judgement. (*Holding up a mirror to him.*) What do you see there?

MURDO. I see my face. There is a touch of the monkey or the ape about it.

SPECIALIST. That you notice that may be a sign of sanity. On the other hand it may be the opposite. Are you not tired of bed?

MURDO. Not at all. In bed we are born and in bed we die.

SPECIALIST. Hm. I see. Do you shave? Do you use Occam's razor?

MURDO. I use an ordinary razor. Do you yourself shave?

SPECIALIST. Naturally. Specialists must shave. GPs need not. They are generalists and can hide in the undergrowth.

MURDO. So what do you think is wrong with me and can it be cured for love or money?

SPECIALIST. For money certainly. You must take two of these tablets every day. They are a nice colour: I chose it myself. Also they are very cheap.

MURDO. Will they give me back my will to work?

SPECIALIST. I can't say about that but their sale will help the drug company. Their name of course is unpronounceable.

Pause.

MURDO. You have no idea of how to cure me. Cure me of what? Metaphysical absurdity. Maybe you are the patient and I am the doctor. Maybe it is I who am cured. To be cured is to lie in bed and watch the world. Where are you going next in your big car? To bring deceit to someone else?

SPECIALIST *takes out a watch which he dangles in front of him.*

Are you trying to hypnotise me?

SPECIALIST. Watch the watch. It is quite an expensive one. Your eyes are closing, closing. Your hands are on a spade. You are about to dig. Oh my God you cut my foot there.

MURDO. What happened?

SPECIALIST. My imagination was too strong. I thought you cut my foot with the spade.

MURDO. What spade?

SPECIALIST. Never mind. Idiot. (*Hands him a brush.*) Here is a spade. Dig with it.

MURDO (*raises his leg but can't push it down*). No wonder I can't push it. What you have given me is a brush, not a spade. Do you think I'm a fool?

SPECIALIST. Very puzzling. You are an enigma. Or you are very clever. Take the tablets I gave you.

Scribbles on a pad.

MURDO. What are you writing?

SPECIALIST. I am writing that you are perfectly sane but
cunning. You can tell the difference between a spade and a
brush. Your disability pension is stopped from today's date.

MURDO. I don't have a disability pension.

SPECIALIST. You mean you took to your bed without a
disability pension. You really are a fool. In any case loss of
money will make you more metaphysical. Lack of money and
the metaphysical are closely linked. Rich people are never
metaphysical. My job is to cut off any benefits you may be
getting. That way you won't bother the state and you can be
as metaphysical as you like.

Suddenly MURDO *removes the* SPECIALIST's *glasses and
smashes them against the wall.*

MURDO. Get out of here and I hope you smash your car, you
blind shark.

SPECIALIST. You bloody mad man, I hope you die of
schizophrenia.

SPECIALIST *stumbles out.* MURDO *shouts after him.*

MURDO. Do you think the practice of medicine consists in
cutting off benefits? I hope you land in a ditch, upside-down
preferably.

JUDITH *enters.*

Oh hello, Judith. Did you meet a half-blind specialist on your
way in?

JUDITH. There was a stumbling man certainly.

MURDO. Was it my mother who sent for you? She thinks the
cure for all diseases of the mind is marriage.

JUDITH. No it wasn't your mother who sent for me. And I certainly wouldn't marry you if you stayed in bed all the time.

MURDO. Yes, why don't we get married. The groom in bed
with a carnation in his pyjamas.

JUDITH. I saw a man passing when I was coming in. He was
carrying a scythe. Rather odd in May.

MURDO. I know who he is. He is a symbolist.

JUDITH. I really think you should get up. It is not good for you
to be lying in bed.

MURDO. I wish I could get up but I can't. My hands are paralysed.

JUDITH. What nonsense. If that was a specialist what did he say to you?

MURDO. He said I was sane but cunning and that he was going to stop my disability pension.

JUDITH. But you don't have a disability pension do you?

MURDO. Of course I don't.

Pause.

How are your patients these days? I don't suppose you want to take my pulse?

JUDITH. No I don't.

Pause.

Did you hear that other people have been staying in bed as well?

MURDO. Are they imitating me – in bad faith?

JUDITH. I don't know what you mean by bad faith.

MURDO. Well they might just be lazy. They might not be doing it for metaphysical reasons. Anyone can stay in bed, but to stay in bed constructively, that is more difficult. Who are they?

JUDITH. Malcolm MacDonald is one.

MURDO. That fat bigot. If I'm going to have a horizontal following let it be the pure of heart, not fat slobs like Malcolm MacDonald. He can't even spell metaphysical.

JUDITH. Anyway that's what happened. You've started a fashion.

MURDO. Do you think I should take out a patent? After all I am the pioneer.

JUDITH. Really Murdo I don't want to be visiting people who aren't ill. There are plenty of people who are really ill.

His MOTHER *comes in. She looks tired.*

MOTHER. I brought the two of you some coffee. (*She distributes it.*) What did the specialist say to you? He wasn't in a good humour.

MURDO. He said I was sane. I smashed his glasses to prove I was, I hope he crashed his car.

JUDITH. You did what?

MURDO. I smashed his glasses. It gave me great satisfaction. He is a selfish bugger. The trouble with you, Judith, is that you believe that people are more important than money; that's quite old-fashioned.

JUDITH. Look at the unselfish person who's speaking.

MURDO. That doctor was a pure materialist. No sense of the metaphysical at all. Mother, Judith, doesn't want to marry me as long as I lie in bed.

MOTHER. Quite right too.

JUDITH (*to* MOTHER). Are you all right? You're looking pale.

MOTHER. I'm fine.

    JUDITH *gets up*.

JUDITH. I'll have to go.

    JUDITH *goes*.

MOTHER. Well, Murdo, I really don't know what to do with you. I don't understand you and never have but you're my son after all.

    She too goes.

MURDO (*pause*). And so I have my imitators though they don't understand my reasons. In the past we believed in aims and purposes for the human race. Now there are none. We are as random as the Lottery. So where is our energy to come from in order to get up in the morning.

VOICE. Do you know what you're doing, Murdo?

MURDO. I'm doing nothing.

VOICE. Judith is a nice girl, Murdo.

MURDO. I know she is.

VOICE. It isn't good for you to be alone.

MURDO. I thought you were alone. I thought you were the loneliest of us all. From morn to dewy eve you fell and so, eventually, did Eve.

VOICE. You think you're suffering. You don't know what suffering is. You think I'm the Devil. Maybe I'm your conscience. Maybe I won't come back.

MURDO. Goodbye then. (*Takes out his binoculars.*) In the olden days sins were scarlet. They walked about in fire and smoke. You could see them with binoculars. The Devil himself you could see. That buzzard hovering there; in the Middle Ages it might have been an angel. Now the landscape is empty of devils. Good and evil don't accost us on the road or in the field.

VOICE. Of course it may be that you're mad.

MURDO. I thought you said you weren't coming back. (*Pause.*) Did you hear me? Are you there?

No answer.

You must have gone.

Takes out his binoculars again.

That buzzard is diving. Has it seen a rabbit? Nature red in tooth and claw. I'll turn these the other way.

DEATH *comes in.*

MURDO. Why, you're quite small. Why are you here?

DEATH. This time I have a mission. Your mother gave me a cup of coffee. She's very generous. Generosity is the first of virtues. I wish in my line of work I had more opportunity to make use of it. I had a little conversation with your mother. She's a good woman but very puzzled that someone brought up among thistles and sheep should act as you do. Also, she's ill.

MURDO. You are at the bottom of everything. I wonder if the world will ever be rid of you.

DEATH. The world is beautiful because of me. That's the way you should think. Look at these lovely spaces. Who was that pretty girl who left the house?

MURDO. Her name is Judith.

DEATH. A venerable name. A lovely name. A Biblical name.

MURDO. I don't want you to say it.

DEATH. Anyway I have a purpose in coming though also I wished to see you about your metaphysics. Lots of intelligent people take to metaphysics when they are only frightened of me. They talk about ghosts, poltergeists, angels, vampires, but none of these exist. There is only me and my scythe which is, of course, symbolic. People can't stand the bareness without metaphysics. And yet if they look at the world around them it is so beautiful. All the animals, insects, flowers, plants, hills, lochs, mountains. What do they need angels for? Everything is much more straightforward than they think. May, I think, is such a beautiful month.

But I must be getting along. I find this scythe a bit awkward but people expect it of me. I must find a safer logo. I do a lot of walking at this time of year. I'm not quite so busy as I am in the winter so the walking keeps me fit. (*His voice becomes more significant.*) Now, Murdo, you will remember this moment for a long time. It will be the most important moment in your life.

He leans over and looks at MURDO *intently.*

Don't blame me too much. Such things are inevitable.

DEATH *moves quickly away. There's a silence. After a while we see* DEATH *with his arm around Murdo's* MOTHER. *They walk away. There is a sound of faint elegiac music. After a while* DEATH *comes back and pulls* MURDO *out of bed.*

DEATH. Murdo, it is time for you to get up.

There is a struggle but MURDO *stands unsteadily on the floor. The faint music still.*

I'm sorry, Murdo.

DEATH *leaves.* MURDO *stares wildly around him. Then he gives one long piercing scream.*

Time has passed. Perhaps there is a change in the light. DEATH *comes in and looks around him. The bed is now made.*

DEATH. He must be out working.

DEATH *touches the chair. There's dust on it.*

This place needs a woman's hand.

MURDO *comes in.*

MURDO. It's you. I don't know how you have the nerve to come back.

DEATH. I came in to see how you are. The fact is . . .

MURDO. I should kick you out. I'm sure you could have left her.

DEATH. I'm afraid not. The metabolism was not in good shape.

MURDO (*suddenly*). Was it my fault?

DEATH. Her death you mean?

MURDO. Yes, was it my fault?

DEATH. To be honest it's hard to judge these things. There's the physical and the psychological.

DEATH *picks up the blue vase and puts it down again.*

This is very dusty. Mothers must die and fathers must die. You must look on the bright side. She might have ended up senile, or in a home. The death of a mother is of course dreadful. There is nothing worse.

MURDO. Did you have a mother?

DEATH. If I had I can't remember.

MURDO. Why have you come to see me?

DEATH. I don't really know. I feel responsible for you. You are such a romantic. When a mother dies a man retreats into himself. No-one will love him as unconditionally as his mother did. It's good for you to talk even to me. You could talk to me about your metaphysics if you like. I find it entertaining.

MURDO. As a matter of fact I go out and work now. To prevent myself from thinking.

DEATH. That is why a lot of people work. The thing is, of course, I'm always around. Like the sound of the sea around an island, I'm always present. Death has a gift for metaphor, don't you think? The trouble is people try to forget me nowadays. In the Middle Ages I was always there. That was my best time. Plenty of plagues. I see you're wearing a black jersey.

MURDO. It's none of your business what I wear.

DEATH. I don't know if it's a good idea. You should wear a nice flowery shirt to remind you of nature and its normality. There's someone at the door.

It is in fact the MINISTER *who comes in. He enters in a deep, religious gloom. He takes off his hat and sits down.*

MINISTER. I came to see how you were and to offer you my deepest sympathy. We are like the grass and the flowers of the field. Ecclesiastes. Here there is no abiding city.

MURDO. Thank you.

MINISTER. Your mother was a good woman. A regular attender and follower. She would wish you to be the same.

DEATH. How do you know that?

MINISTER (to MURDO). Who is this gentleman?

DEATH. I am an observer with an interest in logic. I represent Murdo till he is himself again.

MINISTER. I think his mother would have wished him to attend church. What do you think Murdo? You caused your mother much suffering. She confided in me and hoped that some day you might see the light.

DEATH. What you are saying there is below the belt.

MINISTER. Sin often is below the belt. Murdo, do you wish this gentleman to be here or should we speak in private?

MURDO. He is always here.

MINISTER. Is he indeed? Well sir you may not have known of Murdo's disobedience but I saw, and the whole village saw it. Now he can repent and go to church.

DEATH. Why?

MINISTER. Why can't you let Murdo speak for himself?

DEATH. You have no right to make an orphan feel bad about the death of his mother. We are who we are. Who is looking after your mother?

MINISTER. If it's any of your business my sister is.

DEATH. For all I know you may have disappointed her by entering the ministry. She might have wanted you to be a National Health administrator or the head of a privatised industry. Why aren't you looking after your mother?

MINISTER. Well I . . .

DEATH. There you are you see. You are inarticulate away from your simple theology. Life passes, life sparkles and passes. Think of a bicycle wheel. It is like that. What do you think it is like?

MINISTER. It is like a pair of scales as you will find.

DEATH. And I think it's like a bicycle wheel. Not much room for compromise there. (*To* MURDO.) I have to go. Watch yourself. Don't be trapped. You are very vulnerable.

DEATH *goes.*

MINISTER. What an ill-mannered individual. Shall we pray, Murdo?

MURDO. If you like.

MINISTER. Are you not kneeling?

MURDO *does not kneel.*

Dear Lord, send down your manifold blessings on this grief-stricken house. Bring him who dwells here to full obedience and grace in thine own good time. For thou art merciful and just, and you sent down your only begotten son to die on the cross. Amen.

I don't think you should be seeing that friend of yours. He is leading you down wrong pathways. Also he has no respect for the cloth. Do you not believe in God?

MURDO. He permits too much carnage. I have seen too many photographs of mangled children.

MINISTER. The ways of God are inscrutable.

MURDO. Have you seen the photographs of the little children, some with no arms and no legs and some in school uniform floating down the rivers of Rwanda?

MINISTER. He said – Suffer the little children to come unto me.

MURDO. Oh this is dreadful. I think you should go.

MINISTER. If that is what you wish.

MINISTER *turns at the exit.*

I think you will need me some day.

MURDO. God forbid. (*Thinks, laughs.*) That's a bit of a paradox. Those who have no imagination are the ones who should die. It is best to be vulnerable like a snowdrop in the spring.

MURDO *puts his head in his hands. Enter* JUDITH, *brightly dressed.* MURDO *springs to his feet.*

JUDITH. Why are you wearing that black jersey? It makes you look thin. And why is this place so dirty?

JUDITH goes and gets the brush and brushes quickly.

MURDO. I have had two visitors.

JUDITH. What two visitors?

MURDO. The Minister and Death.

JUDITH. Who?

MURDO. Death. The man with the scythe.

JUDITH. Is that who he was. Are you all right?

MURDO. Death was arguing with the Minister. He's very bright.

JUDITH. I would have thought they would have agreed on a lot of things.

MURDO. Not at all. Death is surprisingly cheerful, full of the joys of spring, far more cheerful than the Minister.

JUDITH. That's interesting. Move over.

JUDITH brushes around his chair.

That window needs cleaning.

JUDITH gets cloth and brings it back.

Here's a spider's web. Do you want to see it? It's quite perfect.

MURDO. If there's a fly in it I don't wish to see it.

JUDITH. Don't bother then. I see you've been out working. What were you doing?

MURDO. Not a lot. If I stay in the house Snoopy next door comes in with scones.

JUDITH. I'm sure she means well.

MURDO. Not at all. She has an insatiable curiosity. How does she have the energy for it.

JUDITH. Well you have your books and she has her curiosity.

JUDITH stands back from the window.

Always make sure that your windows are clean. If you have an untidy house no-one will call on you. Not even Death. I'll put up fresh curtains for you some time.

MURDO. You're not working today?

JUDITH. Not on a Saturday. I've my own work to do. Why don't you make a cup of tea while I finish cleaning the window.

MURDO *goes and* JUDITH *cleans.*

How odd. Talking about Death taking a fancy to him. Certainly there was a man with a scythe. I saw him.

JUDITH *stops and thinks, the cloth in her hand.*

Really, really strange.

JUDITH *looks in the window as in a mirror, tidies her hair a little bit, then begins cleaning again. After a while* MURDO *comes in with two cups of tea.*

JUDITH. Your window is much cleaner. You should get a clearer view of everything.

MURDO *puts down the tea.*

JUDITH. As a matter of fact I like to see you doing that. You should learn to cook, iron your clothes and write your own Christmas cards. Maybe your metaphysics protected you from all that.

Pause.

Deep down your mother didn't want you to get married.

MURDO. What are you talking about?

JUDITH. Why else did she let you stay in bed but to protect you. You are still your mother's boy though. This time I've cleaned your window. There is no reason in the world why I should clean it again. Next time you can do it yourself. And why should I brush your floor for you? This tea is not terribly good.

There's a knock at the door. When MURDO *goes to the door it's the* INSURANCE MAN.

INSURANCE MAN. Excuse me. I was at the house the other day but everyone was in bed.

JUDITH. I wasn't.

INSURANCE MAN. By the way I sell insurance. Life insurance, accident insurance, endowment, and many other kinds. What if you or your wife were to die suddenly?

JUDITH. I'm not his wife.

INSURANCE MAN. Oh . . . What if you or this lovely lady who is not your wife were to die suddenly?

JUDITH. I'm not a lovely lady.

INSURANCE MAN. I beg to differ.

MURDO. What is the point of insurance if I have no dependants?

INSURANCE MAN. Everyone has dependants. We are all dependent on each other. You may not be married to this lovely lady but perhaps you may consider her as your dependant.

JUDITH. I hope not.

INSURANCE MAN. I wouldn't like you to drop dead, sir, and your bones to be of no financial use to anyone. Foresight is everything in this life. Without it man would not be where he is now.

Enter DEATH.

DEATH. You've got it all worked out haven't you?

INSURANCE MAN. Who are you?

DEATH. It doesn't matter. You depend on me for your statistics. A cold-blooded way of working.

JUDITH. It is indeed.

DEATH. Thank you. We haven't met. (*He shakes her hand.*) I think Murdo will have told you who I am. I look on him as a slightly retarded son. (*Turns to* INSURANCE MAN.) The advantage you take!

INSURANCE MAN. I'm merely a servant of my firm. Naturally we want people to stay alive so that they can pay their premiums. I myself work hard. I travel from one end of the country to the other. I am insured with my own firm. What if I were to drop dead while selling insurance? I work so hard that I hardly ever see my family who are all insured. However, I do not complain. (*To* DEATH.) Are you insured, sir, if I may ask?

DEATH *laughs*.

DEATH. That is a very complex question. You couldn't afford to insure me. I think that is the short answer. I see that you have a B.M.W.

INSURANCE MAN. That is true sir. I work on commission.
In short then, none of you is taking insurance so my visit has
been a waste of time. I hope you are suitably sorry for me.

MURDO. There would be no point in my taking insurance.

JUDITH. Nor me.

DEATH. Nor me.

INSURANCE MAN. Well, I did try. I have fulfilled my part of
the bargain. I can't persuade you out of compassion?

MURDO. No thanks.

DEATH. No thanks.

JUDITH. No thanks. Have you any insurance against dead
mothers?

INSURANCE MAN. No, not that one. We are not sentimental
here. However I did my best.

JUDITH. And you are well dressed.

MURDO. If a little depressed.

The INSURANCE MAN *does a little dance. Then they all
dance.*

DEATH. Dancing about the insurance tree
Is a funny dance for you and me.

JUDITH. For to get the money you must die
And in the cold your bones must lie.

MURDO. And men will wear a shirt and tie
And your happy wife will weep and cry.

DEATH. And they'll sing psalms, a policy
Will come in handy for the wifey.

MURDO. She'll have, I'd say, a second life
For there'll be an end to daily strife.

JUDITH. She'll dress in an expensive gown
When they lower her husband down.

DEATH. Oh death is what is necessary
For our dance around the insurance tree.

They stop dancing.

JUDITH. I'm afraid I have to go.

INSURANCE MAN. And I too. Empty-handed as I am.

DEATH. And I too.

They go.

MURDO. I must have a drink.

MURDO *pours himself a drink.*

Judith is very outspoken. I thought I was intelligent but it
turns out that I'm stupid after all. Mother didn't like me to
drink . . . However, I am alone now and I can drink. I drink,
therefore I am. Did Kant drink? Did Schopenhauer drink?
Probably not. Kant, I think, would have had mineral water.
Is it true, as Judith says, that my mother still exerts an influ-
ence over me? She did make my meals, wash my clothes,
and iron them.

NEIGHBOUR *comes in.*

NEIGHBOUR. I came to see how you are.

MURDO. I'm fine.

NEIGHBOUR. I see you are. No sooner is your mother dead
than you start drinking.

MURDO. Do you want a drink?

NEIGHBOUR. No thank you.

MURDO. I did see the gleam in your eye. You do really want a
drink.

NEIGHBOUR. To think what your mother would say if she saw
you now. She was so good to you. I'm surprised at you.

MURDO. I'm not surprised at you.

NEIGHBOUR. I must go. You are not in a fit condition to talk
civilly.

NEIGHBOUR *goes. On her way out she surreptitiously takes
the blue vase.*

MURDO. Some day in May
She'll come and say
Doleful the man
The sun shines on today.

I'm fit as a trivet
On drams of Glenlivet
But on Glenmorangie
I can't think of a rhyme.

MURDO *goes. The stage is empty. Light changes. It's mid-morning.* MURDO *is drinking tea,* JUDITH *comes in.*

JUDITH. I've brought you some curtains.

MURDO *goes out and brings in a ladder.* JUDITH *begins to take down the old curtains.*

JUDITH. I can sniff whisky. Were you drinking?

MURDO. Last night a bit. However I've discovered a new breakfast – porridge and mandarin oranges. It's very refreshing.

JUDITH. Is that all you had for your breakfast?

MURDO. I wasn't all that hungry.

JUDITH *works at the curtains.*

JUDITH. You can hold the ladder.

MURDO *holds ladder.*

Have you finished with your metaphysics now? I can tell you that all your followers have got out of their beds.

JUDITH. You're not holding the ladder steady. I don't suppose you've ever put up curtains.

MURDO. Never.

JUDITH. In reality this is one of the things we humans do. We put up curtains. You'll have to learn this yourself. You can't have the same curtains forever.

MURDO. I like the colour. Blue was always my favourite colour.

JUDITH. I can't be coming over here all the time to help you.

MURDO. Snoopy called. I offered her a drink but she didn't take it even though she wanted it. I could see the gleam in her beady eye.

JUDITH *throws the old curtains down at him.*

JUDITH. I'll wash these for you. Now give me one.

MURDO *fumbles about but finally finds one.*

You remind me of a nestling. Unprotected and naked.

MURDO *is looking up at* JUDITH *while she works at the curtains.*

MURDO. I suppose we could call this a lyrical interlude.

JUDITH. What are you doing? You should be watching what
  I'm doing.

MURDO. I am, I am.

  MURDO *watches for a while.*

JUDITH. Now give me the other one.

  MURDO *does so.*

From here you look as if you haven't shaved properly.

MURDO. Judith . . . I . . . I . . .

JUDITH. What are you stuttering about? You never used to
  stutter.

MURDO. I was just going to say – do you like your job?

JUDITH. Of course I like my job. I help to bring children into
  the world. (*Pause.*) Do you want me to cook you some
  breakfast? I don't suppose you have any bacon and eggs.

MURDO. I'm afraid I'm short of both.

JUDITH. There's so much you have to learn and I don't have the
  time to teach you. As a practical person you're a nincompoop.
  You're like an alien. There, that's finished.

  JUDITH *steps down from the chair.*

MURDO. They're very fine. Very blue and perpendicular.

  MURDO *looks at them again.*

They are really. I welcome them to my house. (*Suddenly.*)
  Do you think I took up metaphysics because I couldn't do
  anything else?

JUDITH. So you've made a great discovery.

MURDO. When I was young my father was shouting at me
  continually. Went about like a fireball. One day he fell down
  and had a stroke. He never read any books and he didn't want
  me to read books. One day he asked me to go up to the roof
  and clean the chimney. I couldn't do it. I was paralysed.
  Maybe it was after that, that I began to read metaphysics.
  My father was a very impatient man. Do you remember him?

JUDITH. Yes I do.

MURDO. He was very red-faced. One time I was reading a book
  about Robin Hood and he tore it up. What did you think of
  him?

JUDITH. I never thought of him at all. (*Pause*.) What are you going to do about the chimney now?

MURDO. I don't know. I'll have to think about it.

JUDITH. Poor Murdo, that's your trouble, you have to think about everything. I thought there was a blue vase over there.

MURDO. Was there?

JUDITH. Did somebody take it?

MURDO. I never noticed.

JUDITH. Really, you don't know anything. I bet that one next door took it. Did you leave her here on her own?

MURDO. I'm not sure. I may have. I think mother may have promised it to her.

JUDITH. Well did she?

MURDO. I don't remember. Oh I do remember now. She was weeping at the funeral. Uncontrollably. And then suddenly she stopped and asked if she could have the blue vase. I was so surprised that I didn't know what to do. She said that my mother had promised it to her.

JUDITH. And had she?

MURDO. She may have. I don't know.

JUDITH. Really you . . . I shall have to see her about it.

MURDO. You'd better not do that.

JUDITH. Why not. She's no better than a thief, Did you actually give it to her? Or did she take it?

MURDO. I think she probably took it. I can't remember actually giving it to her.

JUDITH. I'll see her about it. (*Looks about the room.*) Has anyone taken anything else? I don't think anything else is missing.

MURDO. You think it's important, that blue vase. Maybe it has some symbolic importance.

JUDITH. Don't be stupid. It was naked greed on her part.

MURDO. But a vase and a blue vase. It's symbolic.

JUDITH. Oh be quiet.

MURDO. Blue for heaven and eternity. And the vase like Keats'
vase. Are you actually going to confront her?

JUDITH. Of course I am.

MURDO. I could never do that. What will you say to her?

JUDITH. I don't know yet. Something will come to me at the
time.

MURDO. I think that's amazing. That sort of confidence.

JUDITH. Rubbish. Anyway I have to be going. And don't drink.

JUDITH *takes the curtains with her and gives one more
admiring look at the blue ones. Then she goes.*

MURDO. I think I love her. She's so sensible. But why should
she bother with me. I've always been too shy to speak to her.
And that's another reason why I became a metaphysician.
(*He looks over at the clock.*) Imagine Kant. He used to go
for a walk every day at the same time. The townspeople
used to set their clocks by him. He never married. A lot
of philosophers never married. Now I wonder why that is.

Pause.

It's hard to know why Judith never married. Maybe deep
down she's shy too, though she's not metaphysical. She drives
about the countryside and she's very popular. But how should
I, as a metaphysician, face her in the watches of the night?

Pause.

And so Kant went for his walk and thought about the
universe. Did he never think of women at all? Maybe he
thought women disturbed the universe. (*He uses a thick
Teutonic accent for Kant.*) And his gaze was down at the
earth while he thought about the heavens.

He paces up and down.

Maybe he looked up at his chimney. And he never looked to
left or to right though a murder might be committed on his
left hand side and a rape on his right hand side. Good
evening, he would say to them, as they murdered or raped.
Nice weather for the time of year. In his most metaphysical
voice. Or he might say it to a thief who was putting his hand
into his pocket and robbing him. It is a fine metaphysical
night and the moon and the stars are out. And he would say

to the police, I can't say I noticed anything. Murdered you say, just by the roadside? I have never murdered anyone in my life. (*Laughs.*) So there is Kant wearing a hat and he goes forward into the universe. Noticing nothing at all. Not even the brambles. Or the workers. Though they might cast a few light quips after him. 'Effing idiot,' they would say in their best lager-lout voices, 'You don't know your arse from your metaphysics.' And they munch their thick sandwiches and talk about women. None of this he notices. What a man. What a hero. What a fool. The fact is, Kant should have stayed in his bed as well. And Lord, he was never in love as I am. How can I prove my love and will Judith love me back? She seems so self-confident, so complete in herself. Last night I dreamed of her. I dreamed I was putting slates on the roof and writing on them at the same time. Now that my mother is dead I am permitted to love. Is that not the answer to the riddle?

DEATH *comes in with a bottle of whisky.*

DEATH (*he puts the bottle on the table*). I feel very sad.

MURDO (*gets glasses*). You feel sad.

DEATH. I feel sad and I have to get drunk. (*He pours out whisky for both of them.*) It builds up. The pity.

MURDO. You feel pity?

DEATH. Slainte.

MURDO. Slainte.

DEATH. Of course I feel pity. Do you think I like killing children for instance? Do you think I like to see them die? Everywhere. All the weight of my unpopularity. I am necessary, but that doesn't make my work any lighter. Today there was a woman who chose death so that her child could be born. Many people are nobler than me and that is hard to take.

MURDO (*ironically*). You're acting on orders.

DEATH. You might say that. Nevertheless, sometimes I feel responsible.

MURDO. What would you say if I said I wished to die?

DEATH (*pouring whisky out for them*). I feel like that myself sometimes. Why do you want to die?

MURDO. I'm in love with Judith and she doesn't take me seriously. She thinks of me as a little boy.

DEATH. Love and death are, of course, allied. The number of poems that have been written about us!

MURDO. That's not much use to me. If I could marry Judith I should be happy, I'm sure about that. I didn't know that when my mother was alive. Do you think I'm only a boy?

DEATH. Well, I have this theory. There are some people who can read books and there are others who can read the world. When you're reading a book you can go back and check the sense. You may not have time to do that when you're reading the world. The fastest readers of the world are the ones most likely to survive. Behind the physical is the metaphysical. Isn't that a wonderful theory?

MURDO. Very clever.

DEATH. And true.

MURDO. You are not the most modest among us.

DEATH. So you see I have my theories but I do not let them distract me from the job in hand.

MURDO. Judith is very beautiful. How did I not notice it before.

DEATH. You weren't lonely before. You had your mother.

MURDO. I would hate it if Judith married someone else. She could give my life some direction. She was going to ask for my blue vase back. From Snoopy.

DEATH. Have you lost a blue vase?

MURDO. Yes. But I never noticed I had lost it. A lovely blue vase. The colour of eternity.

DEATH. Sometimes you talk a lot of rubbish. (*Pours out another drink.*) I hope I don't have an accident with my scythe. Maybe I should put a red light on it. Excuse me, I have to visit your toilet.

DEATH *staggers out.*

MURDO. How odd. Death in my toilet. I don't seem to get drunk at all. Since my mother died I have been drinking but I never seem to get drunk. She didn't like me to drink. My father never drank. And of course my brother doesn't drink.

DEATH *comes staggering in.*

DEATH. I'm ashamed to say I was sick in your toilet. I think I must be suffering from stress.

MURDO. Now I've heard everything. Would you like an Anadin?

DEATH. No thanks. It's all right for you. You've never taken responsibility for anything.

MURDO. That's true.

DEATH *pours out more whisky.*

DEATH. You have no idea of the sights I have seen. School children macheted to death. (*He bangs the table.*) I hate the human race.

MURDO. I understand.

DEATH. Of course you don't understand. You have seen only one death, and that was peaceful.

MURDO. When I was young I saw a red coffin and people in red velvet suits dancing along with it. And there was music. But probably that was my imagination. Imagination is an antidote to death.

None of this helps me with Judith.

DEATH. I will speak to her.

MURDO. Do not frighten her. If you frighten her I will kill you.

DEATH (*laughs*). That is highly unlikely. And yet it would be nice to die. To be at peace. Not to see the faces.

DEATH *throws his glass across the room in a sudden rage.*

MURDO. Calm down. That's bad mannered.

DEATH (*stands up*). Kill me, kill me then.

MURDO. Don't be silly. I have nothing to kill you with.

DEATH. What am I talking about. Of course you can't kill me. Not even if you had explosives.

MURDO. I could give you some sleeping tablets the doctor gave me.

DEATH. They would be no use. Nothing is any use. Some nights I don't sleep at all.

MURDO. I'm really sorry for you. (*Drinks whisky.*) You'd better watch your temper. I make allowances but not everyone would.

DEATH. You are becoming a shupershilious bugger. Do you think you are shuperior to me, eh?

MURDO. I was only offering some advice.

DEATH. Shupershilious bugger.

MURDO. Maybe you should be going home. And put a notice on your scythe: WATCH OUT FOR DEATH OR HE MAY RUN YOU DOWN. (*He laughs.*)

DEATH. Bloody shupershilious bugger. I could kill you like that. (*He waves an arm.*)

MURDO. Why don't you?

DEATH. That would be too easy for you. Shupershilious bugger. (*Mutters again.*) Shupershilious. Bugger!

DEATH gets up, falls, gets up again and staggers out muttering to himself.

MURDO. What a quarrelsome character. He must have been drinking before he came here.

There's a scream from outside and then the NEIGHBOUR *comes in.*

NEIGHBOUR. Who was that man? He nearly killed me.

MURDO. I am sure he's sorry for it.

NEIGHBOUR. Not at all. He didn't even apologise. Ridiculous. What was he doing with a scythe anyway?

MURDO. What are you doing with a blue vase?

NEIGHBOUR. What . . . what . . . what are you talking about?

MURDO. I have to say this to you. Otherwise I have no chance with Judith. I have to say this face to face. No evasion. (*He is slightly drunk.*)

NEIGHBOUR. What are you talking about?

MURDO. The blue vase. (*His voice rises almost to a shriek.*) The blue vase.

NEIGHBOUR. What blue vase? Oh that vase that your mother promised me?

MURDO (*still nervous*). Have you any evidence of that?

NEIGHBOUR. I don't have a signed contract if that is what you mean.

MURDO. Well there you are.

NEIGHBOUR. There I am what? What do you mean? Your mother and I were always good friends.

MURDO. You may have been but she wasn't. The blue vase had a sentimental value.

NEIGHBOUR. What sentimental value?

MURDO. I bought it . . . (*In a rush.*) for my mother's fiftieth birthday. You can have something else if you like. You can have . . . a pan.

NEIGHBOUR. I don't want a pan. I have plenty of pans. Are you saying that you want the blue vase back? Is that what you are saying? You gave it to me yourself.

MURDO. I didn't think at the time.

NEIGHBOUR. Of course you had only got up from your bed. Maybe you weren't compos mentis. I shall go and get the blue vase. No-one can say that I kept something when it was not given freely.

MURDO *does a little dance and punches the air with his fist. He is very excited.* NEIGHBOUR *comes in.*

NEIGHBOUR. There you are. There's your blue vase.

MURDO. I hope you understand. It has sentimental value.

NEIGHBOUR. I do understand. Very well indeed.

NEIGHBOUR *stalks out.* MURDO *kisses the vase.*

MURDO. Wonderful. I stood up to her. Judith can't say I didn't stand up to her. The blue vase. There is something significant about it, something symbolic. When the gods go, blue vases remain. It is really quite pretty. I wonder where mother really got it from. I shall tell my grandchildren about that exchange between myself and Snoopy. The Battle of the Blue Vase. (*Stops.*) What grandchildren? After all it was not a major confrontation. It was a mere skirmish. On the other hand, for me it was an Iliad.

JUDITH *comes in. She is carrying curtains.*

JUDITH. I managed to have your curtains washed and dried.

MURDO. Do you see anything? Anything significant, anything symbolic?

JUDITH. What are you talking about? Have you been drinking again?

MURDO. As to that, my friend Death called and was sick in my toilet. What an honour. But apart from that do you notice anything significant? Turn your eyes that way. (*Pauses.*) It is indeed – the blue vase.

JUDITH. What did you do?

MURDO. I had a direct battle with Snoopy. Across the blue vase we gazed with hostility at each other. And in my case with triumph. I think I need a drink.

JUDITH. No you don't need a drink.

MURDO. O.K. then. I fought her to a standstill. It was vulgar but a comprehensive defeat for Snoopy.

JUDITH. I don't believe it.

MURDO. I said to myself, Judith will be proud of me. Language and ideas flowed from me. I was inspired.

JUDITH. What did you say to her?

MURDO. I told her that the blue vase had sentimental value. I said I had bought it for mother's fiftieth birthday. I lied of course.

JUDITH. And how did she take this?

MURDO. She became haughty and then she went and brought me the blue vase.

JUDITH. Poor thing.

MURDO. Poor thing. What are you talking about?

JUDITH. I don't think you went about it in the right way. Still apart from that it was a good effort.

MURDO (*sulking*). I thought I did very well. It's not every day a metaphysician descends to the vulgar. Do you think Kant fought over a blue vase?

JUDITH. Probably not. But then you aren't Kant are you?

MURDO. That's pretty wounding. On the other hand Kant isn't
me either.

JUDITH. Don't expect praise all the time. Still you did well.
I'm sure your mother wouldn't like Snoopy to have the vase.

MURDO. Mother won't know whether she has it or not.

JUDITH. I suppose that's true too. The main thing is that you
shouldn't drink too much. I suggest you put this bottle and
that glass away.

MURDO. All right. But I really do think I should have been
praised more. A laurel leaf or two would have been in order.

MURDO *goes away with bottle and glasses.*

JUDITH. He did this for me obviously. There is more to him
than I thought. It is possible I shall be able to mould him. He
showed courage when he confronted Snoopy. I think he is in
love with me and I like him. He has a gentle nature, all he
needs is direction. He is of course also frightened of me. (*She
goes over to the blue vase.*) It really is nice, a deep, deep blue.
Funny thing, Murdo's eyes are deep blue as well. I think
maybe he should become a teacher, maybe with younger
children. They are more imaginative. It's not too late for that.
He is not the usual kind of crofter.

MURDO *comes back in.*

MURDO. To think that I used to he a metaphysician.

JUDITH. We were all something different at one time. In my
dreams I was an air hostess.

MURDO. In the blue of the sky. You could have been one.

JUDITH. Yes, married to a pilot with straw-coloured hair.
However, I eventually thought it was too high for me.
My father was against my becoming a nurse. He thought
I wouldn't be able to stand the blood. But I could, and much
better than he would have done. You know, Murdo, what I
have learnt is that life is beautiful. Never forget that. And
never take to your bed again. Anyway I'll have to be going.

DEATH *comes in.*

DEATH. Don't go. (*To* JUDITH.) I've come to apologise to
Murdo.

MURDO. What for?

DEATH. I lost my temper. I threw a glass on the floor.

MURDO. That doesn't matter.

JUDITH. You always seem to be visiting Murdo. Why is that?

DEATH. I have taken him under my wing. Murdo is one of the
 questioners. Murdo, I wonder if you'd leave us for a moment.
 I have something to say to Judith.

MURDO. Fine. Don't be long.

 MURDO *goes*.

DEATH. Judith, I'm worried about Murdo. He's very lonely and
 that brother of his never visits him. He's in love with you.
 He was saying to me that he might kill himself. I don't want
 that to happen.

JUDITH. Why don't you want it to happen?

DEATH. I told you. I like him. There's something of the holy
 fool about him. He's an innocent. There's not many of them
 about. Do you love him?

JUDITH. I won't desert him. He had an argument with Snoopy
 next door. I think it was because he wished to prove himself
 to me.

DEATH. I nearly cut her legs off with my scythe.

JUDITH. That would have been something to see.

MURDO. Can I come in?

DEATH. Of course. It's your house.

 MURDO *stands over at the window, picks up the field glasses
 and looks out.*

MURDO. Oh God!

DEATH. What are you seeing?

MURDO. There's a cat springing on a baby rabbit.

DEATH (*puts his hand on* MURDO's *shoulder*). There's nothing
 you can do.

MURDO (*shaking the hand away*). You bastard.

JUDITH. Murdo.

DEATH. Let him speak.

MURDO. It's not so much the deaths themselves but the pain. And then they often happen in the middle of a life's work. When there is much left to do.

JUDITH. You have to accept all that.

DEATH. If there were no death the world would be choked with the living.

MURDO (*goes over to the vase*). I suppose there is always the blue vase. It is the colour of the sea.

JUDITH. Or the sky.

Murdo's BROTHER *enters.*

BROTHER. I came to invite you for your tea but I see you have visitors.

JUDITH. I was just leaving.

DEATH. And I.

JUDITH and DEATH *go.*

BROTHER. Why didn't you come to see us?

MURDO. I didn't feel like it. Anyway I thought you would blame me.

BROTHER. For what?

MURDO. For mother's death.

BROTHER. I did at the beginning but now you're on your feet and you've forgotten all that bed nonsense. That was Judith Cameron, wasn't it?

MURDO. Yes.

BROTHER. And the fellow with her?

MURDO. A friend of mine.

BROTHER. Odd-looking fellow. I was speaking to Snoopy and she says you're acting in a peculiar manner. Something about a blue vase. And that you're drinking too much. She says someone nearly cut her legs off with a scythe.

MURDO. He was unlucky.

BROTHER. Are you?

MURDO. Am I what?

BROTHER. Drinking too much.

MURDO. No. Are you still building a lot of houses?

BROTHER. Yes. I'm pretty busy.

MURDO (*suddenly*). You're younger than me but you always beat me when we fought. You were more daring than me. You had a great head for heights You used to climb cliffs. And you cleaned the chimney.

BROTHER. And you were mother's favourite.

MURDO. I'm trying to understand why I read so much and especially metaphysics. Something very strange has happened to me. At one time I used to think that I was more intelligent than you, because I knew about Kant. Now I realise that you are more intelligent than I am. You could read Kant if you wanted to but I couldn't build a house. You succeeded in marrying.

BROTHER. I succeeded. What are you talking about?

MURDO. Well, you did. You took that leap. And not only that but you have children. I don't understand it. And the children don't like me.

BROTHER. That's not true.

MURDO. Yes it is. They stand and stare at me with their thumbs in their mouths. They instinctively feel there's something wrong with me. They can smell Kant coming off me.

BROTHER. What a lot of rubbish you talk.

MURDO. No I don't. What is your secret? How do you under-stand everything so quickly? How do you know how to deal with your children? And build houses?

BROTHER. I'm beginning to think Snoopy was right.

MURDO. She's another oddity. She set her heart on that blue vase. It was important to her. Now why is that? Can you explain it? Extraordinary. And I didn't even miss it.

BROTHER. Well, you are a bit unworldly.

MURDO. That doesn't explain anything. Anyway I won't come over for my tea. I have to learn to cook for myself. I've discovered a new delicacy, porridge and mandarin orange slices. Very refreshing.

BROTHER. Whatever you do don't set the place on fire.

MURDO. Anyway thanks for calling.

BROTHER. I didn't come over before because I thought you might be blaming me.

MURDO. For what?

BROTHER. For not visiting you more often. The fact is Lorna didn't like Mother.

MURDO. Mother missed the children.

BROTHER. I know. It's been rather awkward and she used to phone such a lot.

MURDO. Lorna likes nice things. That's why you have to work so hard.

BROTHER. I must be going. I've a lot to do. (*Stands awkwardly for a bit.*) Look after yourself.

MURDO (*looking after him*). Et in perpetuum frater ave atque vale. And forever and forever farewell, my brother. I don't understand plans for houses but you do. And you tell your children the way they should go. Very strange. Such confidence. Such extraordinary confidence. (*Pause.*) I really can't understand it.

KANT *comes in perhaps wearing a cloak.*

MURDO. Who are you?

KANT. My name is Immanuel.

MURDO. Kant.

KANT. The exact personage. No, rather changing from moment to moment.

MURDO. There were so many things I wished to talk about. You spoke of the starry heavens above and the moral law within.

KANT. I did indeed.

MURDO. I'm not however going to discuss that. Were you happy as a bachelor?

KANT. That is a trivial question.

MURDO. Well this is a trivial age. People no longer have any shame.

KANT. No shame!

MURDO. Shame has vanished from our age. It is a refugee. You lived a reasonably long life for your time. You took regular walks. Were you happy? You never married.

KANT. No I didn't marry.

MURDO. You're not very communicative are you?

KANT. You ask me whether I was happy as a bachelor. I answer to you yes I was. But I had a great consuming idea. Are you a bachelor?

MURDO. Yes, but I'm not happy.

KANT. You are, as they say, in love with someone.

MURDO. Yes, she is very sensible, practical and pretty and younger than me. Your philosophy has made me unsuited to her.

KANT. I am sorry to hear that. Sometimes I was not happy. The starry heavens are vast and we are small. I used to look at them and think, I am much alone though I am a professor.

MURDO. I am not suited to be a bachelor though I have discovered porridge and mandarin orange slices. However, that is not a big consuming idea. I thought I was happy but that was when my mother was alive, I have found out a lot of things about myself since then. In retrospect.

KANT. In retrospect?

MURDO. Yes, little events explode in my mind. I thought at one time I was intelligent. Now I know that I'm stupid.

KANT. I always thought I was stupid. Once I met a woman on the street in the twilight and she said to me 'Do you want a good time?'. I said that I would study the concept, which I found interesting, good in connection with time. She wore a short red skirt. She took me to her tenement through whose roof I saw the starry heavens. I took off my watch and placed it beside me.

MURDO. And?

KANT. And then I realised who she was and I ran away. She shouted names after me, I will not repeat them. I think I was frightened of her. I did not go back for my watch.

MURDO. Oh well, I'm glad that at times you could be as stupid as me. What do you think of my blue vase?

KANT. It is pretty. It is blue. (*Picking it up.*) Though of course in certain lights it may be green. Then again if one is colour blind it may be grey for all I know. It is a sensory enigma.

MURDO. My next door neighbour almost stole it from me. Have you ever argued with a woman about property?

KANT. No, I do not think so. Though my landlady once said I should change my socks and my knickerbockers. But she liked me, I think. You see I was never drunk. Drink prevents us from seeing the moral law.

MURDO. I think it is not easy to be a bachelor nowadays. Or to have a consuming idea.

KANT. Maybe not. It was good to talk to you. That is an interesting use of the word good.

KANT is about to go away with the vase.

MURDO. My vase please. (MURDO *takes vase back.*) I think I shall go to bed. I am tired.

The stage darkens; noises and shrieks of the night in the midst of which one can hear the phrase, 'The starry heavens above and the moral law within.'

Morning. MURDO *enters. He pauses for a moment.*

MURDO. I know what I'm going to do.

MURDO goes out. The stage is empty. An urgent drum beat starts. After a while there's a scream and NEIGHBOUR *rushes in. She hunts around frantically for the telephone, finds it. Then dials.*

NEIGHBOUR. 999. What? What? What? Ambulance. Address. Edgemoor Cottage. Edgemoor Cottage, that's the address. His name is Murdo. He fell from the roof. Come at once. Edgemoor Cottage.

NEIGHBOUR *rushes out. After a while* DEATH *and* NEIGHBOUR *come in carrying* MURDO.

NEIGHBOUR. Should we have moved him? I don't think we should have moved him.

DEATH. It is lucky I was passing. Put him down. Go and tell Judith.

NEIGHBOUR. What shall I tell her?

DEATH. Tell her that he fell. From morn to dewy eve. No, tell her that he fell.

NEIGHBOUR *goes.*

DEATH (*bends down*). I can't hear anything from you, Murdo. What a cavalier fool you are. You shouldn't have tried it. Cleaning chimneys is not for you.

During this scene one may hear the noise of an ambulance klaxon, at first faint, then stronger.

DEATH. Of course I know why you did it.

JUDITH *rushes in.*

JUDITH. Is he all right?

JUDITH *bends down over him.* DEATH *moves away.*

What happened? Pray God he will be all right.

NEIGHBOUR. He was standing on the ladder looking up at the sky. Then he shook his head. And then he fell down.

JUDITH. Will he be all right?

DEATH. Yes he'll be all right.

Ambulance klaxon stronger.

JUDITH. Murdo, Murdo, what a fool you were, like a knight of old. But I love you for it.

Suddenly MURDO *raises his head.*

Look, he's all right. He'll be all right.

Two AMBULANCE MEN *come in.*

DEATH. All right, lads.

JUDITH (*to* DEATH). I don't want them to be rough with him. I'll go with him to the hospital.

They go out. DEATH *comes back in. One can hear the ambulance klaxon diminishing. Pause.*

DEATH. So we have true love triumphing again. Which is very good.

NEIGHBOUR *comes in.*

NEIGHBOUR. You were the one who nearly cut off my leg the other day.

DEATH. I am very sorry.

NEIGHBOUR. Do you think he'll be all right? I wouldn't want anything to happen to him, though he took back the blue vase.

DEATH. He'll be fine. Judith and he will get married. I hope to attend their wedding.

NEIGHBOUR. You may not he asked.

DEATH. They always say in the marriage service, 'Till death do you part.' I shall stand at the side, not between them.

NEIGHBOUR. It was strange. He looked up at the sky as if he didn't know where he was.

DEATH. That is why metaphysicians should never climb ladders.

NEIGHBOUR. Well if you think he'll be all right I have work to do.

NEIGHBOUR *goes.* DEATH *remains thoughtful. After she has gone* DEATH *picks up the blue vase and looks at it.*

DEATH. It's very pretty right enough.

DEATH *lays the vase down with a smile and goes.*

End.